AF571893

# BRIDGE ACROSS THE SEAS

*By P.B. Innis*
*and*
*Walter D. Innis,*
*R. Admiral USN Rtd.*

**BRIDGE ACROSS THE SEAS**

by P. B. Innis and Walter D. Innis, R. Ad. USN, Rtd.

copyright © 1995 P. B. Innis.
All rights reserved. No part of this book may be reproduced in any form, except for quotations in a review, without permission from the publisher.

Devon Publishing Co., Inc. Washington, D.C. 1995
ISBN 0-941402-12-6

*War is an all consuming fire*
*Devouring victor and vanquished alike*
*Unless the Flames of Victory*
*Are contained by the magnanimity of Peace.*

# FOREWORD

The Spring of 1945 witnessed some of the hardest and most continuous fighting on land and sea that history had ever recorded. At that time the United States and her Allies were driving Japan to her knees and every kind of weapon and every kind of warfare was focused on the capture of Okinawa and large scale air attacks on the Japanese Islands. All of this was in preparation of a final assault on the Japanese homeland itself.

Much has been written about the carriers, the battleships, the cruisers, the submarines and the aircraft that were in constant action against a fanatical foe, who had introduced the Human bomb, the Kamikazi. This weapon inflicted heavy damage and, in several instances, succeeded in sinking ships. At the same time many of the U.S. Army Air Corps B-29 aircraft returning from the attack on Japan, were forced to land in the sea thus activating large scale rescue operations.

If one could have overlooked at one time this scene of violence, he would have observed numbers of small ships busily providing life support in many forms to our personnel in serious difficulty. It is one of these smaller ships, the USS BERING STRAIT, that I think deserves far more recognition than the three Battle Stars she finally did receive. The BERING STRAIT was assigned every kind of combat mission one can imagine. She escorted larger ships through submarine infested waters. Again and again she brought every gun to bear on hostile aircraft, she rescued the crews of downed aircraft who otherwise might have perished and she excelled at supporting large seaplanes assigned to her control.

I have a special interest in the BERING STRAIT since she was commanded by an old friend, Commander Walter Innis. We were flight students together at Pensacola, Florida, in 1935. Commander Innis was a man of outstanding professionalism. It was his motivation that enabled him to quickly train raw recruits into a high state of readiness.

But let me start at the beginning.

The first assignment of the BERING STRAIT in the Pacific War Zone was radar picket duty to warn friendly forces of enemy aircraft approaching Saipan. This was a duty not normally assigned to sea plane tenders like BERING STRAIT, but the mission was conducted in an outstanding manner. The training conducted by Innis en route from the U.S., paid off. The next mission involved taking position to conduct rescue of ditched aircraft, the majority of which were U.S. Army Air Corps B-29s returning from attacks on Japan. This mission involved the rescue of over fifty airmen. The Commanding General commended Innis for this action and noted that several of the airmen rescued were already back on flying duty.

The invasion of Okinawa began on April 1, 1945, and the combat fury intensified. The Japanese increased their Kamikazi attacks over a wide area and frequently the BERING STRAIT was a target, firing every gun aboard at the suicide bombers. Only the high state of the training of the crew enabled her to avoid serious damage. While the air action was going on the BERING STRAIT was constantly rescuing downed airmen from the sea. According to official reports, the planes under BERING STRAIT control, carried out 268 missions during April, May and June 1945, rescuing 105 men who represented 39 different squadrons - 26 Navy, ten Marine Corps, 2 Army Air Corps and one Royal Fleet Air Arm. The carrier based squadrons came from 23 ships including the HMS Formidable.

Pilots and aircrew men were not the only beneficiaries of the capabilities and fighting spirit of the crew of the BERING STRAIT. The destroyer Brain was hit by two Kamikazis on May 27, 1945 and large numbers of her personnel were flown to safety and much needed medical attention. Frequently, during this period, BERING STRAIT planes escorted damaged aircraft to safety or directed other ships to the rescue of survivors in the water. Additionally, the BERING STRAIT went to General Quarters 154 times, sometimes 5 or 6 times a day. She splashed several planes including a Kamikazi just before it plowed into the sea.

Following the occupation of Okinawa the action quieted down except for a few typhoons which forced evasive action. On September 26, 1945, BERING STRAIT set sail for Japan to participate in the occupation. She remained in the port of Sasebo until December 30th when she sailed for San Francisco arriving on January 21st, 1946 and, immediately, her inactivation commenced.

BERING STRAIT had spent only a little over a year as a commissioned ship in the U.S. NAVY. But what a year!

## POSTWAR

The spectacular life lived by BERING STRAIT was not to end on the scrap heap. She was transferred to the Coast Guard in September 1948. She operated with the Coast Guard for the next 23 years, conducting law enforcement, weather lookout and rescue missions. She served in the Vietnam War conducting coastal surveillance.

On January 1st, 1971 she was transferred to the South Vietnamese Navy and renamed TRAN QUANG KHAI. When South Vietnam fell to the Communists, she was formally acquired by the Philippine government and renamed again as DIEGO SILANG. She served with the Philippine Navy until the late 1980's.

Flying the flag of three nations over a life span of 35 years, this scrappy little ship participated in two wars and in peacetime spent many years on the high seas, providing security and safety for thousands of people.

Tom Moorer,
Admiral U.S.N. Rtd.,
Editor

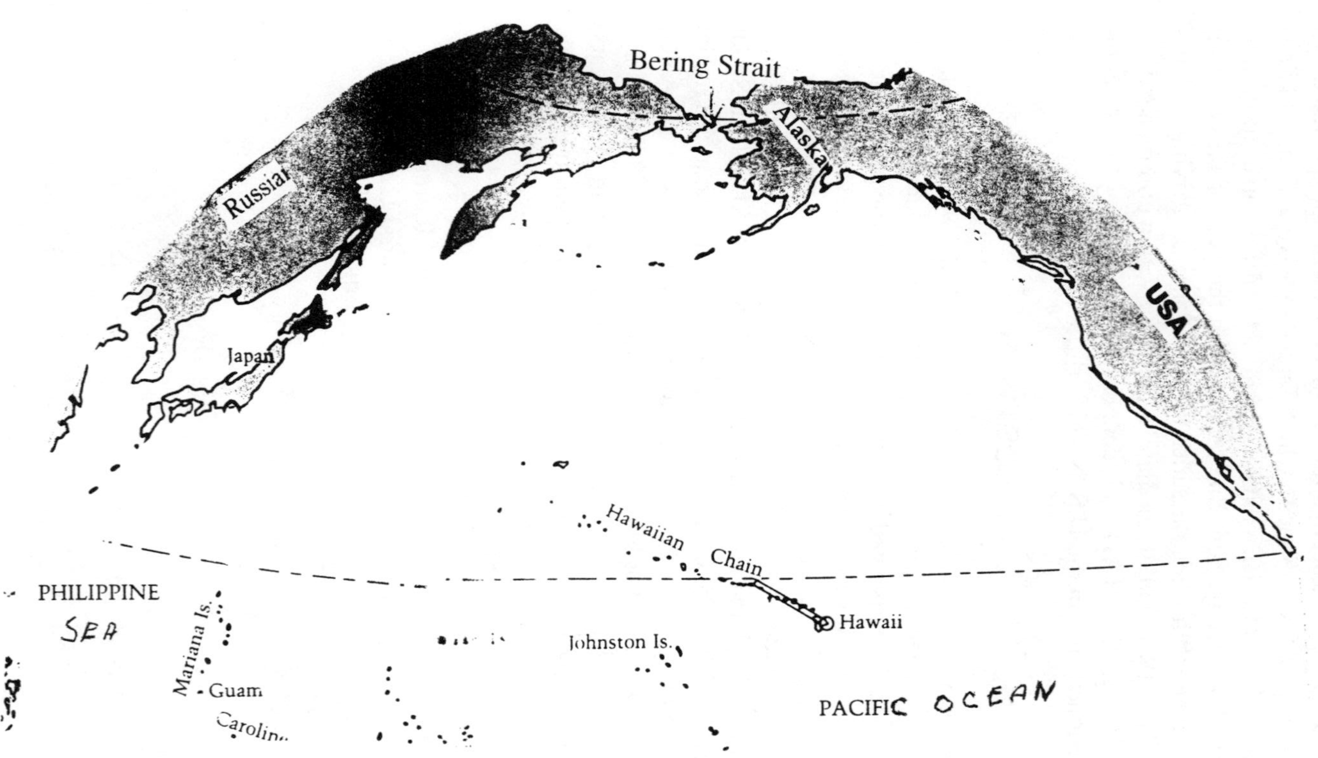
USA
Alaska
Bering Strait
Russia
Japan
Hawaiian Chain
Hawaii
PACIFIC OCEAN
Johnston Is.
Mariana Is.
Guam
PHILIPPINE SEA

# CONTENTS

# BRIDGE ACROSS THE SEAS

BY P. B. INNIS AND
WALTER D. INNIS, R. ADMIRAL USN RTD.

In September 1991 a Japanese lawyer came to Arlington National Cemetery and knelt at the tombstone of a U.S. Naval officer. Saying a Buddhist prayer, the lawyer reiterated his gratitude and his intention to follow the Golden Rule in all his dealings with America.

Why did he come? Why did he make such a promise?

This is the story. It began nearly fifty years ago in the Pacific where the brave, little picket ships were out alone intercepting kamikazis and picking up ditched B-29 crews.

It continues through the battles for Iwo Jima and Okinawa and the Occupation of Japan.

It tells of the amazing goodwill of approximately 4,000 American sailors in the Korean War and its affect on commercial affairs with Japan today.

It tells how one of the same little picket ships went on to serve with the Coast Guard in Vietnam, was turned over to the Vietnamese Navy, escaped to the Philippines when Saigon fell and then, under the Military Sales Act became a ship of the Philippine Navy.

As President Bush wrote, "It is truly an honor for the Department of the Navy to have played this role in building a 'Bridge of Peace'."

# SHAKEDOWN

## EN ROUTE TO PEARL

**"Prepare to Ditch."**
The order echoed with deadly intensity throughout the crippled B-29. Seconds later she hit the water with a crash that split the plane in two, spewing men and debris into the towering waves.

There was no moon, not even a star showing through the blackness as the airman struggled to get his head above water.

God! we're done for! We don't stand a chance in this. If the Japs don't get us the sharks will- even if the Dumbo picked up on our Mayday, they'd never find us. Desperately he shouted into the screaming wind trying to locate the rest of the crew, but the wind only sent his own voice back to him.

He hated the sea with a terrible hatred. That's why he'd joined the Air Corps. "Godamnit, I'll not let you get me." he shouted as a wave crashed over him sending him down in the depths of the raging blackness. Struggling desperately, his lungs bursting for air, he knew he'd never make it. Then, suddenly, everything was quiet and, opening his eyes, he saw he was in his own bed safe at home in Kentucky, far away from the Pacific Ocean, fifty years after the plane crashed off the coast of Japan in World War II.

It was an old, familiar nightmare, but each time the terror and horror of that night was just as real and he thanked God that he woke up just before the sailors beat off the sharks and pulled him aboard. They'd saved his life and he'd never forget them nor their ship.

He got up to make himself a cup of coffee. By now he was wide awake. Always, after the nightmare he found he couldn't get back to sleep. It brought back too many memories. Memories of shot up planes spiralling down to a fiery death, of bloated bodies floating on the sea, of — "Stop it!" he shouted at himself and took a gulp of the coffee. Downing it brought back the taste of that good old Navy java they gave him when they hauled him out of the water. Laced with brandy it was. He'd never forget how good it tasted. God! they'd been lucky. If that ship hadn't been there, I wouldn't be here, he thought.

The Bering Strait they called her. Funny name for a ship Vaguely he remembered reading about a Bering Strait in an old book his Dad had given him when he was in High School. His Dad had been in the Navy and hoped he'd follow after him, but he'd always wanted to fly. He'd kept the book for his Dad's sake, even though it was all about the sea.

He took the book down from the shelf where it was mixed up with a bunch of paperbacks and, finding Bering Strait in the index he read;

"Long ago, aeons before Polaris became the North Star, there was a place where East and West not only met but was firmly joined by a bridge of land reaching from Siberia to Alaska.

"In time, animals, birds and plants crossed to and fro and later, the ancestors of the original inhabitants of the American Continent immigrated from the East across this land bridge. Then with the melting of the glaciers and movements of the earth's crust, this land bridge split apart and the waters of the rising Arctic Ocean swept through forming the narrow body of water known as the Bering Strait separating Russia from the North American Continent.

"Since then this body of water has separated East from West with waters 25 fathoms deep. It was named for Victor Bering, a Russian explorer who crossed the Strait in 1728."

What the book didn't tell was that ten thousand years after this split between East and West, on the 19th of July 1944, a ship, the first to be named the USS Bering Strait, was put in commission at Lake Washington Shipyard, Houghton, Washington, with Walter Deane Innis in command.

The USS Bering Strait AVP 34, was a seaplane tender of the 'Barnegat' class with secret orders which would take her into the war zones of the South Pacific and the China Sea where the war was still raging against Japan.

Although no one would have believed it at the time, after many adventures and a strange twist of Fate, the USS Bering Strait was to become a bridge linking East and West once again.

But all that was well ahead of her, and as the ceremonies began, it was mostly excitement and pride that filled the hearts of the shipyard workers and the officers and men who would sail in her.

Being wartime, there was an added poignancy to the Chaplain's opening prayer asking Divine protection for the ship and its crew and an added fervor to the National Anthem as the ship's flag was raised for the first time. Up to now, she had flown no flag of her own and had been under the jurisdiction of the shipyard commander, now she was an operating vessel of the United States Navy.

After the usual official speeches, a representative of Pan American Airlines presented a flask of seawater complete with seaweed, which they had just flown in from the waters of the Bering Strait. This flask stayed with the ship throughout her wartime career.

Innis felt lucky to get the brand new USS Bering Strait as his first command. Somehow everyone present knew the Bering Strait was a 'Happy Ship'.

Whether its true or not, most sailors believe a ship has her own special personality. Some have the reputation of being happy and lucky and others seem unfortunate from the day they are built. No one really knows what makes the difference though hard-bitten seamen say its nothing but strict discipline and hard work that makes a 'Happy Ship'.

While Innis had already seen years of war service-beginning in the Atlantic Neutrality Patrol, most of the crew were inexperienced. Many had never seen the sea before and knew next to nothing of the Navy. It was going to be hard work to make a good crew out of these men, but the shakedown cruise, was a good test of crew as well as every part of the ship. By the time they reached the war zone, the worst and the best would be known about all of them.

It is hard for anyone, especially men used to the wide open spaces of the Midwest, to live in the cramped quarters of the ship and to sleep in the limited space allotted. Tempers could get short, fighting could break out and some might even try to jump ship. But somehow, it would be done. They knew that in battle the lives of all on the ship and the ship itself, depended on it.

Building up morale is a slow business. There is an awful monotony at sea and on the shakedown most of the crew were finding their sealegs and suffered badly from seasickness. Looking at the sea day after day was not what they had expected. Where was the action, the excitement of battle they'd heard about?

Although it was summer, the weather was cold, wet and foggy, but then something happened which relieved the monotony and lifted everyone's spirits a bit.

On the 11th August, Sam Bender S2c, was on lookout from midnight to 0400 hrs. It was a foggy night with no moon. Visibility was nil. Sam, who had reached the ripe old age of 19 years, had good strong nerves, but for some reason he felt almost panic stricken as he strained his senses trying to keep alert to any danger to the ship. The darkness and the clammy damp of the fog enveloped him like a shroud and the low moan of the foghorn sounding at regular intervals, did nothing to raise his spirits. This was the first time he'd been on lookout and he wished to God he was somewhere else.

How am I supposed to see anything in this stuff? What do they think I am? A goddamned cat or something? He looked at the illuminated dial of his watch. He'd only been on duty for an hour. Three more to go! Suddenly he felt a light touch on his face.

Spinning around he tried to pierce the darkness his heart beating fast, he waited listening intently. But there was nothing but the sound of the foghorn and the usual sounds of the ship.

I must have imagined it. This goddamned fog is getting to me, he thought. Kentucky never went in for fog. There might be a bit of mist in the early morning, but that was gone by sun up. Wonder how they're doing back there. All asleep in their beds by now. He felt an awful longing to be back home in Kentucky. Just to see the place again- the farm, the animals - everything. Dad for ever telling him what to do and Mom- God ! what I'd give for a piece of her pie right now!

He'd been in a big hurry to get away and see some action, but the old home looked pretty good from where he stood now. Maybe there'll be a letter when we get to port. Mom was a good letter writer. She — then he felt another touch on his face and he knew he hadn't imagined it this time. Someone had definitely touched him. He turned quickly and challenged the air, but there wasn't a sound. Was some smart aleck trying to be funny and give him a hard time? Or was someone testing his nerves? Well, he'd show them he was no sissy. He could stand lookout with the best of them.

Sam looked at his watch again. Still an hour and a half to go. Then it would be over and he could get some sleep. But supposing there was something or someone who shouldn't be around? Ought he to sound the alarm? But for what? How can I say someone touched my face so I sounded the alarm ? They'd think I'm crazy. If I'd been knocked down, I'd have something to show for it. He decided to stick it out and say nothing. But he sure was glad when his watch was over.

It was in the chow line at lunch that he heard there was a stowaway on board.

"Have you seen the stowaway, Sam? They say he must have sneaked in last night. Weren't you on lookout? Did you let him on board?"

Sam's heart almost stopped. Was that what touched his face? A stowaway! God! Would they put him in irons?

"Where is he? When did he come aboard."

"He's up on deck somewhere. Nice looking fellow."

"I thought stowaways were thrown overboard or something."

"Not this one. He's a friend. Why don't you go and take a look at him? You'll be surprised."

But up on deck there was no sign of a stranger.

"Where's this stowaway I've heard about?" Sam asked a sailor as he went back down the ladder.

"He's around here somewhere. Flew in on his own. Must have known we're a seaplane tender." and the man laughed as if it was a big joke.

Much later Sam discovered that the stowaway was a bird ! A song sparrow ! The bird had been sighted by the Watch at 0700 hrs making an unauthorized landing on the fantail. It was thought that the bird, not being qualified for instrument flying, had made a forced landing in the fog which had surrounded both ship and shore when the Bering Strait left the building yard for shakedown. By the time the fog lifted they were well at sea, far from the bird's home port.

"Let's give it a name. If its going to join the crew we've got to call him something.

"This started a tremendous discussion about names suitable for birds, beasts and babies. After considerable disagreement, the bird was named Jerry Sparrow and made a member of the crew.

Sam was never allowed to forget his first night on lookout. Remarks on his eyesight and his ability to recognize flying objects went on for weeks. But he didn't mind too much. Secretly he enjoyed the bird. His mother always threw out food for them. She liked to keep them around in winter.

"Snow's hard on the birds." she told him. "There's not much food and the water's all frozen up and, anyways, they're company when you and your Dad aren't around.

"Jerry conducted daily flight operations, giving the ship almost continual air coverage throughout the hours of daylight. On completion of his flights, he always made a standard approach (without benefit of a landing signal officer) and never missed making a perfect landing.

Just before the ship reached Alameda a message was received that Seaman James Ferrell's mother had passed away.

"I can't believe it." Ferrell said, "My Mom was always worrying about me getting killed, I never thought she'd be the one to go."

The same thing was in the mind of his shipmates when they heard . Somehow, no one expected those they left behind to go before they did.

"You'll get some leave, won't you, Jim ?"

"Skipper says I can go ashore when we dock and pick up the ship again in San Diego."

When the boat shoved off taking Ferrell ashore, Jerry, the sparrow flew off with them and Sam thought, well he's gone AWOL, we won't see him again. But lo, and behold, three days later Jerry returned accompanied by another song sparrow of more modest coloring.

Jerry had found himself a mate and had obviously decided to join the Navy and see the world!

The crew named the female Berry and she became as versatile as Jerry on wingovers, approaches, landings and all other air tactics employed by heavier than air types. Except for objecting strongly to gunnery practice, both birds were happy and comfortable on board until one sad day when Berry was found dead on deck.

Jerry was beside himself. The very next day he went AWOL

and was never seen again. Both Jerry and Berry were missed. Their cheerful twittering and merry patrols had eased the tension of the long, boring days at sea.

*On October 9*, the Bering Strait arrived at Pearl Harbor. Now there was no complaining about monotony. Days and nights were filled with one task after another. The wrecks in the harbor were a grim reminder of the reality and brutality of war and most men made the opportunity to write letters home when ever they could, fearing it might be their last chance.

After establishing a seadrome at Kubio Bay, the ship carried out training exercises with detachments of Martin "Mariners" and tended a succession of flying boats from Patrol Squadron (VPP) 25.

Knowing that they were likely to be at sea on Christmas Day and thinking it would cheer things up a bit, the skipper got hold of a small tree which could be fixed up like a Christmas tree. This little tree was kept in a pot on the bridge and tended very carefully. It was the source of much speculation in the enlisted mess.

"What's the old man put a tree up there for? That ain't no place for a tree."

"Maybe its some kind of fruit he likes to eat."

"He's always watching over the thing. Never knew no other skipper to keep a tree on the bridge." Seaman 1st class Hukkanen said.

Hukk, as he was known to all aboard, was one of the more experienced men. He had served on the USS South Dakota and survived the sinking of the USS President Hayes. Hukk ran the boatswains locker up in the peak and mostly, the men took notice of what he said.

"Think he's losing it Hukk?"

"I wouldn't say that? Seems to run this ship pretty good. Most skippers have some weird idea or another."

Most of the month of November was spent at NAS Kaneohe training an Air Sea Rescue Task Group consisting of the ship and the seaplane detachment of Rescue Squadron (VH) 2 and it was here that the potential Christmas tree vanished.

Scuttlebutt had it that some visitors were coming aboard and there would be a movie.

"Think we'll get a chance to see it after?"

"That's what usually happens. It's a long time since we've seen a movie, hope its a good one." Charlie Cates answered.

But to the disgust of the crew, the visitors came and went taking the movie with them. Only the officers had a chance to see it. That night the tree vanished and it wasn't until thirty years after the war ended, that Hukk admitted he'd crept up to the bridge and deep sixed it because the men were so mad they didn't get to see the movie.

# CHRISTMAS

## DECEMBER 1944

Then on the 1st December, in obedience to COMAIRPAC Secret Movement Order # 010236, the Bering Strait was under way for Kwajalein, Marshall Islands.

This was it! At last they were to have a go at the Japs. This was what they'd been waiting for. By this time the morale of the crew was so high they thought they could take on anything afloat.

Looking back, Gordon Jarvis, Gunnery Officer, recalls a day the ship received information that a Jap destroyer was in the vicinity. Jarvis reported to the skipper that this destroyer had six inch guns. As the Bering Strait had only 5 inch guns, the other ship had the advantage.

"We'll sneak up on them and take them by surprise." the skipper said.

As General Quarters sounded throughout the ship, men dropped whatever they were doing and rushed to their battle stations.

"This is no drill. This is for real." sounded in their ears through the noise and clamor of the bells and buzzers. Fast and furiously reports came to the bridge, "Guns manned and ready, Steering manned and ready- Engine room manned and ready- Ready- Ready, Ready. Excitement was intense. This was what they were here for. This was their first test. But they were sure they were more than equal to it and were ready to show what they could do.

"TARGET SIGHTED STARBOARD."

Eagerly guns were swung round to point at the target which was now clearly visible.

Tense with mounting excitement men waited the order to FIRE, their fingers on the firing keys.

But the order never came. The Jap destroyer changed course and fled! To this very day the crew are sure the destroyer knew they couldn't stand up to the Bering Strait and were afraid to take them on! No one even considered the possibility that the destroyer might be searching for bigger game!

Every day General Quarters was sounded at dawn and twilight, these being the times when the enemy is most likely to stage a surprise attack, and after crossing the International dateline on the 5th, the ship zigzagged her way to the Marshalls.

On Christmas Day 1944 the Bering Strait, along with PC 1082 and PC 572, was escorting USS Situla and four merchantmen to Saipan. Positioned 3,000 yards ahead of the convoy the Bering Strait created a smoke screen protecting the convoy from the Jap subs which had been reported in the vicinity.

A special Christmas card had been designed for the Bering Strait by A. Dupont, USN and both officers and men had sent this off to their families and best girls before they left Hawaii knowing it would be their last chance to send mail for a while. Because there was no chaplain aboard, the skipper conducted a short service. Two members of the crew read passages from the Bible telling of the birth of the Prince of Peace and of the song the angels sang to the shepherds as they watched over their flocks in Bethlehem. Then all joined in singing Christmas Carols.

"That Silent Night thing always hits me in my gut. We always sang it at home at Christmas while my sister played the piano. She wasn't that good but we always got through it."

"Do Japs keep Christmas?" Sam asked.

"No they have some religion of their own. Be just like them to try and sink the lot of us on Christmas Day." 18 year old Signalman Adam Reiss remarked.

"Well, we're ready for the bastards. Just let them try it."

But the day passed uneventfully and they were all able to enjoy a Christmas dinner as good as any they would have had back home. It was so good that several of the crew had kept a copy of the Menu and supplied it for reproduction in this book.

By Dec 28th the Bering Strait was anchored in Saipan Harbor with watch set at War condition III.

According to protocol the skipper went to call on Vice Admiral Hoover, Commander of the Forward Area. Admiral Hoover was a big, tall, stately fellow every inch an admiral and well respected by the men.

Saipan had been pretty much cleaned up, but signs of the bitter struggle to take the island were still visible. Even the Japanese civilians had fought fiercely and when they saw there was no hope, mothers threw their babies from the cliff and saw them dashed to death on the rocks below, before committing suicide themselves.

"Christ!" a Marine who had taken part in the battle exclaimed. "I'll never forget the sight of those dead and dying kids smashed up on those rocks."

Then, on New Year's Day, began the highest test of morale any ship's crew is likely to get - Orders for radar picket duty. Men on radar picket station were under constant stress. Subject to sudden attack from enemy bombers and kamikazis they were standing at General Quarters for hours on end with the "ship buttoned up." Sleep had to be taken when and where they could get it. A few consecutive hours was the greatest luxury for those on picket station.

Picket ships were small destroyers or AVPs which rolled and pitched mercilessly in heavy seas. As Samuel Elliot Morison wrote in his book THE TWO OCEAN WAR, "Although your historian himself has been under kamikazi attack, and witnessed the hideous forms of death and torture inflicted by that weapon, words fail him to do justice to the sailors who met it so courageously."

Like the brave men of the Merchant Marine, sailors of the picket ships never received the recognition they deserved.

Serving as Fighter Director ship to intercept Japanese planes operating between Iwo Jima and Truk, in Operation Michigan, the Bering Strait was on station until the 28th of January.

Returning to Saipan for logistics and repairs, Orders were received to relieve USS Fanning (DD-385) on Air Sea Rescue Life guard Station.

## WAY TO IWO-JIMA

### FEBRUARY 1945

At 12 noon on Sunday, the 4th of February 1945, the Bering Strait was underway for its Air Sea Rescue Station with orders to pick up survivors from any ditched aircraft.

When the mission was known there was some considerable discussion among the crew. They wanted some real action - a chance to get a few Japs.

"Hell, we'll be nothing but a sitting duck out on that goddamn ocean all by ourselves. We'll be sunk long before them bombers go anywheres." Bat always considered it his duty to point out the worst of every situation. What irritated everyone was that there was always an uncomfortable amount of truth in what he said so he was usually told to shut up.

"Well, its a pretty big ocean. The Japs might not notice us out there. They'll have their hands full fighting off the bombers."

"Who's going to pick us up if we get hit?"

"You'll have to swim home, sailor, or start walkin' on water or something."

"Why did we get this stinking job?"

"God knows. Don't ask me."

"I never thought I'd end up on a Dumbo, for God's sake."

"Well, there's not much we can do about it now, so you might as well shut up and stop griping."

"O.K., O.K. What you're saying is, someone's got to pick up those flyboys if they get shot up and all I'm saying is, I wish it wasn't me. What they need is a base close to Tokyo."

"Yeah, but 'til they get one its up to us."

"Everyone knows those B-29s have been a waste of money.

What have they done so far? The Navy's took all these islands without any help from them and we've had to spend too much time and space bringing spare parts and supplies for them and on top of all that, I heard the pilots can't get the hang of flying the damn things and they've crashed more than the Japs have knocked out of the air." Bat had had it.

"They say they can carry more bombs than any other plane."

"What good's that if they don't hit anything?"

"Don't ask me. Ask the Skipper, he's working on some plan to make sure we rescue everyone of them that ditches anywheres near us."

"All I can say is, I hope we're still around when the time comes, that's all."

In spite of all the griping, the whole crew were ready and willing to turn to and when the time came, they proved this by picking up more downed airmen than any other ship.

Once the Marianas were in the hands of the Allies, all eyes were turned on the conquest of the mainland of Japan. The Joint War Planning Committee in Washington agreed with General Henry H. Arnold that the new B-29 bombers could strike Japan and bring the country to its knees. The hope was that intensive bombing of Japan would make invasion unnecessary and save many lives.

The B-29 had a range of 3,500 miles carrying a four ton load of bombs and by Fall of 1944 there were 500 planes and their crews ready for action. The B-29s first started operating from China, but logistical problems made this unsatisfactory. A new bomber command, the XX1st, under Brigadier General H. S. Hansen, was formed, to operate from Saipan and Tinian.

High altitude precision bombing attacks against Tokyo were made but high winds and cloudy conditions over the targets prevented any real success. Inadequate maintenance facilities and the long over-water flights which consumed so much fuel, caused increasing loss of planes. In January 1945, Major General Curtis LeMay relieved General Hansen but still there were as many bombers lost to operational difficulties as there were to enemy fighters or anti aircraft guns. So, it was decided that an intermediate airbase was absolutely necessary to reduce the dangers of the long flights.

Iwo Jima, strategically placed half way between Saipan and Tokyo, was chosen as the most valuable stepping stone. Its airfields would provide a base for fighters and an emergency landing field for B-29s.

Naval strategists had been eyeing Iwo Jima for some months, considering it as a base for landbased air power which would augment the carrier's striking power when attacking the Ryukyo Islands.

Apart from its strategic position, Iwo Jima had little to recommend it. It is a desolate volcanic island 4 1/2 miles long and 2 1/2 wide described by the Japanese as a place of "sulphur, no water, no sparrow and no swallow." It is shaped like a tear drop and it certainly brought endless tears of sorrow to the next of kin of the incredibly brave men who gave their lives to gain control of it.

D Day was set for February 19th 1945. Although Iwo Jima was subjected to constant aerial bombardment and three days of naval gunfire to reduce the island's defenses before landings were attempted, it was not until D Day itself that it was realized that very little damage had been done to the Japanese defensive positions. Only after desperate fighting and incredible bravery on the part of the Marines and all taking part, was the island taken. In command of the operations was Admiral Spruance. Vice Admiral R K. Turner commanded the Joint Expeditionary Force and Lt. General "Howling Mad" Smith of the U.S. Marine Corps commanded the Expeditionary Force.

*Japan.*

In Japan, well aware of the danger to their homeland if Iwo Jima fell into the hands of the Americans, the War Lords chose Lt. General Tadamichi Kuribayishi to defend it to the death.

Kuribayishi was an experienced soldier. He had organized the 1st. Imperial Guards Division in Tokyo and fought in the invasion of Manchuria and China. Also, he had gained a respect for and some understanding of Americans during a two year stay in the United States.

The General found the Japanese forces on Iwo Jima to be of poor calibre, but he planned a remarkable defense which would cost the Americans dearly. The few civilians on the island were evacuated and the "Courageous Battle Vow" that "Each man would kill ten of the enemy before dying." was made by every fighting man.

With strict discipline, Kuribayishi began a tremendous system of tunneling in the rock. Walls of concrete entrenched and protected the 75 mm mountain guns and the new rocket guns. Tanks were buried so that they could not be spotted from the air. Mount Suribachi, the inactive volcano on the south of the island, had a seven story gallery hollowed out to conceal artillery, mortars and machine guns.

Kuribayishi's H.Q. was created at the north end and consisted of 500 feet of tunnels some 75 feet underground. This was where the final resistance would take place.

Meanwhile the B-29s continued the exhausting and dangerous flights to bomb Japan and the Bering Strait stood its lonely watch below.

*Tinian Island. Feb 10 1945.*

In the evening of Feb. 10th 1945, B-29s of the 505 Bomb Group, were roaring down the runways of Tinian Island. Their mission - to bomb the Nakajima Aircraft Factory, Ota, Japan. This factory built one of Japan's finest fighter planes, the Nakajima Ki-84. It was hoped to do enough damage to stop production for a while.

Unfortunately, the mission did not start off well. Two of the planes aborted before takeoff and one failed to gain lift and crashed into a large mound at the east end of the airstrip. Bursting into flames as the bombs exploded, the plane was completely demolished and all the eleven crew men were killed instantly. Parts of the plane were found all over the island.

Just before the crash three planes took off successfully. Their crews were in high spirits. They were doing what they had been trained to do and they were going to do it well. Although there was low cloud cover, it was fairly clear above ten thousand feet and things looked good. Fortunately, there was no way they could know that they were bound together by a tragic twist of Fate which would send their planes to the bottom of the sea.

The first of these three planes was B-29 no K-375, otherwise known as Deacon's Delight. The Pilot was 1st Lt. J. J. Halloran; co-pilot, 2nd Lt. F. A. Kays. Then there were, 2nd Lt. Paul M. Shuford, 2nd Lt. Howard Atkin; T/Sgt. Sam Burch; Sgts. Philip Knutson; Sol Serkin; Sigmund Lewandowski; Cpls. Floyd Larson;

Donald Lehman, Bernard Gallinger; also a passenger named Petersen was mentioned in the ship's log.

Next to take off was B-29 K-43 known as "Heavenly Body" Like the crew of Deacon's Delight it was also this crew's first trip to Japan. 1st Lt. O. F. Lowry, was the Pilot; co-pilot was 2nd Lt. F. L. Sult; 2nd Lts. B. Townsend; R E. Hansen; R. M. Weigel; T/Sgt C. J. Blackwell; Sgts. M. J. O'Conner; L. B. Mooty; E. M. Holt; W. R. Hupman; and Cpl. C. Q. Morton, completed the crew.

The third plane was B-29 242- 824 known as "Homing Bird" from the same group. The crew consisted of Melvin G. Cash 1st. Lt. Commanding. 2nd Lt. H. W. Wing, co-pilot; 2nd Lts. John R. Slevin; Elmer E. Stapler; W T. Trivette. S/Sgts. James Halsey; Hugo C. Drum. Sgts. Morris A. Palmer; Philip Neverman. Cpls. Stanley A. Odon; Carl T. Ptalzgrat.

All three crews were ready for anything the Japs could dish out and go one better.

*Aboard the Bering Strait*

Far below the bombers, the Bering Strait was steaming independently on Air-Sea Rescue station remaining within 10 miles radius of Lat. 20-00 (N), Long. 143-15 (E) . The ship was dark and Condition III of War Readiness was set. The B-29s were counted as they flew overhead. Watch would be kept until the same number returned or was accounted for one way or another. It would be a long watch as the mission to Ota would take approximately 14 hours.

It was 06.30 when enemy fighters were sighted.

"Sound General Quarters." the Skipper's voice was sharp.

"Aye, Aye , sir." and immediately the ship was filled with alarm bells and whistles and the sound of men running in every direction.

"This is it. We're as good as done for out here on our own with them damn Japs all over the place.." Bat lamented as they ran to their battle stations.

A couple of Zeros flew over too high for the ship's guns to hit them. Then they turned and dived down one after the other firing at the ship with all they had.

"Get the bastards. Get 'em." and the ship's five inch guns let them have it.

Climbing at full power the Zeros pulled out, but not before one received some flak from the ship. A trail of smoke plumed out and he began losing altitude. Suddenly, the Zero burst in flames and spiralled into the sea. Cheers rose from the ship as they watched it sink. There were no survivors.

"That's one less. Better watch out for the other. He might be hanging around waiting his chance to try again."

But all was quiet, the skies were clear and at 0710 the ship was secured from General Quarters and Condition III set as she commenced patrolling on station.

*En Route to Tokyo*

At this stage of the war the B-29s flew in loose formation from Tinian until they were near the coast of Japan then they closed up. High level bombing was still the practice of the Air Corps so they crossed the coast at 28,000 ft. Up to now the flight had been uneventful then suddenly the planes were buffeted by such high winds that they were practically standing still in the air.

"God! we're only making about 60 groundspeed with an air speed of 260. I've never encountered winds like this." Pilot Lowry of Heavenly Body exclaimed. "Must be 200 miles per hour."

"It'll make us a good target for flak. I'll be glad when we're out of here." answered Sult.

"I knew winds were to be expected, but this is like a hurricane. The weather briefing never said anything about a typhoon, did it?"

"No, only that high winds were usually encountered over Japan."

At this time there was not much knowledge of the circumpolar winds ( jet stream) which occur at high altitudes.

"Zeros! Zeros at eleven o'clock. Zeros 12 o' clock. Christ! there's swarms of them." the intercom was crackling.

A zero zoomed past them and hit a B-29 to the left. It went down in trail of smoke and flame.

"That's Walt Schroeder's plane, he————" the thud of flak hitting the plane drowned the rest of the sentence and Sult and Lowry were too busy to think about anything but avoiding the Zeros and getting to the target. They didn't even notice the two B-29s colliding just off their right wing when the Japs dived right at them.

Flak was all around the 'Heavenly Body' now they were getting close to the target and the plane shuddered as they took several direct hits.

"Bomb bay cables severely damaged, sir, doubt if doors will open." Bombardier Hansen reported.

"Any hope of repair?"

"We'll give it a try, but I doubt it."

"Do your best. Salvo if you must."

Hansen and Weigel, flight engineer, worked feverishly trying to splice the severed cables in the bomb bay but the damage was too great. All they could do was get the doors open and let the bombs drop hoping they'd hit somewhere near the target.

As soon as Hansen shouted, "Bombs away." the plane turned and headed for home making as much speed as possible.

At first there was a feeling of triumph aboard the Heavenly Body as they left the target area. In spite of the heavy flak, the high winds and the swarm of enemy fighters, the plane was still in the air and no one was injured. With any luck they'd make it back.

Then it was realized that the bomb bay doors were still open. Although Weigel and Hansen did their damnedest to get them shut, it was no use. So, taking a terrible risk, Weigel climbed out on the bomb doors and forced them closed. No sooner had he settled down again, when he discovered that it was impossible to transfer fuel from the #2 tank. This tank supplied the fuel for the return flight. Unless they could get at it, they were done for.

The control line to the selector valve was cut by flak.

"About all we can do is to try working on the valve with a pair of pliers." Weigel said in reply to Lowry's questions.

"For God's sake get it moving. How much fuel have we got left?"

"About two hours, not more, that's if the gauges are accurate. They're known to read a bit high."

"Keep me informed of progress."

"Sure will, sir."

In spite of all the engineer's efforts, nothing could be done to transfer the fuel and with only one engine operating, the skipper made the decision to ditch. Immediately, navigator Townsend and radio operator Holt worked out their position prior to sending out distress signals. The crew attempted to jettison equipment, but , as the bomb bay doors were inoperative, very little could be thrown out.

Central Fire Control Hupman saw to it that most of the ammo

was fired as the crew assumed ditching positions.

Hupman had two choices of ditching position, one was under the forward blister where the navigator shot the stars, or he could go and sit against the rear bulkhead. Hupman said he never knew why he chose the forward blister, but if he hadn't he would never have gotten out.

There was an ominous silence as the plane dove through the thick cloud cover to the heavy seas below. The landing lights were on but it was impossible to see anything and at approximately 130 mph the plane struck a heavy swell. The force of the impact was so great that the plane broke into three pieces. Water rushed in and it sank in less than five minutes.

Hupman was lucky, the fuselage cracked in front of the tunnel allowing him to inflate his Mae West and shoot to the surface. Floundering around he felt a cord in the water. Must be something at the end of it, he thought, as he pulled himself along it. It turned out to be the cord attached to a five man life boat which had broken out when the plane broke up. Grabbing at the sides of the life boat he tried to pull himself aboard, but his life jacket kept him away from it. Yelling and cursing he was finally pulled aboard by Sult and Townsend who were already in it together with Hansen.

All of them had swallowed a lot of the plane's fuel and salt water and were badly bruised from being thrown around when the plane hit. Sult had a bad cut on his leg and Hupman had injured three fingers. The waves were over five feet high and kept washing over the raft and they had to keep bailing to stay afloat.

Claude Blackwell, tail gunner, had been swept out when a rush of water entered his compartment. Inflating his one man dinghy, he began searching for other members of his crew. He saw the other raft, but the mountainous swells prevented him from reaching it. Then Blackwell heard Holt, the radio operator calling for help and started paddling in the direction of his voice. As he got near he saw Weigel was already close by in a one man dinghy. Holt had lost his so they decided to try and get close enough to get Holt out of the water and support him across their two rafts.

"Get a hold of my raft." Weigel shouted to Holt, "We're going to try and get you between us until we can find the five man or the seven man."

"O.K." Holt gasped, his mouth full of oil and water. Somehow, between them they got close enough for Holt to hold on. Then came the hard part. Each time they tried to get him up between the two rafts, the waves threw them apart.

"It's no go." Holt cried. "Look out for yourselves, I can't make it."

"Hold on, we'll make it together." and waiting for the next swell to pass they got him up between them.

Meanwhile the other men were trying to get close enough to join forces, but the rough seas made it impossible and, after a while, they gave up trying. All the men were sick , soaking wet and chilled to the bone. Weigel began coughing up blood and to their horror they saw this was attracting sharks.

"God help us. I don't know how long we can last if we're not rescued pretty soon." they looked desperately around hoping for a light or the sound of a plane, but the sky and the sea were empty.

Silence settled over them, each wondering if he would ever see home and family again.

*Aboard Homing Bird*

Shortly after Heavenly Body left the target area, Homing Bird was crossing the coast of Japan en route to the target area. Although the same flight-stopping winds were encountered and the flak was even heavier, the crew managed to drop their bombs right on target, but not before flak had ruptured the #3 gas tank and knocked out the #2 engine.

"Manifold pressure's down to 50 inches." Wing commented.

"Yeah, and we can only make 2600 RPMs on three engines. We can't keep formation. We're on our own." Cash replied.

"How about———.

"Zeroes at ten o clock. Zeroes coming in." Already guns were blazing away as Cash started avoiding action. Then just as suddenly as they had appeared the Japs were gone.

"Scared 'em off this time."

"There's plenty more around ."

"We're ready for them." gunners voices came through loud and clear. It was this spirit that enabled Homing Bird to fight off thirty attacks before they were well out to sea.

Meanwhile fuel was transferred from the damaged #2 engine to #3 engine and once out at sea, #3 engine was feathered and the remaining fuel transferred to #4.

"I reckon we've got enough gas for about four hours." the flight engineer advised.

"That'll leave us a long way from home. There's nothing else for it, we'll have to ditch." said Cash, as he got the radio operator on the intercom and instructed him to send out their position. "Let's hope to God there's a Dumbo around."

*Aboard the Bering Strait*

Still steaming independently on Air-Sea Rescue station as before, time passed slowly on the ship. An error noticed in the gyro compass had been corrected and an exercise in steering casualty drill performed. Watch was set, Condition III.

As usual, Bat was complaining, "If you asks me, being out here is nothing but waste of time.

If one of them planes gets hit, it'll be over the target and that's where they'll ditch. Right next to the coast of Japan."

"How do you know they went to Japan? There's plenty of other targets around."

"It stands to reason. We've got to standby all night and all day. If they wasn't going a long ways we wouldn't be standing by that long. Japan's where they went, if you ask me."

"Well, nobody asks you, right."

"Mores the pity. If I had my——— What's going on? We've changed course!" before anyone could answer, the Exec's voice came over the PA system, "Now hear this, hear this, all hands to rescue stations on the double."

*Aboard the Deacon's Delight*

Ten minutes before reaching the target area, Deacon's Delight was attacked by Jap fighters. With all guns flaming they returned fire as they continued on to the target. Now flak was increasing and this scared off the fighters but not before they hit the Delight's #3 engine. But this didn't stop the Americans from dropping their bombs directly over the aircraft factory.

"Bombs away." brought a cheer from the crew as the plane turned for home.

But the Jap fighters were waiting for them, and in spite of evading action, K-375 was hit several times. #2 engine was damaged and a fire broke out in the radar room. Halloran thought for a while that they would make it back to Tinian as the damage did not appear too severe. Then he noticed oil pressure dropping rapidly in #3 engine which was promptly feathered.

Three minutes later #2 engine became useless. Because the oil fuel line had been shot away, it was impossible to feather it.

"Doesn't look good." Halloran said to Flight engineer Burch, "Got any suggestions?"

"We can increase RPM's on #1 and #4 ? And how about jettisoning all equipment and firing the ammo. That'll reduce the weight and conserve gas.?"

"Right, that ought to help. With any luck we might make it back to Tinian." and telling the crew how things looked, he instructed them to throw out all loose equipment, flak suits, helmets, food kits, bombsights, the radar set which had been wrecked by 20mm gunfire and to fire most of the ammo from the machine gun belts.

But worse was to come. Icing conditions forced the plane down to 6,000 ft. fuel was very low. Navigator Paul Shuford was doing his damnedest to keep the plane on course. Though enemy fire had destroyed every mechanical means of navigation, Loran, radar, radio compass, Shuford reported to Halloran that he was confidant they were still on course.

By now, Halloran knew there was nothing else for it. They would have to ditch. Calling the crew he gave them the choice of bailing out and taking their chances on their own or sticking with the plane and ditching together. Unanimously, the crew voted to stick together and ditch.

"I'll get you as close to Uncle Sam as I can and, God willing, we'll get picked up."

He knew their chances were slim. Although an Air Sea Rescue Task Force was established with AF bombers, Navy planes and ships posting a rescue line along the route to Japan, hundreds of airmen and planes were lost and never heard of again. The Pacific is a pretty big ocean and the Japs still controlled a large part of it. Also, it is hard to spot a plane or a life raft in daylight under the best of conditions when an exact position is given, but at night and in a rough sea they would need an awful lot of luck. Especially as the navigator had to depend on his own judgement and skill and had no other way of checking their position.

"All tanks empty, sir, I've sucked out the last drops." the Flight

Engineer reported.

"Thanks, Sam." Halloran acknowledged and reaching over he switched on his emergency signalling equipment.

The crew were already in ditching positions except for the radio operator who had tried to open the astrodome by pulling on the strap and now was trying to break it open with an axe.

Twenty year old Corporal Larson, left gunner, looked out but all he could see was absolute darkness. Not even a star was to be seen. How could they be found at night, he wondered. It was an awful big ocean and there were sharks. He was scared but he didn't show it. Later, he said he knew they had the best pilot ever and he'd do his best for them.

Desperately, Halloran tried to pierce the darkness in hopes of seeing some sign of life below, but there was nothing but impenetrable blackness. Then, suddenly a search light swept straight up into the sky a few miles west of them. There was no way of knowing whether it was a friend or foe, but with no gas they were beyond caring. "Here we go. Hang on." shouted Halloran, aiming the plane straight into the light. The time was 2308.

As the crew said later , they were in luck. Down below was the Bering Strait! The ship's radio operator had picked up the plane's emergency call. Immediately the skipper ordered full speed ahead and changing course, the ship raced to the crippled plane. At the same time the skipper ordered the ship's searchlights to be beamed skywards risking revealing the ship's position to the Japs, in the hope that the B-29 would see the light and know help was on the way.

Circling the ship twice, Halloran came into the wind and ditched a thousand yards ahead of the Bering Strait. The plane hit tail first with a terrific thud, then settled on the waves.

Immediately, the plane filled with water. Desperately, every man scrambled out of their assigned exits fearing the plane would sink and take them with it.

The Bering Strait's searchlights were now deflected on to the sea alongside, and the ship's lifeboat was racing towards the wreckage of the plane.

In eleven minutes the whole crew were safely aboard the ship. Sgt. Serkin was the only one injured. He was taken to the sick bay with a badly lacerated leg requiring 17 deep and 17 skin stitches.

The rest of the crew were given medicinal brandy, a hot shower and a good meal before they thankfully fell asleep.

Meanwhile, between 0 to 0300 hrs that night, Sunday 11th, the sailors had the motor whale boat and the personnel boat out picking up all floating material from the ditched aircraft. Next the ship opened fire on the plane trying to sink it, but the empty 'Tokyo' fuel tanks were full of air and kept it afloat.

Halloran, who had been watching, asked the skipper why he didn't let the plane take its time, "When the air is out of those empty fuel tanks, it'll sink on its own."

"We've got to sink it now. All trace of it must be removed so no other ship or plane wastes time looking for survivors. I'll have to ram it." and so Deacon's Delight was rammed and broken in half. First the engine and wing section sank and then the tail, and they watched with an awful sense of loss as she slowly disappeared beneath the waves.

"Well, we'd better get some sleep while we can. You've had a long day." the skipper said to Halloran. "Yes, I'm ready to turn in and thanks to you we've got a bunk to sleep in." their eyes met exchanging a look which would only be understood by those whose lives were in danger every hour of the day.

It seemed to the crew of Deacon's Delight that they had just gotten to sleep when they were startled out of their slumbers at 0630 by gongs clanging, alarms bells ringing and orders roaring over the PA. "What's going on for God's sake." a sleepy airman muttered.

"General Quarters. Jap planes sighted." a sailor shouted running to his battle station.

"Christ! you'd think the whole Jap Army and Navy were after us by the noise they make. But they sure get you up and running." Kays said, making his way back to his bunk when he discovered the Japs were not attacking the ship and it was not about to sink.

At 0708 the ship was secured from General Quarters and normal routine was in force once more. But it didn't last long , at 1130 voice contact was made with a Dumbo plane reporting two life rafts at a position about 55 miles distant, close to Iwo Jima which was still in Japanese hands. Course was changed and for the next four hours the ship steamed on to rescue the survivors.

"Wonder who they are? They're lucky that Dumbo plane found

them and sent their position." Knutson remarked to one of the sailors.

"Hope we get to them before the Japs do. They're pretty close to Iwo. I knew them flyboys would ditch close to the Japs" Bat answered.

*Aboard the life rafts of Homing Bird*

In spite of a fifty knot wind and a swell of eight feet, the crew were able to get out without serious injury when the plane hit the ocean. Five men managed to get into one of the two seven man rafts and six got into the other. They paddled away from the aircraft and made themselves as comfortable as they could for the night. In the morning they discovered that they had lost touch with each other in the darkness, but they were able to make contact again and decided to tie the two rafts together. The dye marker was poured over the side and the men waited anxiously watching the horizon for a ship.

All were nauseous and bruised from the ditching but the charms from the accessory kits in the life rafts, relieved the nausea somewhat.

About 1000 they saw a Navy PB4Y1 coming towards them. Immediately some of the men focussed their signalling mirrors on the plane willing it to spot them.

"Come on, Navy. Come on. We're waiting for you." they shouted and, as if answering, the plane began circling their position.

"They can't pick us up, but they'll send help. " Cash said, as he saw the men's anxiety. "It's only a matter of time."

"Yeah, but the Japs could come too." said Odam, voicing their fears.

Then they saw a life raft dropping from the plane as it flew off. They paddled towards it, but time after time the rough seas forced them away and they realized it was impossible to secure it in the heavy seas.

"There goes the chow." Slevin muttered as the waves washed over the life raft taking their hopes of food and water with it.

*Aboard the Bering Strait.*

Meanwhile, the Bering Strait was steaming towards them on various courses and speeds. The plane had contacted the ship and given the present position of the life rafts.

Hearing that the ship was answering another distress call, the crew of Deacon's Delight were anxiously scanning the sea hoping to sight the airmen or the remains of the aircraft. "Wonder whose plane it is?" Shuford said to Larson.

"Dunno, hope they'll be as lucky as we were."

They stood there side by side, silently urging the ship on. Would they get there in time? Was the crew still alive? Time was going on, it was almost 1550. Soon it would be dark. Then to their relief they heard the order, "Man rescue stations." and they knew something had been sighted.

"Thank God." Larson muttered.

Down in the life rafts, Cash was the first to sight the ship, then all the exhausted survivors of Homing Bird spotted it and raised a great cheer. "Here comes the Navy."

By 1605 the ship was alongside with all engines stopped. "I've never been so glad to see a ship." said Phil Neverman as they were helped on board the starboard gangway.

While the plane crew was being made comfortable with a hot shower, fresh dry clothes and a hot meal, and exchanging banter with the crew of Deacon's Delight, who were more than delighted to see them, the sailors were hoisting all raft equipment and materials on board.

The skipper was anxious to get moving as quickly as possible as they had received warning of a Jap ship in the area. Still at General Quarters, they were under way by 1616. But all was quiet and at 1835, the ship was secured from General Quarters and the Watch set, Condition III.

*Aboard the life rafts of Heavenly Body*

All through that night Blackwell and Weigel somehow supported Holt between the two dinghies beating off the sharks with the paddles.. When morning came they hopefully searched the sea and sky looking for rescue. The big raft was busy pouring sea marker dye into the ocean. "They should spot that from the air pretty easy." Townsend said looking up at the sky, but all was empty and silent.

"Where is everybody? There's not even a Jap around." said Blackwell. The hours passed with terrible slowness, Weigel was weak and sick, coughing up blood now and again which kept the sharks close to their little raft. Then around noon a speck appeared among the clouds. "Is it a plane ?" Blackwell asked.

"Can't tell yet. Hope its not a Jap."

Hardly daring to hope they watched the speck grow larger and saw it was a plane. "It's Navy! I can see the markings." Holt shouted. and sure enough they saw it was a seaplane with US Navy markings.

They all began shouting and waving afraid it might not see them, but they need not have worried. It waggled its wings as it came nearer and dropped a small package attached to a parachute

The men paddled towards it with all their remaining strength afraid they might lose it. Pulling it out of the ocean, they found it contained cans of water, Charms and cigarettes.

"Thank God, this means they know where we are and they'll send help."

It was about 1510 that afternoon, when a ship, the USS Robert E. Smith, appeared on the horizon. The plane had given the location of the life rafts and soon the ship was along sides.

Sult, Townsend, Hansen and Hupman were picked up first. Then Weigel, Blackwell and Holt were located. As they were being helped on board, one of the sharks that had been bothering them for hours was found skulking under their life raft.

After a quick, hot shower they were led to bunks in the sick bay and given soup laced with brandy. They all said later, that they went to sleep immediately and didn't wake up for hours.

When they did wake up they had another drink of the same and didn't really know what was going on until they were given a good dinner and slept right through until Monday 12th. Feb.

On Monday 12th, The first thing the plane crew asked was, "Any news of the rest of the crew."

"Sorry fellas , nothing so far. With this weather and this sea it doesn't look good. But you'll be transferred to the Bering Strait this morning and she might have some news."

The men were silent, they had hoped something might have come in during the night.

"Well, the Dumbo might have some news. There's still a chance they've been picked up." Francis Sult said, but without much conviction. The force of the impact when they hit the water made it almost impossible for Lowry to escape alive, and if the others had managed to get out, they would surely have heard or seen something of them during all the time they were waiting to be rescued.

But they didn't have much time to conjecture, by 0928 they were in the motor whaleboat transferring to the Bering Strait which was to be their home for the next five days.

Suddenly, right out of the blue as they were all enjoying the first steak they'd had in a long time, Ernie Holt exclaimed, "It was my 21st birthday yesterday and I forgot all about it!"

# ON STATION

## FEBRUARY 1945

With 28 survivors on board as passengers things were a bit tight on the Bering Strait. But somehow quarters were found and the crew did all they could to help the exhausted airmen settle in to the strange new life on board ship. Food and sleep were what they needed most. All agreed the chow was the best they'd had in a long time. On Tinian all they got was tinned stuff. Water was short and they had to make do with a mere trickle from a leaky pipe for a shower. Most of them fell dead asleep after dinner, but Dick Hansen for some reason, couldn't lie still. The unaccustomed sound of the ship's engines as they changed course and speed disturbed him, though he couldn't think why. After all, the planes at Tinian made a lot more noise. Finally, about 0130, he got up and went on deck. A look out recognized him and Hansen asked why the ship was moving so slowly and changing course so often.

"Looking for survivors. Another plane ditched in this area so we're making a parallel search." The man kept his eyes on the water as he answered.

"Do you know the call number?" Hansen wondered if the plane was from his squadron.

"No, sir, I don't. The Old man, I mean the Skipper or the OOD might."

"Is the Captain on the bridge?"

"Yeah, he likes to keep an eye on things when we're searching."

Suddenly the running lights went out and the ship began changing course.

"Better get below, sir. Might be in for trouble."

Realizing the look out was politely telling him to get the hell out of the way, Hansen went below and turned in. Next morning he heard that it was an unidentified aircraft in the vicinity that had caused the order to turn off running lights and although the search continued throughout the night, no sign of survivors was found.

Tuesday, February 13 th was spent steaming as before on various courses and speeds. From 1200-1600 hrs the ship was again on parallel search for survivors. Then that evening just after the ship had secured from General Quarters and War Condition 111 set, an Emergency signal was received from a B-29. The plane had been shot up and feared it would not be able to reach base.

"God, I hope they're as lucky as we were." McComber said. Anxiously, they all waited, saying a silent prayer as the 24" searchlights were turned on to aid the distressed plane.

"Isn't that dangerous?" one of the airmen asked Bat. "Supposing a Jap spots us."

"Yeah, its dangerous, but the skipper thinks it helps you flyboys ditch." Five minutes later news came over the PA. "Plane reports - made it to base."

The same thing happened at 2338 and course was changed and speed increased as the ship tried to contact and identify another distressed plane. But when contact was lost and no more flares seen, searchlights were turned off.

It was always a let down when contact is lost. The horrible thought of being ditched and alone in the dark emptiness of sky and sea with sharks waiting below, was the worst nightmare of most men out there.

For the air crews the sea was a foreign element - the air was their friend and support. That was why they were aviators. They loved the freedom of the skies, the exhilaration of rising above it all, of leaving all the crud of the earth behind. Even in war all this still existed.

For the sailors, of course, the sea was their element. But the sea was like a capricious, temperamental lover whose beauty and mystery held them captive in spite of her cruelly violent storms and tempests which could drown them in the depths of her being.

By and large, the Army, including the Army Air Corps, looked on the Navy as "Fancy Dans" who had everything easy compared with themselves who had to rough it and bear all the burdens. Sailors had good, regular chow and decent quarters.

In return the Navy considered the Army and Army Air an uncouth lot who simply bulled their way through and managed to get promoted twice as fast as they did.

As Bat pointed out, "We might have the chow, but you have the girls. I hear that you flyboys and the GIs get the pick of the girls on them islands. We haven't had a girl for I don't know how long."

"That's right." said Hukk, "If you ask me, I'd take girls over chow any time."

"And another thing, you lot get a change of scenery.

We're stuck out here looking at nothing but sea day after day doing the same old things in the same old place."

"That's why you pick us up. You won't often see good-looking guys like us around."

So the good natured banter went on and it was enlightening to both to get to know more about each other's service. By the time the ship put in to Tanapang Harbor, Saipan, on the 15th Feb., to put the passengers ashore, these Army and Navy men had a healthy respect for each other and had made lasting friendships.

Sailors were able to go ashore for a couple of beers and to feel dry land under their feet for an hour or two, but there wasn't time for much else.

In preparation for the landing on Iwo Jima on D Day Feb 19th, Navy Air and the B-29s were making more bombing raids on Tokyo to reduce the number of Japanese planes available for use against the Iwo landings. On February 16th, anxious to reduce the number of Kamikazis threatening the fleet, aircraft of Task Force 58 bombed Tokyo and destroyed more than three hundred planes on the ground.

For logistical purposes the Bering Strait was moored in Tanapang Harbor, but on the 19th the she was back steaming on station keeping a lookout for Kamikazis. The ship had been attacked twice, when she received a distress call from B-29 Happy 41, of the 871 Squadron, 497 Bomb Group, saying they were about to ditch.

No bearings were given but a Dumbo plane sighted the wreckage and was able to give a position report to the ship. This was fortunate because the damaged plane hit the water with such force that it broke up and sank, trapping five men who drowned in the wreckage.

Arriving at the scene, 12 miles north of Pagan Island, the Bering Strait turned on the search lights, sighted the survivors and hove-to in the midst of them. One had been swimming without a life jacket for two hours, another had only the use of a partially inflated boat, but five, Captain C. H. Smith, Lt. A. E. Austin, Cpls A. W. Fletcher; B G. Budd and N. S. Garrick, were saved. All were very weak and sick. The men were spotted in the darkness because they had tiny lights pinned to their life jackets which they had stolen from the Navy "on personal initiative."

Happy 41's survivors were disembarked two days later at Saipan very thankful to put their feet back on solid ground and the Bering Strait steamed back on station.

Meanwhile the terrible struggle for Iwo Jima continued. General Holland Smith said that "Iwo Jima was the most savage and most costly battle in the history of the Marine Corps." Every inch of ground had to be fought for under the most exacting and bloody conditions.

Then, in the early hours of February 23 there was a break through. A patrol consisting of Sgt. H. O. Hansen, PlSgts. E. I. Thomas, J. R. Michaels and Cpl. C. W Lindberg led by Lt Harold G. Schrier, scaled Mount Suribachi. Scrambling over the rim of the crater, some Japanese on the opposite side fired on them and a short but fierce fight developed. Just as it ended, about 10:20 a.m., a piece of iron pipe was found and a small flag tied to it. This was quickly raised and photographed by Sgt. Lou Lowry. As this flag was too small to be seen from the beach another Marine went aboard the LST 779 and asked for the biggest flag they had.

Joe Hopkins, Captain of this ship, brought out a somewhat tattered flag that had flown over a heavy cruiser and this was carried up to the summit, attached to another iron pipe and raised by five Marines and one Navy corpsman.

This second raising was the source of the famous picture taken by Joe Rosenthal and the inspiration for Felix de Weldon's magnificent Memorial sculpture in Washington D.C. This commemorates and honors all those Marines who fought in the battle for Iwo Jima. Men of all ranks fought with uncommon valor. Deeds of heroism were common. Twenty two Marines won Medals of Honor.

Never to before gotten are the corpsmen who gave their lives giving aid to the wounded. As an example of their bravery are these abbreviated citations of two Navy corpsmen, Pharmacist's Mate Third Class, USNR, Jack Williams, born in Harrison, Arkansas, who, while serving with the 3rd Battalion 28th Marines during operations against the enemy on Iwo Jima, "by his courageous determination, unwavering fortitude and valiant performance of duty, served as an inspiring example of heroism, in keeping with the highest traditions of the U.S. Naval Service. He gallantly gave his life for his country."

Pharmacist's Mate First Class. U.S. Navy, John Harlan Willis, born in Columbia, Tennessee, as Platoon Corpsman serving with the 3rd Battalion 27th Marines during operations against the enemy on Iwo Jima was awarded the Medal of Honor "for conspicuous gallantry and intrepidity at the risk of his own life above and beyond the call of duty. Willis calmly continued to administer blood plasma to his patient, hurling back 8 grenades before the ninth exploded in his hand and instantly killed him."

The island was not finally secured until the 26th March. The Japanese fought even after all food and water was gone, knowing there was no hope of escape or possibility of reinforcements.

The count of Japanese killed and sealed up in caves was 20,703. The Marines lost 215 officers and 4,339 men killed in action and 60 officers and 1,271 men dead of wounds.

Was it worth the enormous loss of life? This question has often been asked. The consensus is that the taking of Iwo Jima shortened the war and saved the lives of thousands of Army airmen.

By the end of the war approximately 2,500 B-29s had landed on the island saving the lives of thousands of crew.

Leonard Carpi a B-29 pilot in the Pacific, now a successful dental surgeon who completed 35 missions over Japan, says "We received battle damage several times and I thank the Navy for being available to us and the Marines who acquired Iwo Jima. Iwo jima saved my life seven times. We could never have made it back to Tinian those seven times."

# IN THE UNITED STATES OF AMERICA

## FEBRUARY 1945

As the war dragged on the families of servicemen were growing more and more anxious about their loved ones, especially those who had been in the Armed Forces since the beginning of the war and who were in the far off Pacific. The new B-29 bomber, was supposed to bring Japan to its knees, but so far it had only brought great losses of airmen and planes with very little to show for it.

It seemed as if the war would never end. Tears that had been shed silently and in secret could no longer be hidden. Every knock at the door sounded like a death knell. Families who had loved ones flying the B-29s knew the odds of being lost in the vast Pacific and they had heard of the harsh treatment given to prisoners of war in Japan and they couldn't help fearing the worst.

"Oh, God, bring him home safe. I don't care if he's wounded, we'll take care of him. Just bring him back." was the prayer constantly uttered by them all.

On the evening of February 18th, Samuel Hupman, father of Sgt William Hupman, of the Heavenly Body, received the following telegram,

THE SECRETARY OF WAR DESIRES ME TO EXPRESS HIS DEEP REGRET THAT YOUR SON SERGEANT WILLIAM R. HUPMAN HAS BEEN REPORTED MISSING IN ACTION

SINCE TEN FEBRUARY IN PACIFIC OCEAN AREA IF FURTHER DETAILS OR OTHER INFORMATION ARE RECEIVED YOU WILL BE PROMPTLY NOTIFIED.
THE ADJUTANT GENERAL.

Sam Hupman knew what was in it before he tore the envelope open. White-faced and heartbroken he handed it to his wife.

"I don't believe it. My Bill isn't dead. He can't be. He's only 20 years old. It says, missing in action, it doesn't say he's dead."

Putting his arm around her Sam said, "It's a good big ocean, mother."

"I know that, but they have those Sea Rescue and Air ships or something waiting for them. It said that in the paper, and, don't you remember, Bill told us about it in one of his letters?"

"Yeah, I remember that, but its eight days since he was posted missing. You'd think he would be picked up by now."

"I've heard of people being picked up weeks after they been ship wrecked." Mrs. Hupman wasn't ready to give up hope.

"Well, there's one thing we can do. Bill gave us the address of some of the men in the same crew. I'll call and ask them if they know anything."

And so they contacted two other families only to find they had received the same news about their son. In fact all members of the crew of Heavenly Body were reported Missing in Action.

They read the telegram over and over, Bill's mother insisting that they wouldn't have mentioned "further details" if they were sure he was dead. But as the days and then a week went by, even she was lost hope.

One night Sam found her in their son's room holding one of his school books, sobbing bitterly as she turned the pages. Just then there was a knock on the door.

"Don't answer it, Sam. I just can't talk to anyone now."

Friends and neighbors had been coming by to try and help but all Bill's mother wanted now was to be alone with her memories.

"I'd best go see who it is. You stay here. You don't have to see anyone. I'll say you're taking a nap or something."

Sam hurried down to the open the door and found it was Western Union with another telegram. Sam's heart turned over. Was this it? Were they confirming Bill's death? He opened it quickly and for a moment he couldn't believe what he saw. Then he raced up the stairs two at a time, "It's from the Air Corps. He's alive! He's O.K.! Look!" and he handed the telegram to his wife.

Hardly able to believe it, she took the telegram and slowly read it aloud.

AM PLEASED TO INFORM YOU YOUR SON SERGEANT WILLIAM R. HUPMAN RETURNED TO DUTY.
THE ADJUTANT GENERAL.

While no one knows for sure what happened to Lowry, Morton, O'Connor and Mooty, it was presumed that they died on impact when the plane broke up, but the rest of the crew were safe.

Later a letter from Bill arrived and the Hupmans learned what had happened to them.

After five days on board the Bering Strait during which time they said they had the best food they'd had for a year, they were put ashore at Tanapag Harbor, Saipan. From there they were flown back to Tinian. Only to find that their tents had been taken down and all their belongings including clothing, put in the warehouse because they had been posted Missing in Action and no one expected them to return alive.

"Mom," Bill wrote, "I'm sure glad you couldn't hear what we said while we were trying to find our stuff. It should have burnt their ears off. We never did get all our stuff back.

"They were all pretty good to us though and the flight surgeon went over us pretty thorough to see if we were fit for flight duty.

"Then we were sent to Hawaii for two weeks R.& R. Families in Hawaii had signed up to take airmen on leave and they are seeing to it that we have a good time."

By February 26 the crew was back on duty in Tinian getting ready to fly again.

Sometimes families waited for many long months hoping to hear that loved ones were alive and well, only to be told they were presumed dead.

The hardest wait was when a family had been told that a relative was a prisoner of the Japanese. Stories of the hardships and atrocities suffered by prisoners in the camps, terrified those with loved ones fighting in the Pacific.

Many prisoners were in camps on lonely islands and were often moved from one camp to another so there was rarely much news of them.

Lt. David Witts, USA, who was in the 2nd Emergency Sea Rescue Squadron, 13th Army Air force, operating in the Pacific from July 1944 - July 1945, tells how Captain Clarence L. Solander a pilot in this same squadron, was flying a special mission when he was successful in picking up seven persons. They were Corporals, William J. Belchus, USA; Alberto D. Pashee, USA; Rufus W. Smith, USMC; Pfcs Edwin A. Petry, USA; Eugene Nielsen and one civilian, Thomas F. Loudon, all of whom had been prisoners for nearly three years.

These men were taken prisoner following the fall of Bataan and Corregidor in May 1942. First they were confined in a camp near Manila and later transferred with a group of three hundred to Puerte Princess, Palawan in 1943. Later 150 of these men were transferred elsewhere leaving 150 behind who were employed building roads and air strips in the area.

Early in December 1944, US Bombers began to range over Palawan bombing the air strip and installations there.

"That's when they started beating us up. Them Japs had a mortal fear of our four engine bombers and they'd take it out on us each time they came over. It was pretty bad, I can tell you - what with the rotten food and everything else, we wondered if we could stick it out."

"That old fella, Louden, though, he was a sharp one. He'd been a trader in Bataan and some of those islands for years. He could speak the lingo and understood some Japanese. He told us that there was a guerilla group on the island and if we could escape and get out, they'd help us.

"Well, we kept looking for a chance. We thought the best time would be when our bombers were over, but them Japs kept a close eye on us day and night.

"Old Louden, though, managed to get out. One morning we found he was gone. Somehow he gave them Japs the slip and got away."

It was lucky that he did. On the 14th. of December 1944 the

Japanese called an Air Raid alert and herded all the prisoners into protecting trenches. But this time there was no air raid. As soon as the prisoners were all lying in the trenches, trucks were driven in and gasoline was pumped over them and ignited.

Some died quickly, others screaming in agony struggled to get out of the flaming mud of the trenches only to sink back to their death. A few who got out and scattered desperately through the flames and smoke of the furnace, were mowed down by the machine guns stationed in and around the camp.

No pity, no mercy was shown. All had to be killed so none would be left to tell the tale.

By some miracle, a few managed to escape into the jungle. Among them, the men that Captain Solander picked up. As one of them said,

"We went as fast as we could through that jungle. Some of us had bad burns, but we didn't take no notice then, all we wanted was to get far enough away before they came after us.

"God! it was awful. I'll never forget the screams and the smell of burning. We could still smell it out there in the jungle.

"With all the screaming and the flames and the confusion, we hoped they hadn't seen us get away, but they did and it wasn't long before we heard them coming behind us.

"Some tried to hide under the low bushes and vines and stuff, but the Japs got them and shot them right there. I don't know why we were lucky - we were ahead. We gained a bit of time while they were getting the others out and shooting them and they might have thought they'd got us all. Anyhoo, we moved on as quiet as we could 'til it got dark.

"We had nothing. We knew we couldn't last long without water. We'd sweated so much that we were all dried out and our burns were giving us hell, too. Most of our clothes were burned off and we had no protection against the thorns on the vines and the insects that are everywhere on those damn islands.

"I began to think the guys the Japs got were the lucky ones. They went quick. None of us could sleep. What with the pain and thirst and listening for the Japs, we couldn't rest. It seemed years 'til morning.

"Then, soon after it got light, just as we was starting up, we heard someone coming. You'll never believe this. We couldn't. It was old Louden! The old guy from the camp! "God! Were we glad to see him!. Well, that old guy, and he was 75 years old, mind you, had heard the shots and guessed there was something going on and come to take a look.

"He shared out the water and food he had with him and then led us to the guerilla camp up in the hills."

Here the man had to pause for a bit as he was overcome by the memories, but he continued, "Hell, I still can't talk of that old guy without breaking up. Well, he'd got an old patched up radio transmitter there in that camp and he sent out the message that fixed up the rendezvous at Brookes Point - allowing time to lead us there. He knew what he was doing all right.

"Them guerillas gave us some clothes and did what they could for us, but they didn't have much. Old Louden was anxious to get us going, he knew the Japs were after him and he was afraid that they might have picked up his radio transmissions.

"He said he'd guide us to Brookes Point as we'd never find our way over the mountains and through the jungle on our own. He didn't seem to worry about the distance - it turned out to be about 75 miles and that's a lot longer in the jungle than on a good road, I can tell you.

"Anyhoo, he got us there and were we glad to see that plane!" It seemed no time at all until they had us back at their base and we saw the good old Stars and Stripes once again. I'll never forget that sight and what it meant to all of us. When we was captured at Bataan our flag was in the dust. All we could think of when we got off that plane was to thank God that we lived to see it flying high above us.

The crew of the plane, "Playmate" 42, of the 2nd Emergency Rescue Squadron, 13th Army Air Force, never forgot the gratitude of these men or their pride when they saw the hundreds of fighters and bombers assembled on the airbase back at Moratai. Then they were sure that we'd soon have the Japs finished off.

# TINIAN ISLAND

## MARCH 1945

March 1945 saw a change in the method of attack on Japan.

High altitude precision bombing of priority targets by B-29s had been attempted time after time but with limited success. The Navy's daring low level air raids on Tokyo had made great headlines in the U.S. making General LeMay desperately anxious to prove that his B-29s could do just as well if not better then the Navy.

To bring the war home to the Japanese people and prove to them that their homeland was not safe from destruction as they had been told, a series of low level incendiary attacks by B-29s on the urban areas of Japanese cities, was planned.

By 1944 scientists of the Army's Chemical Warfare service had developed a more advanced type of incendiary bomb, the M-69.

It weighed 6 lbs and contained napalm. When napalm is set on fire it flows like a river of flame destroying everything in its path.

As most Japanese buildings were of wood, bamboo and paper, it was felt that this type of bomb would prove eminently destructive.

On the night of the 9-10th March, 32 aircraft of the 9th Bombardment Group, 313 Bomber Wing, were on their way with all other units of the XX1 Command to attack the urban areas of Tokyo with incendiary bombs. Among these were two B-29s from the 505 Bomber Group. One named by its crew ' Domino 7' from the 1st Squadron and one from the 482nd Squadron with ' Gordon II' painted on its side.

Both crews were young and enthusiastic and eager to do a good job on this mission which would test the new and untried method of attack. Guns and extra fuel tanks would not be carried and they would fly in at 5000 ft. They had not been told about it until the pre flight briefing and it added a new and dangerous excitement to the flight.

"The engineers weren't too happy about the bomb bay tanks being removed. It sure does cut down on fuel. But we can land on Iwo if we're short." Pilot MacCaskill of 'Gordon II' remarked.

"Yeah, thank God for Iwo. Clearing the Japs out of there has already saved a lot of lives." Cliff MacComber answered, but I think the predictions are that the fuel will last and cutting all the extra weight means we can carry a much heavier bomb load."

"That's true and the more we drop at one time the better.

If this works out it should shorten the war."

"God, I hope so! It's gone on too long."

Heavy turbulence kept conversation at a minimum on the long trip, but this cleared up as they neared Japan. It was about one thirty a.m., that they got sight of Tokyo - it was a sight they would never forget. The city was nothing but a mass of flame and smoke rising up higher than Fujiyama itself.

The lead planes had arrived about 11:45 and flown over the city seeding one napalm bomb every 100 feet making an enormous cross of flaming fire to guide in the main body of B-29s. By now these were stacking up above the city from 10,000 ft. down to below 5,000 ft.

"Christ! the whole city's on fire already. They'll never put that out." Ernie Deutch of Domino 7 exclaimed.

"There'll be nothing left of Tokyo by the time we've all dropped our load. There's never been anything like this." Don Reed answered. "LeMay said he'd destroy Tokyo and he's done it."

"Thank God they don't have any fighters out. They'd easily get us in this light."

"Yeah, and there's not much flak so far."

"Don't talk too soon. Look at that." A B-29 got a direct hit and exploded in a tremendous ball of flame as it fell into the fires below.

"God! that's one of ours."

"Yeah. The A.A. seems to be concentrated in the center of the city. We'd better watch that as we go in."

Guns and ammunition had been removed from the B-29s to make more room for bombs on General LeMay's order, so they were thankful that so far, no Japanese fighters were in sight.

Plane after plane flew over the city scarcely a minute apart, each dropping clusters of incendiary and oil bombs. The bomb bays were fitted with an intervalometer, a timing mechanism which was coordinated with the bomber's ground speed and set to drop the clusters every fifty feet. While the target area included Tokyo's industrial and commercial districts it also included a residential area where approximately 100,000 people per square mile, were packed in.

As Domino 7 made its bomb run across the city, the fires fed by a fierce wind, turned the city center into a holocaust.

Suddenly the great plane was tossed in the air by a thermal updraft and just as suddenly it dropped a thousand feet into the flames.. Desperately the pilot struggled to gain control in spite of being thrown against the metal and nearly knocked out, but just as he was leveling off, flak came streaking up and hit the starboard engine. Immediately it faltered and died.

"God, let's get out of here fast."

"Do'ya think we can make it?"

"We'll give it a damn good try." Captain Hargrove answered firmly.

*Aboard Gordon II*

Meanwhile Gordon II had arrived over Tokyo and was being tossed around by the turbulence as the thermal drafts increased.

"Christ! It looks like Hell itself down there." "They don't need any more bombs on that lot." McComber answered. "But we've got to unload anyhow."

"Yeah, its a good thing its automatic. With all this turbulence I can't keep the damn plane on course."

"Bombs away. Captain." the chief bombardier shouted through the intercom. "For God's sake get us out before we're roasted alive."

"We're on our way." and the plane turned and started for home, passing more B-29s as they went.

"Christ! they're still coming!" and they were. For nearly three hours the B-29s kept coming. Even though the turbulence and smoke kept them from the center of the city, they bombed the outskirts and any place there was a dark spot. Those who came late say they have never forgotten the smell of burning flesh that the smoke brought into the cockpit. Smoke surrounded them, blackening the silver paint of the fuselage with soot..

The stench clung to their flight suits for weeks. Some said they can still smell it to this day.

No sooner had Gordon II set course for home when the plane was caught in a burst of heavy flak. Pressure inside the plane began falling and an ominous oil leak appeared in no 1 engine.

"God! we're riddled with holes." McComber exclaimed.

"Yeah, and we've got an oil leak. I'll have to cut that engine. It must have had a direct hit." the pilot answered .

"Check if anyone's injured will you and see what the damage is back there."

"O.K."

Damage to the plane was considerable but no one was seriously injured.

"Will we be able to make it back, skipper?"

"We'll need a lot of luck to get back to Tinian, but we should be able to ditch near enough to Dumbo to get picked up if no more damage shows up." and picking up the intercom the captain ordered the radio operator to contact Dumbo.

"I want to be sure we're in communication should we need to ditch."

A few minutes later the radio operator reported, "No luck yet, Captain."

"Keep trying."

"Right, I'm doing my damnedest, sir." and he was. In addition to everything else, the radio operator was praying silently for help from somewhere. He hated the sea with a terrible hatred. It was too wet, too rough, too unpredictable and there was too much of it. That was why he picked the Air Corps not the Navy. The farther away from the sea, the happier he was. He couldn't bear the thought of a watery grave. To be stuck in the element he hated for all eternity was too much. He deserved something better. Hadn't he always done his best? Weren't there angels or some sort of things that hang out in the air to save people? Oh God, send one or two or make one of those Navy Dumbos answer me.

But there was no answer from above or below.

*Aboard the Bering Strait*

On the night of the 9-l0th March, the darkened Bering Strait was steaming independently on life guard station Lat. 18-00 (N) Long. 145-15 (E) with Condition III War readiness set. Everyone knew something big was going on, but they were not sure what it was.

The first two watches were uneventful then at 0806 the screen showed an Emergency I.F.F. ( Interrogatory Friend or Foe) in the 30 mile range. But , in spite of every effort, it was impossible to make voice contact . Forty minutes later Emergency I.F.F. appeared again, this time in the 65 mile range, only to fade so quickly from the screen that again voice contact could not be made.

"God! I hate to think of them out there trying to get help and not being able to reach us."

"Maybe they reached a Dumbo plane or some other ship and don't need us."

"Let's hope so."

"There's not much we can do if we can't raise a voice."

"Yeah, that's true."

*Aboard Gordon II*

Time was running out for Gordon II. By 1130 it was obvious the plane was in bad trouble. The skipper was struggling to keep the plane in the air until they contacted Air Sea Rescue, but so far they had had no luck.

"If we don't make contact soon we'll just have to take our chances and ditch." the skipper said grimly. "We'll stay airborne as long as we can, but be prepared to ditch."

Like most airmen, what he most dreaded was ditching his plane. Especially in the open sea mostly controlled by enemy air. Next to being forced down over Japan and being taken prisoner, this was the worst that could happen. The plane could break up so they wouldn't have a chance to get out the life rafts and would have only the Mae West to depend on. He was exhausted and so were all the crew, after being in the air for so many hours they didn't have the strength to keep afloat for long.

Well, maybe one of the Dumbo planes would spot them and there was still a chance they would raise the Dumbo ship. And it was daylight thank God.

But by 1220 he knew this was it and grimly he gave the order, "Prepare to ditch."

*Aboard the Bering Strait*

At 1223 Emergency I.F.F. again appeared on the screen and at 1226 both radar and voice contact was made with the distressed plane.

"Its the Gordon II and its preparing to ditch right away, sir."

"What's the bearing?"

"1120 (t) distance 20 miles."

Immediately the ship changed course and went full speed ahead. All Air Sea Rescue stations were manned ready for action.

At 1232 the plane was sighted 9 miles away bearing, 120 (t). Course was changed and at 1236 the plane circled the ship.

"Look's as if he's going for an upwind ditch landing."

"That wind's whipping up the sea, I hope they don't have trouble."

"There they go." they watched anxiously as the plane hit the water sending up mountains of spray.

"God, its breaking up!" the skipper exclaimed seeing the plane break in half from the force of hitting the water. "Stop all engines. Lower the boat."

Immediately the motor whaleboat was lowered into the water.

Hopefully there would be survivors. For a few moments there was only wreckage to be seen. Then there were a few heads bobbing in the water . The wind and waves made it difficult for the survivors to try and swim towards the boat, but the sailors were ready to haul them in and by 1243 the first one was dragged out of the water and into the whaleboat. By 1248 Captain Bernard MacCaskill, Lt.Col. Clifford MacComber, 2nd Lts. Carl Gustavson and Joseph A. Ptazskowske, T/Sgt. Robert Aspinall, S/Sgt Galen Westmoreland, Sgts. Leon Melesky, Marvin Binger, and Julius Rivas survivors of the Gordon II were rescued and welcomed aboard the Bering Strait as passengers. Two of the crew had not been seen since the crash and it was feared that they were killed on contact.

While the survivors were being made comfortable and their injuries attended by the medics, the crew of the whaleboat started recovering the equipment from the plane crash at the same time keeping a lookout for the two missing airmen. The plane had already gone to the bottom which saved the ship the trouble of sinking it. By 1348 all equipment was recovered and the whaleboat hoisted in and the crew was ready for chow, but they were out of luck.

In the meantime another report had come in and course was changed to investigate a ditching at position 18 -39'30"(N), 145 - 59'(E). At 1530 contact was made with a plane identified as B-29 air sea rescue, call number Daredevil 14. This plane reported investigating a ditched plane in distress.

Steaming at 17.7 knots the Bering Strait changed course to make the rescue. A report of Zeroes (Japanese planes) in the vicinity at 1510 made it necessary to set General Quarters until 1842 when watch was set at War Condition III.

Rescue at night is a nightmare. Not only for the ditched crew, but also for the rescuers. Its hard to enough to sight survivors in choppy seas when the sun is shining, but in the darkness of night it is almost impossible. There is the added danger of running down survivors. The fact that this crew had been in the water for some considerable time before they were sighted, meant they were so exhausted they could easily give up and sink to the bottom.

The Bering Strait was well aware of all this and so the ship would risk itself by turning on a searchlight for a few moments or firing a flare to let the survivors know that help was on the way and encourage them to hold on a bit longer.

At 1995 the ship fired a single green flare and two minutes later a light appeared on the horizon bearing, 210 (t).

Changing course, the Bering Strait fired another single green flare and then a light was sighted at bearing 2150 (t) It was the Dumbo plane Dare Devil, circling over survivors. The Bering Strait continued firing flares at regular intervals and the plane acknowledged by showing their white landing light.

"Thank God that Dumbo plane's still around we'll be able to sight any survivors in that white light. Have the masthead and side lights turned on."

"Aye, Aye, sir."

By now all Air-Sea Rescue Stations were manned once more and, shortly after, a light was sighted on the surface of the water. "Looks like it might be a life raft."

"Yeah. Look, there's another flashing light."

"Lower the whale boat."

"Aye, Aye, sir."

Immediately the whaleboat hit the water the motor was started and on its way to a life raft that showed up in the light from the Dumbo overhead.

"Looks like there's four or five men there."

"Yeah." slowing the motor, the whaleboat moved alongside the bobbing life raft and willing hands grabbed the men by whatever was nearest, hands, hair, legs and pulled them aboard.

The searchlight swept over the sea and two more lifeboats showed up paddling towards them. In five minutes Domino 7's entire crew, Lt. Muriel Hargrave, 2nd Lts. Ernest Deutch, Donald Reed, William Brabham, M/Sgt. David Nesmith, S/Sgt. John Schoonmaker, Sgts. William T. Cook, Edward Albraicht, Richard Giliman, and Cpl. Thomas A Cerro, were in the whaleboat and hoisted aboard the Bering Strait.

"Thank God for the US Navy. Are we glad to see you."

"And we're glad to welcome you on board. We've got some friends of yours who'll be more than glad to see you. We picked them up a bit earlier."

So, forgetting for the moment everything they'd been through, the two crews drank the health of the Dumbos in some medicinal brandy the medics had thoughtfully provided.

Up above the ship the Dumbo plane, seeing all safe, signalled its return to base and the Bering Strait's weary crew hoisted the whale boat back on board ready for another day.

At 2147 the ship was darkened, secured from Air-Sea Rescue Stations and the watch set at War Condition III.

After each rescue the skipper discussed the circumstances of the rescue with the survivors to get their input and any suggestions for improvement. These were shared and discussed with the C.I.C. team and Communications; with the Medics; the First Lt. responsible for the deck force being trained in hoisting boats, rigging embarkation nets etc.; the Gunnery Officer, in control of searchlights and defensive action; the Mess Treasurer and Supply Department whose job it was to see that bunks were prepared and clothing, small stores, toilet articles were brought out for issue and hot food prepared. In turn each passed the information throughout their department and asked for comments, so that the entire ship was organized for Air-Sea Rescue and every man had his station.

This readiness was absolutely necessary as time makes all the difference in saving life. The mission from Tinian to Tokyo took 15 hours if all went well. This was a gruelling and extremely fatiguing flight for the B-29 crews even in the best of circumstances and when they were shot up and damaged so badly that they had to ditch, the pilot needed every possible assistance. From these discussions and the experiences of the ship's crew, the skipper drew up some guidelines for Surface Air-Sea Rescue which were later issued by the Commander Forward Area for use by ships in the Central Pacific and also made available to other areas. see page

It was March 16 before the 20 B-29 survivors were disembarked at Saipan by the Bering Strait. Meanwhile, they were made comfortable on board the ship as she steamed to a new Air Sea Rescue station 20 00 'N, 144 30' E to relieve USS Cook Inlet (AVP 36). The rest and good food gave the airmen a chance to recover from their ordeal before they were back on duty again.

Back in Saipan the crew of the Bering Strait were in hopes of some R&R.

"Do ya think there's a chance we might get to that island, what's it called. Begins with a U - Urinal or something. There's girls there I heard, and we're due for a bit of R&R."

"You mean Ulithi. They say its set up just for the comfort of us poor sailor boys. But I can tell you there's not much chance. I heard there's something big in the wind and I betcha we'll be out there knocking off Kamikazis again."

"I want to be somewheres with girls and beer and palm trees for a bit. We've had our luck. It can't last much longer. Chances are against us. It's not like we got back up and plenty of air cover. We ain't got nothing out there on our own." Bat lamented.

"Well, we're still afloat and that's something and there's a whole lot of mail coming to the ship. Though I don't know as anyone's going to write to an old guy like you, Bat."

"Who're you calling old? I'll have you know I've got more women back home coming after me than you'll get in a lifetime."

"I heard as you haven't even gotten a wife, so I don't think you'se as good as you makes out. Sounds like no woman would have you."

Bat's face darkened and for a moment it looked as if he was

going to knock the boy down, then he said quietly, "Knock it off there, we'll be underway as soon as all supplies are on board."

Only the Skipper knew that Bat's wife and child had been killed in an accident on their way home after seeing Bat off from his last leave and he still couldn't bear to talk about it.

On March 17th the Bering Strait arrived in Apra Harbor, Guam, and according to COMFWDAREA's secret despatch # 120845 (March), she was detached from Task Unit 94.7.2 and reported to Commander Fleet Air Wing ONE (CTG 50.5) for duty. No chance of R&R for anyone. Immediately preparations were started for operation ICEBERG, code name for the invasion of Okinawa.

Aviation tools and part of the necessary supplies for supporting six PBM-3R seaplanes were received and on the 19th the Bering Strait was underway for Saipan providing an antisubmarine screen for USS Hamlin (AV-15).

Later that day the PA system blared out, "Now hear this. This is the Captain speaking, the following message has been received from the Commanding General addressed to USS Bering Strait-

> 'SINCE YOU HAVE BEEN OUR GUARDIAN ANGEL OF THE SEAS YOU HAVE RESTORED TO US 50 CREW MEN. MANY OF THEM ARE FLYING AGAINST THE ENEMY AGAIN. WE ARE GRATEFUL FOR THE SPLENDID WORK YOU HAVE DONE AND WISH YOU ALL THE BEST OF LUCK.'

You earned this commendation by your hard work and dedication to duty, I know you were hoping for a bit of R & R or a chance to go ashore, instead we are ordered to an even more difficult task. But I know we can do an even better job than before and hasten the time when we can go home to our families."

There was a great deal of discussion among the crew as to what such a commendation meant.

"Does it get us any extra pay?" asked Jim Ferrell.

"No such luck, but its a good mark for the record."

"Well, that's better than nothing."

"You're the lucky one, Vern," Ens. Jarvis said to Gunner's Mate, Vernon Belseth, "you'll go ashore at Saipan for transportation stateside. You're slated for a course at the Training School in Washington."

"I do! Thank you, sir," a bright smile lit up his face, he'd been hoping for this. "Anyone else going with me, sir?"

"Not as far as I know. You're the only one."

Jarvis had been in the shipyard working on the ship before she was commissioned, and as gunnery officer, he knew Belseth and most of the crew pretty well. Belseth had shaped up and gotten his sealegs quickly and was ambitious. Jarvis was sorry to see him go, but he deserved a break.

"Good luck, Belseth, work hard." and returning the man's salute, Jarvis went on his way.

"How do you rate such luck?" Belseth was asked over and over in the Mess when the news was heard. "We're off to God knows where as a target for those damn kamikazi s and you're slated for a school statesside. You got some pull somewhere."

"I'm naturally brilliant, haven't you noticed?"

"Most likely the brass is glad to get rid of you."

"He's reserve. They always get the breaks." the good natured hazing went on, but while they were envious, they all wished him well when he went ashore on March 22.

By the 23rd of March all the personnel and equipment of Rescue Squadron 3 ( VH-3) was aboard. all stores and supplies stowed and all logistic preparations for Operation Iceberg, completed and they were underway for Kerama Retto, Nansei Shoto and the attack on Okinawa.

# TOKYO

## MARCH 1945

Ariko Mikata had lived with her family in a village fifteen miles south of Tokyo all her life. Ariko was seven years old by American reckoning or eight years by Japanese reckoning which counts a child one year old when it is born.

Ariko had been fearful for a long time and, after her friend Yuko's house had been destroyed when the Americans bombed the city, she was too terrified to sleep.

On this particular night, March 9th-l0th, Ariko was so afraid that she begged her mother to let her sleep with her and Auntie.

"Very well, my daughter, but only tonight. What would Papa-san say if he heard you. He wouldn't like to think his daughter feared the Americans."

Ariko hung her head and bowed meekly. Her father was in the Imperial Navy and was never afraid. She knew she was not behaving well, but she couldn't help it.

"You must ask Auntie. She might not want you to share her mat."

"Please let me, Auntie. I will be very quiet and still."

Old Auntie, a little mouse like woman who never had an opinion of her own, said anxiously, "We must do as Mama wishes, my little one."

"Come then, Ariko, but its just for tonight." and her mother turned to go to the sleeping room.

"Can I have some rice, Mama? I am hungry."

"There's only a little left. We must keep that for tomorrow. Perhaps I'll be able to get some more from Uncle Hito in the morning."

Ariko bowed again. She hadn't really expected anything more

to eat. For the past six months she had gone to bed hungry. Even if her mother had enough money to buy more food, it was hard to find any in the shops. Ariko knew that going hungry was a sacrifice everyone must make for the Emperor and for their country. Soon the victorious Armies and Navies of Japan would kill all the Americans and everything would be comfortable again and there would be plenty to eat Most of the children in the city of Tokyo had been sent to the country away from the bombing and most of the schools were closed. But Mrs. Mikata thought that as they were fifteen miles from the center of Tokyo, they were safe enough so there was no need for Ariko and her brother to be sent away.

The family usually went to sleep early so they wouldn't feel the emptiness gnawing at their stomachs. Sleep took away all pain and fear. But it seemed as if they had only been asleep for a few minutes when they were awakened by the heavy drone of planes overhead and great flashes of light in the sky.

"Mama! Mama! what is happening ?" Ariko cried.

"It is the Americans. Try and go back to sleep. I will watch over you."

But before Ariko could lie down again, her brother Kiko, came rushing in, "Mama, Tokyo is on fire! the whole world is on fire. Look! Look!."

Ariko and her mother jumped up from the sleeping mat and pulled back the bamboo curtain. The whole sky was lit up with flames punctuated with explosions of light as the incendiary bombs ignited the napalm dropped from the B-29s. Ribbons of flame danced across the sky when the wind caught the burning napalm as it fell to the ground.

"It's the fire devils. We'll all be burnt up!" Ariko was terrified.

Desperately her mother pulled the child to her wondering what to do. Then Auntie Siko suddenly cried out , "It's coming here! The fire is coming this way. We must go to the sea and save ourselves in the water. Hurry, hurry before the fire comes."

"But the house, all our things. We must try and take some with us."

"Come." Old Auntie insisted taking charge for once in her life, "Come, there is no time. Look." and she pointed to the street where crowds of people could be seen by the light of the flames, fleeing from their burning homes. Bicycles, carriages, people pulling handcarts, all crowded along the road trying to beat the flames roaring behind them.

"Quickly, put on your kimono and shoes." Mama said and without stopping to gather up any belongings, their mother urged them into the street. "Hold on to me and Auntie. Whatever happens do not let go or we will never find each other again.

Shaking with terror they obeyed, clinging to their mother's kimono. They were almost knocked down by the crowds rushing by then they were caught up and carried along with them.

Ariko stumbled badly in her old fashioned wooden shoes. Her leather ones were worn out long ago and there were no more to be had. Tears rolled down her cheeks but she didn't notice them. People pushed passed them unheeding of anyone or anything but getting as far as they could from the flaming inferno behind them. It was all Ariko could do to cling to her mother. The noise of the planes, the crack of anti aircraft fire, the roaring of the flames and the shouts and screams of injured people and the crying of babies, battered her senses so that she was hardly conscious of anything but keeping hold of her mother.

It seemed to go on for hours, their breath came in sobbing gasps as they desperately tried to keep their footing in the crush. By now Mama was almost carrying Old Auntie whose strength was giving out. Then a plane roared overhead almost touching them and an incendiary bomb dropped into the crowd of people far behind. The bomb exploded in a blast of flame and the people surged forward trying to escape the fire so that Ariko and the those close to her were forced into the crowd ahead.

Screams of fear and pain mingled with curses as some fell to the ground and were trampled underfoot. A man fell on Old Auntie forcing her from Mama's grasp and before they could save her, she vanished beneath their feet.

"Help! Help, my sister —" but Mama's cries were lost in the tumult and they were carried forward against their will unable to do anything to help Old Auntie even if she were still alive.

Then, suddenly, the skies were silent. The planes were gone leaving fire, death and destruction behind them. Fanned by a fierce wind a firestorm developed in the center of the city. Most of the houses in and around Tokyo were built of wood, bamboo and paper, so they were highly flammable and were quickly consumed by the flames in spite of the desperate effort made by the few firefighters. The Japanese had not expected such vast quantities of incendiaries and oil bombs to be dropped and their amateur firefighters armed with handpumps and buckets could make no impact on the firestorm. By morning sixteen square miles in the heart of Tokyo were devastated and the people now knew that their Gods were powerless to protect them. The American Gods were too strong As the ashes cooled, the government tried to determine the number of dead. Accounts varied from 100,000 to 197,000. It was said that an accurate report was impossible because the conditions were too horrible to mention.

Carried along by the crowds, the Mikato family travelled many miles before they were able to sink down in a field and rest.

In the distance they could see the city still burning and they feared their home would be gone. They had no food but they were not hungry. The horrors of the night were too close to their minds "Where is Auntie, Mama? Will she be able to find us?" Ariko asked.

"I fear she will not be able to find us. It is possible that she has gone to our ancestors. She was old and not very strong and this terrible night was more than she could bear."

Ariko was silent, she loved Auntie, surely she would not leave them now When daylight came the sky was so filled with smoke and ashes that the sun was hidden. Some people sat staring ahead neither speaking or moving. Some wandered among the crowd looking for lost relatives. Others started walking back to the city hoping against hope that their house would be still there or there would be something left that they could salvage.

It was afternoon before Mama Makito summoned enough strength to start the walk back to see what had happened to their home. Some rescue workers had brought water in buckets so they could drink, but there was no food to be had.

Fires were still burning and the sky was filled with smoke and ashes. A horrible smell of burning flesh hung over everything from the bodies of people and animals who had not been able to escape. The road they had travelled on from the city was littered with bodies of those who had been trampled underfoot or burned to death. They were completely unrecognizable. Mama looked at everyone to see if Old Auntie was among them. Perhaps a shred of cloth from her kimono or a shoe would tell where she lay, but there was nothing she could recognize They passed groups of people standing silently looking at the ashes of all their worldly possessions. Stunned by their loss and at the bitter knowledge that their sacred homeland was no longer inviolate.

As they came near to their street, they saw that all the houses, except for two large ones built of stone, were gone. Many were still smouldering, their own among them. There was nothing left. Nothing at all.

"What shall we do, Mama? where can we go?"

We will find somewhere. We will have to go to your grandmother in Kyushu, I think. We will have to get tickets to go on the train part of the way and then walk the rest."

"I could help build the house again, Mama," Kiko said."

It is very hard to get tickets on the train and they cost much money."

"There is nothing left to build the house with. It is not possible, my son, and the Americans will come again you can be sure. We will have to go. If we cannot get tickets we must walk."

So with only the clothes on their backs and the few yen their mother had hidden in her kimono, they set out on foot for the long journey south.

Ariko never forgot that night. For years afterwards she would dream that the flames were pursuing her, coming closer and closer and just as she was about to be burnt alive, she would wake up screaming.

# OKINAWA

## PREPARATIONS FOR 'ICEBERG'

Okinawa, 60 miles long, is the biggest island in the Ryukyo chain, with the Pacific on one side and the China Sea on the other. As it is only 400 miles from Kyushu, the island on the south coast of Japan, it was to be the springboard for the invasion.

Once Okinawa had been an independent kingdom but it was taken over by the Japanese in 1879, 26 years after Commodore Perry landed there in 1853. In 1945 there were about half a million Okinawans on the island. These were mostly small farmers cultivating little fields among the steep limestone hills and groups of pine trees.

American intelligence estimated that there were approximately 70,000 Japanese troops ready to defend Okinawa and they were expected to fight to the death as they had on Iwo Jima. Heavy casualties were feared as the Japanese had airfields on Okinawa and nearby islands as well as 55 on Kyushu. It was known that over 2,500 planes could attack the invasion force.

The defense of Okinawa was under the command of Lt. General Mitsuru Ushijima, an experienced officer whose plan was to let the enemy invasion come ashore and move inland where they could not receive cover or support from their ship's guns and then attack and destroy them. In the meantime, kamikazis would be attacking and sinking the ships of the invasion fleet.

Vice Admiral Kelly Turner USN, had planned a preliminary operation to secure Kerama Retto, small group of islands about 15 miles off the coast of Okinawa. These islands would provide protection for an eight by four mile stretch of water, known as Keramo Retto Passage, which could hold over fifty large ships. With the islands secured, ships could refuel, repair damages and drop anchor with far less chance of attack from enemy surface or air fire. Also, it would provide a haven for the care of the wounded.

What Admiral Turner did not know was that the Japanese had made the Keramas a base for renraku tei, suicide boats each equipped with two 264 pound depth charges. The pilots of the boats had orders to ram into US ships, preferably those laden with personnel or essential supplies and sink them.

Meanwhile the Bering Strait was steaming towards the Keramas in company with Task Group 51.20, to play their part in "Operation Iceberg."

On March 26th, commanded by Lt. General S. B. Buckner, five battalions of the United States 77th Infantry Division were put ashore to secure the Keramas before April lst, the date the invasion was to begin. Ironically, the code name was "Love Day."

The Japanese had not expected any attack on Kerama Retto and had moved most of the troops that had been based there to Okinawa, so there was not much opposition. But, warned by experience on Iwo Jima, the Americans were searching caves and inlets where Japanese might be hiding out when they came across a new and deadly weapon.

"What the Hell's this thing." P2c Jack Lowe exclaimed, gingerly walking around a plywood contraption about 28 feet long and five wide.

"Careful, don't touch it. Might explode."

"Looks like a boat."

"Made of plywood! How long would that last in the water?" "It's got an engine, so its meant to move."

"Fishing boat, do ya' think?" "Could be, but why in here?" "Say, lookee here. These here are depth charges. This ain't no fishing boat. This thing could sink a ship."

Altogether the troops found and destroyed about 360 of these suicide boats hidden in caves and secluded inlets in Kerama Retto.

This operation alone, saved the lives of many men. Later, it was learned from captured Japanese papers, that these boats were meant to travel in threes alongside an enemy ship. Then, when they got close enough, the pilots would trip the explosives and try to escape before everything was blown apart. They did not expect to survive the explosion. Like the kamikazi pilots, they were prepared and willing to give their life for the Emperor.

At 1108 on March 28 the Bering Strait was safely anchored in Kerama Retto Passage to the relief of all aboard.

"Well, we got this far in one piece," muttered Bat, "but judging by the way them damn kamikazis are sinking our ships, I don't suppose our luck will last much longer. Stuck in this place we'll just be a sitting duck again."

"If you'd been topside with me, you wouldn't be such a wet blanket, Bat."

"What d'ya mean? What do you know I don't know?"

"Well, for one thing, there's more ships than you'll ever see in your whole life up there. The ocean's full of them. Carriers, destroyers, LSTs you name it, they're all there. Them Japs won't know what hit'em once we get started." Sm2c Hall answered.

"Can't be soon enough for me. Are you sure they're all ours?"
"Of course they are. Except for some Royal Navy. They brought along four carriers, a couple of battleships and a whole bunch of destroyers. There's some from other countries too."

"How do you know so damn much?"

"I hear things up on the bridge. I'm the Signalman up there and don't you forget it."

"O.K., O.K., keep your hair on. Just asking."

Spirits were high on the ship. There was a feeling of excitement and expectation. Something big was about to happen. This might be the battle that would finish off the Japs and they'd get home at last.

They didn't want to hear Bat's belly aching. They felt invincible. Secretly, they might have moments of doubt and write quick letters to loved ones at home in case they didn't get back, but these moments were short lived.

Hall was hoping there'd be mail. Ann, his girl, had said she'd wait for him no matter how long it took, but there hadn't been mail call for too long. He was not the only one hoping for mail. Ensign Snow, regular Navy, who reported aboard the Bering Strait in July 1944 directly from Officer Training School, was anxious to hear from his wife, also named Ann. They'd been married twelve years and a friend had told him Ann had been sick. Snow was a strong, earnest officer who did everything by the book and considered the Navy the best outfit in the world, but there were times when he longed for home.

For officers and men alike, mail was the lifeline to all they'd left behind. It gave assurance that the good old US of A was still there - that loved ones hadn't forgotten them.

Pin ups, girlie mags, movies and fantasies helped, but they couldn't take the place of the real thing. It was months since they had touched a real, live girl.

But they didn't have much time to worry about it. There was work to be done. Sonar searches had to be continued at anchor.

Though the Passage had been swept by the mine sweepers there was always the danger of a stray mine. Also, the water was full of trash and the Japanese had been known to hide under a bunch of garbage with a grenade under their arm ready to throw on the ship when they got close enough.

In preparation for the arrival of Rescue Squadron Three (VH3) the Seaplane Base group was busy establishing seadrome facilities and all the while there was the roaring of planes flying over and the sound of guns in the near distance reminding them of what lay ahead.

"Any chance of going ashore, Chief." Sam Bender asked.

"I heard as the Captain was talking about the men going ashore for a looksee and couple of beers, but he hasn't given the order yet. There's still a few Japs hiding out." Chief Millard answered.

"Well, I sure would like to put my feet on dry land for a bit with an ice cold beer in my hand."

"You're not the only one. Though I don't suppose there's much to see but some dead Japs and a few palm trees. They say the folks— then he was interrupted by the welcome sound of "Mail call" coming over the squawk box and all else was forgotten.

On March 29 the Rescue Squadron, commanded by Lt. Commander W D. Bonvillian, USN, reported aboard with six PBM-3R seaplanes.

Innis and Bonvillian were just settling down in the Captain's cabin to discuss plans when there was a knock on the door.

"Come right in." the Captain said.

"Just picked up, sir." and the signalman handed the Captain a distress signal from a B-29.

"Well, we'll have to continue this later, Commander. Are your crews ready for take off?."

"Yes, sir." and in a few moments two planes ,piloted by Lt.'s Kouns and Eddy, took off to the rescue. But in spite of a thorough search the mission was negative.

Tension mounted as "Love Day " approached and it was almost a relief when General Quarters sounded and men raced to their battle stations.

Already the ships with longer range guns were firing at two Jap planes approaching from the east. Flying together they dodged the fire then suddenly changed course and one came directly towards the Bering Strait.

Guns swiveled round and, as the plane came in range, the ship let him have it with all they'd got. But to the disappointment of the whole crew, the plane got away with no observable damage.

"We'll make up for it next time, lads." Gunnery Officer Jarvis said. "Any rate we scared them off."

# LOVE DAY

## EASTER SUNDAY 1945

April lst, Easter Sunday dawned with a clear sky. By this time four more squadrons had joined the Bering Strait in the group.

They were VPB 208 from USS Hamlin; VPB 18 from USS St George; VPB 21 from USS Chandeleur and VPB 27 from USS Yakutat, USS Onslow and USS Shelikof.

"Well, this is the big day. We'll be lucky if them damn Japs don't get us with them kamikazis and to think back home they'll all be eating Easter Eggs." Bat muttered.

"This is safe place, I heard." a quiet voice answered.

"Who gave you that tale, Blanket?" Hukk asked skeptically.

"Chief told me." Blanket was an Indian and while he had great courage when there was action, he suffered from too much imagination in between.

"Sitting ducks again, that's what we are. This time we don't even get to go on rescue. All we do is keep them planes ready to fly." Bat was even more pessimistic than usual.

"Hey, shut up, Bat. There goes the P.A." suddenly all was quiet as they waited for what they knew must be an important message, "Now hear this, Captain speaking. The invasion of Okinawa started at dawn today. Air massive kamikazi attacks on all ships are probable. Heavy casualties are expected.

"Planes must be kept ready for take off at all costs so that distress signals can be answered without delay. Thanks to the splendid work of all hands, we've been lucky so far but we can't afford to let up. The safety of the ship and all aboard depends on each man continuing to do his best."

"Sounds as if we're in for a bad time." Hukk said.

"That's what I've been telling you." Bat answered.

"So long as we get a chance at them, I don' t care what they try." Blanket was excited at the thought of action.

Later that morning a call came in from Commander Bonvillian, who was piloting PBM-3R "Mariner" on an assigned search. The plane had intercepted a message that survivors from a crashed Grumman TBF from Squadron (VT) 29 were taking to a raft on the shore of Nakagusuku Wan, Okinawa.

Calling the ship Bonvillian requested permission to attempt the rescue of the survivors as they were only fifteen minutes away.

"Let's hope we get them before the Japs do." Bonvillian said as the plane increased its speed to 140 knots and in 14 minutes they sighted four friendly fighters circling a raft with three men in it.

The raft was in very shallow water about two hundred yards off shore.

Gunfire aimed at the raft was coming from shore positions but so far it had not been hit.

"Say, Skipper ,there's a couple of Japs launching a boat back behind the raft. They're out to get them."

"Pass the word to the fighters. They'll take care of them."

answered Bonvillian as he circled for landing. Obviously they did as the boat was not seen again.

The three men in the raft were paddling desperately towards the deep water as the plane circled. They knew that a Jap plane could attack any moment, but the 15 knot wind made it hard going.

The plane circled over them expecting to be able to land alongside, then Bonvillian exclaimed, "God! look at those coral heads. We can't land here, we'll be ripped apart. They'll have to come to us in the deep water."

"They'd better put a move on. Our luck won't hold much longer."

"It's the wind that's against them. I'll make another pass, maybe they'll be close enough then."

But it was no use. The raft was still in shallow water beyond the coral heads.

Three more passes were made then, finally, the raft reached the edge of deep water. Swiftly the Mariner crew rigged a life ring from the plane's stern and hauled the them in.

By 1230 the three survivors, Ensign L. A. Zemanek; J. F. Thompson, ARM3c; and C. H Plotczyk, AMM3c were safely aboard together with their raft.

"We sure thought we were done for when we had to ditch. The damned AA knocked out our engine. We landed in a rice paddy then carried the raft over to the shore. We reckoned we had a better chance at sea than right there with the Japs." Zemanek said.

"Had you been in the raft very long?"

"Just about an hour. Thank God you came along. Luck was with us today."

None of the three suffered any injuries and on arrival at Kerama Retto they were put aboard the USS St George to return to their squadron.

Meanwhile the Bering Strait had been at Battle Stations from 0140-0214 and again from 0235-0245 under attack from Jap planes. No serious damage was done but they knew it could happen any time and sure enough, the Japs were back attacking from 1914-1940.

That night, as Blanket was turning in, he said, "Thought it be more busy day. Two rescue missions. General Quarters three times that's all."

Very little news came in from the landing beaches. The scuttlebutt was that landings were made without opposition. All the Japanese fighting power appeared to be launched against the ships and several had suffered severe damage and loss of life..

"It's like Iwo." the Exec said in the ward room that night.

"They've set a trap they hope we'll walk into. They'll wait 'til the troops are landed and moving up and then when they get where they want them, they'll attack. Meantime they are going after our ships."

"Well, Buckner's a pretty savvy guy, he must know what's going on."

"Let's hope so. But you've got to get the men on the beaches before the place can be secured. I feel sorry for those poor devils. It's no picnic on ship or shore."

Then the men rose as the Captain came in with a message in his hand, "Relax, gentlemen. Commander, I think you should read this message aloud, as you had a lot to do with it."

"Thank you, sir." Bonvillian took a quick look, smiled and

said, "It's from Commander Task Force 51 addressed to the Captain of USS Bering Strait...' Well Done'."

"It's a good start." Innis said , "Pass it down."

For the next three months the Bering Strait served as coordinating control tender at Kerama Retto, also conducting sonar searches to guard against midget submarines.

April 2 was the beginning of standing at Battle Stations hour after hour, both day and night. The maintenance crew were constantly at work keeping the seaplanes ready at all times. Rescue missions were flown throughout the day. The sight of damaged ships, including Admiral Spruance's Flagship, USS Indianapolis, limping in for repairs, only increased the men's desire to fight and to give everything they had to finish off the Japs. .

On April 4. Lt. Edgar Palm landed near Kikai Jima in answer to a distress signal, and was able to rescue Lt. Cozzons of USS Cabot.

"Did any members of your crew get out, Lieutenant?"

"I saw a couple of parachutes over to the west not too long ago, but I lost sight of them when I hit the water."

"God that AA is getting close." Palm exclaimed as the shore batteries opened up on the plane. "I'll make a search of the area though, we might be able to sight them."

But, in spite of a low level search, no sign of any other survivors was found.

The following day was a very busy one. Lt. Commander R. A. Barrett rescued Lt. Kemp, ARM2c Cory, AMM2c Dulnize of VT-9 Yorktown also Ensign Hudspeth of VF-9 Yorktown, four miles from Miyako Jima.

Meanwhile Lt. E. Mansueto picked up Lt. Grist, of VF-17 Hornet, near Kikai, immediately after he finished assisting DD-801 rescue another survivor near Tokuno Jima. Answering another distress call, Lt. W. D. Eddy Landed at sea near Ishigaki Shima, and rescued Lt. May and ARM2c Cohan, of Yorktown VB Squadron.

While the invasion forces were moving further inland, the Navy surrounded Okinawa to prevent the Japanese from bringing in reinforcements. On April 6th. the enemy began Operation Ten-Go, an enormous massed Kamikazi attack against the amphibious forces.

“Hell! “ exclaimed Bat as he raced to his Battle station, “the whole damn sky is full of the bastards.”

The ships in Kerama Retto were at General Quarters from 03 in the morning for the greater part of the day but no damage was done to them until the late afternoon. Then a wave of kamikazis headed directly towards the southern part of the anchorage.

Immediately all ships began firing, trying to splash them before they could do any damage, but at 1630 a suicide plane crashed into the deck of a ship south of the Bering Strait.

“God! those bastards got that LST.” the Exec exclaimed.

“Yeah, you don’t stand much chance when they come at you like that.” the Captain answered. He’d hardly finished speaking when they were deafened by a tremendous explosion and an enormous burst of flames and smoke covered the area.

“Christ in the foothills! That’s the ammunition ship over at Aka Jima.”

They stayed at General Quarters for three more hours until 1930. Exhausted, Bat spoke the wish of all aboard when he said, “All I want is to hit the sack. I’ve had it for a while.”

But they were out of luck. In ten minutes a couple of Zeroes were sighted and General Quarters was sounded once more. This time the Japs flew over at a high altitude and then for a while all was quiet.

Meanwhile, the famous Japanese carrier, the 67,500 ton Yamato, together with a cruiser and eight destroyers, commanded by V. Admiral Seiichi Ito, was steaming towards Okinawa to finish off any ships not sunk by the kamikazis. At this stage of the war Japan was very short of oil as it all has to be imported. With the loss of so many of their ships, Japan had not been able to replenish supplies and the Yamato had only sufficient oil for a one way trip. However, all the ships had enormous supplies of ammunition and could take a terrible toll of the US and Allied ships and men. Their orders were to “Fight gloriously to the death and completely destroy the enemy fleet.”

Fortunately, a US submarine detected the Japanese force and it was kept under observation by two search planes. On the morning of April 7. Captains of battleships of the Fifth Fleet were sent a signal by Admiral Spruance to be ready for surface action.

Then later, carrier planes from the USS Enterprise sighted the

Yamato and Admiral Mitscher launched a tremendous air attack of bombers and torpedo planes on the Japanese ships.

Visibility was very low because of a rain squall and, as the Yamato had no air cover because of a decision to use all planes against the US and Allied ships, the Japanese were massacred even though they fought desperately turning every gun skyward.

With her battle flag still flying, the Yamato, the proudest ship of the Japanese Navy sank beneath the ocean taking her captain and over 2,000 men with her.

Only four destroyers managed to return to Japan. All the other ships were sunk, their crews going down with them. Among them Yoshio Mikata. There were very few survivors.

The Yamato was more than a ship. It was also a symbol, for Yamato was the ancient name for Japan. The dramatic new seacraft, launched in June 1992, by Japan, is named Yamato 1. Powered by magnetohydrodynamic propulsion (MDP), problems caused by the propeller system are eliminated. It cannot be detected by sonar. Is this the ship of the future? The word Yamato means 'foot of the mountain'. A Japanese legend tells that the land of Japan was formed when the Goddess came from Heaven to the mountain called Fujiyama. Descending from the cloud which had brought her, she formed the land around the foot of the mountain and put it under Divine protection. Kyoto, the ancient capital, was in this area until the mid nineteenth century when the capital was moved to Tokyo. Kyoto, with its beautiful old buildings, was not bombed by the Allies.

The sinking of the great battleship, Yamato, brought home to the Japanese, more than anything else, that their sacred homeland was no longer invulnerable and they must expect invasion.

Now the Japanese had only one battleship left but they kept up the terrible massed kamikazi attacks which were causing horrendous damage to US ships.

Between the 8th and 11th of April, 19 rescue missions were flown by the Bering Strait squadron. On the 12th Bonvillian searched until dark for a survivor who, they found out later, had been picked up earlier. Having no voice transmitters and with weak IFF, Bonvillian was fired on by friendly forces and landed at sea.

Somehow he managed to keep the plane afloat and taxied 40 miles in the darkness to base.

During this time the American troops on Okinawa realized that the days of non resistance on the part of the Japanese were over and not only did they have to overcome their bitter fighting, but they had to overcome some of the most difficult terrain they had encountered so far. Once past the flat beaches and rice paddies they found heavily fortified steep slopes and ridges with mine fields and tank traps at the foot. It took seven days to take less than 7000 yards at a cost of 1,200 casualties. The troops suffered incredible hardships and bravery and self sacrifice became commonplace as the days and nights wore slowly on and heavy rain turned the ground to mud.

The skipper of the Bering Strait was about to leave the bridge just after dawn on April 13th when the news was received that President Roosevelt was dead. The ship had stood at General Quarters twice since 0320 and when the crew heard "Now hear this," coming over the loudspeaker, they groaned.

"What's up now?" Bat muttered "Don't we get a chance to have a cup of coffee?" Then there was dead silence as they heard the brief message." President Roosevelt is dead."

"God! What will happen now?"

"D'ya think the war will be over?"

"Maybe its a Jap rumor."

"Will Truman be any good."

These were the questions being asked on land and sea.

President Roosevelt had been Commander in Chief from the beginning of the war. Could anyone take his place? But there was little time to dwell on these things, the enemy was still there and the Bering Strait was at Battle Stations again as the kamikazis returned. Three ships were damaged, but the Bering Strait escaped except for some slight damage from flak.

During the next three days the suicide plane attacks on shipping were accelerated. The destroyers and other small ships were the main target as they were not so easily protected by US planes as the larger ships. The Bering Strait squadron flew 11 missions rescuing 10 survivors including the Commanding Officer of VC 93, Petrof Bay. Lt Eddy was returning at night from a search mission when he was forced to land at sea by friendly gunfire. He was able to taxi to base with all hands safe.

By now many men were wondering if they'd ever see home

again.

Day after day ships came in badly damaged with flags at half mast for the shipmates killed when fighting off the kamikazis. Old photographs of loved ones were cherished and carried in uniform pockets.

"Did I ever show you this picture of my brother?" Bill Haproff S1c, asked Hukk as they went off duty.

"No, let's have a look at him. He sure is more of a looker than you." Hukk joked." Where's he now?"

"He's in the Navy somewheres. I haven't seen him in 3 years.

I don't even know if he's still alive. Haven't heard from him lately."

"We should get mail tomorrow." said Hukk handing back the photograph. "Well, I'm going to hit the sack before those damn Japs come over again."

"Okay, so'm I."

Bill had no sooner dropped off to sleep when he woke up with someone shaking him and shouting, "Hi there, get up. There's someone here says he's your brother."

Sure enough it was. "Well, old buddy, you never thought I'd find you, did you.'

"How in the hell did you get here? Bill demanded scarcely able to believe his eyes.

"Well, I knew you were on the Bering Strait and when my ship came into Kerama Retto, I asked permission to come see you. My skipper asked your skipper and he sent a boat over and here I am."

By now a whole bunch of sailors were crowding around slapping the brothers on the back, envious of their good luck, hoping some would rub off on them - and it did. A few days later, John R. Spekhart, S2c of the Rescue Squadron, heard that his uncle, Chief Warrant Officer Talmadge, was aboard the USS Mt. McKinley.

"I haven't seen him for eight years. I don't know as I'll recognize him. Think the skipper will let me go?" Knowing he might not get another chance to see his uncle, the skipper arranged the visit with the skipper of the Mt. Mckinley and sent the seaman over in a boat.

48 years later when Spekhart was asked about his experiences in the Pacific, the meeting with his uncle was the first thing he mentioned - next, the horror of the kamikazis.

Day after day the ships fought off attacks and day after day the rescue missions were flown. Often rescues were made under enemy gunfire. One day 4 badly injured airmen were picked up and it was decided to transfer them to the USS Kenneth Whiting as she had a much larger hospital and more medical equipment than the Bering Strait. No sooner had the four men been transferred than the Whiting was hit by a kamikazi and all four were killed.

The last week of April was no easier. The ship stood at Battle Stations several times a day. Twenty five rescue missions were flown, most encountered enemy fire and heavy weather.

The USS Pinckney was hit by a suicide plane causing an explosion and fire. The Bering Strait turned her guns on a Zero attacking her and scored several hits. On the 29th to the delight of all aboard, the Bering Strait scored several hits on a Val which splashed a hundred yards astern of USS Hamlin and exploded.

Then came the news that Mussolini had been hanged from a lamp post by partisans and the following day that Hitler had committed suicide. Surely, everyone felt, the end of the war was near and if their luck held, they'd be alive to tell the tale.

"Them Japs will have to give in now that their buddies are finished. They won't be able to carry on their own." for once even Bat was jubilant.

But he was wrong. There were to be many more months and many more lives lost before the war was over.

Because of the serious losses to the fleet caused by increasing kamikazi attacks and the slow advance on land, Admiral Chester Nimitz, Commander Pacific Fleet and Pacific Ocean Areas, himself, arrived in Okinawa to see what could be done.. The 27th Infantry had been replaced by the 1st Marine Division, as the Infantry's strength had been reduced by 3,250 wounded. The Marines were anxious to make a landing and attack behind enemy lines rather than laboriously continue General Buckner's cautious plan of frontal attack.

Nimitz, in favor of the Marines' plan, pointed out that fourteen hundred ships were supporting the ground forces and ships and men were being lost to air attack every day. Therefore something must be done to put a stop to this. Buckner replied testily that the Navy could not interfere in the land operations.

"Well, if you can't get a move on in five days, we'll have to get someone out here who can." said Nimitz.

Even as they were speaking, a breakthrough was beginning. The Japanese were falling back to another line of defense. But this proved to be the start of even more bloody battles both on land and sea.

Richardson Preyer, Gunnery Officer on board the USS Preston, DD 795, later Congressman, 5th District of North Carolina, has vivid memories of kamikazi attacks during the Okinawa battle. Out of his squadron of 7 destroyers, five were sunk.

On one occasion the Preston was attacked by about 60 Japanese planes. By this time many of the planes flown by the Japanese were older types and were no match for the 2 Corsairs which came to the aid of the Preston. The Corsairs shot down 20 of the Japanese planes and the Preston, herself got several, but still they came at the ship. Then as five Jap planes came directly overhead the Corsairs, now completely out of ammunition, dove at them and cut the tails off two amidst the heavy fire from the ship.

"By some miracle we never hit the Corsairs." said Preyer.

"But one other time we did hit one of our own. We were at the north tip of Okinawa, the Marines were landing there, and we were firing on an airstrip where Jap planes were taking off. A spotter in the Marines was talking the range to us and we were doing pretty well.

"Then a plane that looked like a Zero came in our sights and we shot it down. It turned out to be a Hellcat - the Hellcat and the Zero looked rather alike. The Hellcat was on the wrong bearing. None of our planes were supposed to be there. Fortunately, it was not seriously damaged and we were able to pick up the pilot who was as mad as hell.

"For God's sakes, why don't you look what you're doing." he said, "Now I've lost my plane I won't be able to get to that Movie show that's laid on for tonight."

Emily, Preyer's girl friend, was doing volunteer work with the Red Cross at a submarine base in Brisbane, Australia in 1945.

Submariners who had been in the Indian Ocean for 2 months at a time often came in with bad injuries. Emily remembers writing letters for some who had lost their hands.

To Emily's disappointment, Preyer's ship never put into Brisbane, so they never met in the Pacific, but when they married in 1946, two of the submariners came to the wedding in North Carolina.

The letter given below from a kamikazi pilot, shows his fanatical devotion to the Emperor and to his own honor.

*"Dear Mother whom I honor and my deceased father, watch over me. Grandparents, younger brothers and sisters, I hope you are being fine.*

*Now, I, Maseo is writing this with deep emotion. What more is there to say now, except I pray for your happiness? In regards to my 19 years of life, why regret if the blossom falls when it is still in bud if need be? No further needs be said, just please understand that there are no clouds in Maseo's heart; it is clear and content - nothing to reconsider - no regrets. As a member of an honorable force at sea my only hope now is that I will be of good service. It is nothing more than Maseo's honor and happiness that I was chosen to ride on one of the newest weapons carrying the frantic hopes of all naval personnel and my countrymen, which will contribute decisively to the Great Asia War. I desire that you, Mother and everyone to be proud of me. Please remember Maseo's gallant burning red appearance attacking the enemy task force. Maseo will not be destroyed until the US and Britain are defeated. Even though my body shall be done away with in the South Seas, surely my spirit will continue. I shall be living forever day and night as a spirit fighting for my country: living in your heart, Mother and living in the country land.*

*Mother, please watch your health, you may be lonely, but be of good health. Younger brothers and sisters, help your mother and grow up to be a person who is of service to others. Grandparents, take enough rest, live long and see Japan victorious in the great Asian War.*

*Under the dim light I am writing this in a hurry. Only annihilation awaits me tomorrow, is what i have told my heart to prepare for. Now I am quietly thinking and longing to see the skies over home. Maybe, I will be lucky but I will not overly seek for it, if I still have life I will write again. I will ask my comrade to mail this letter along with the cigarette the Emperor gave me, because I do not have enough time. Praying for your health and happiness, From Maseo."*

This letter is reproduced through the courtesy of Captain Frank A. Zimanski, USN, Rtd. Captain Zimanski received the letter enclosed with one from the pilot's family when the Captain returned the pilots identification tag to them 43 years after his death.

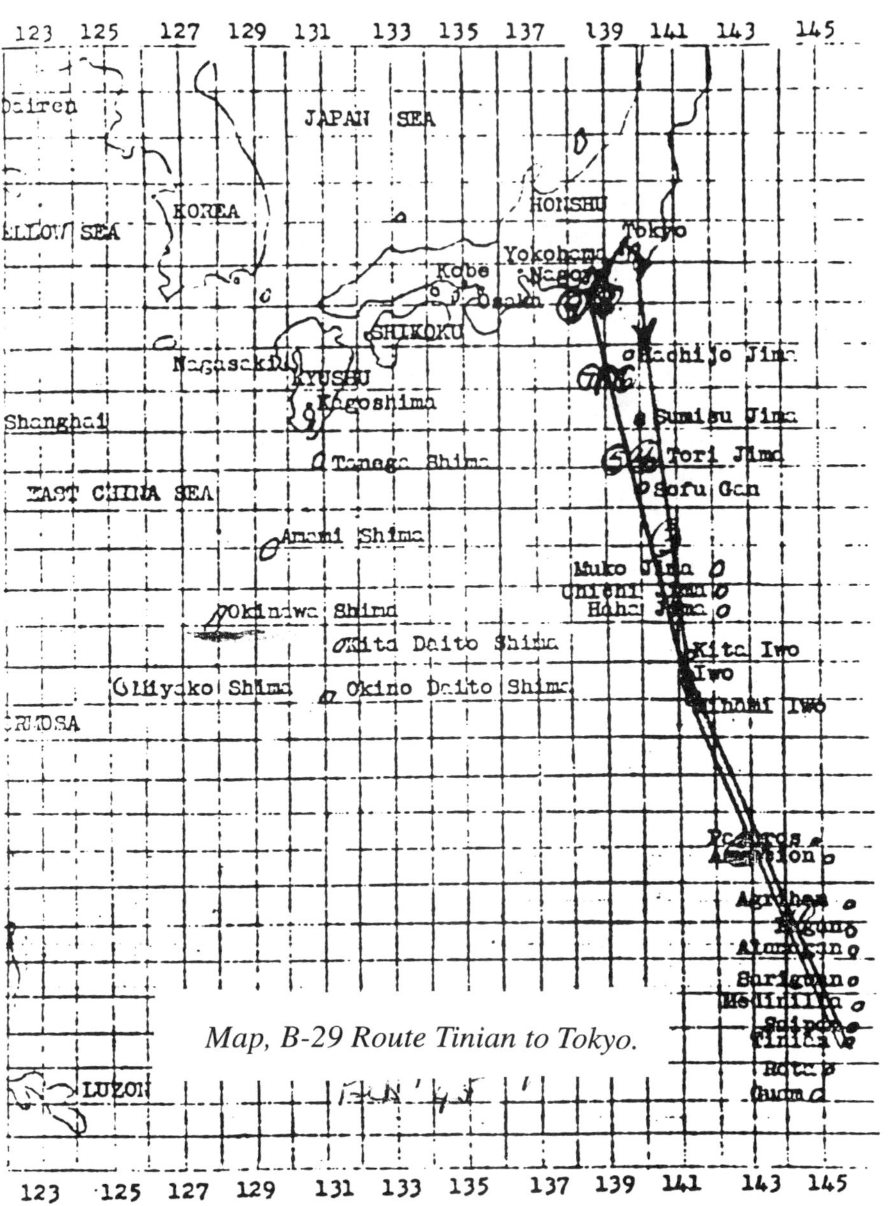


*Map, B-29 Route Tinian to Tokyo.*

*Crew of 484th Squadron, 505 Bomb Group.*

*Innis and Ferris with prisoners.*

*Cave on Kerama Retto used by snipers.*

*Children lining up for candy.*

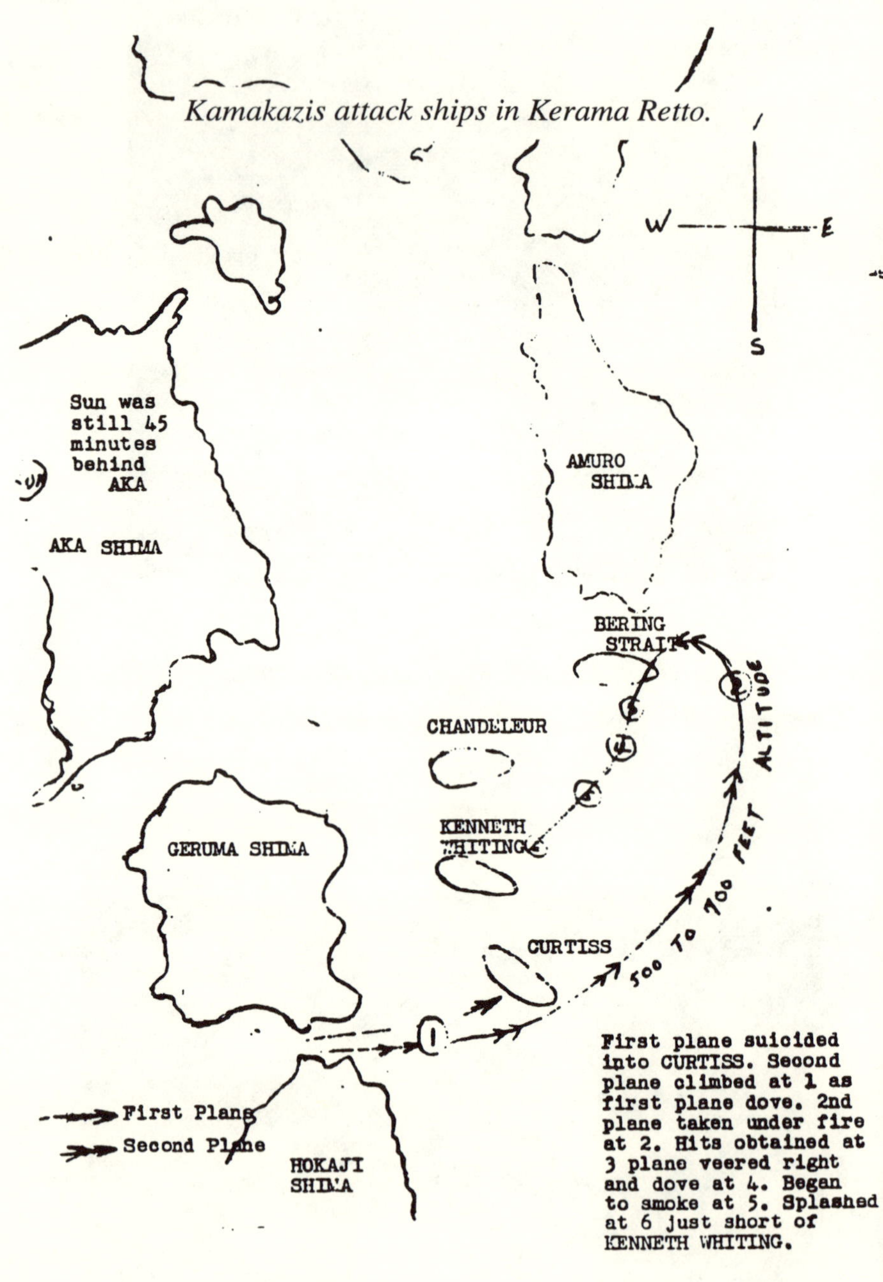


*Kamakazis attack ships in Kerama Retto.*

# KERAMA RETTO

## 1945

The first week of May saw little change on board the Bering Strait. No one got much sleep and what they did get was broken by calls to Battle Stations or distress calls. The exhilaration over the deaths of Mussolini and Hitler had evaporated into exhaustion when nothing was heard about ending the war. The kamikazi attacks continued. On May 4 alone, 7 US ships were hit and 446 sailors killed.

At 0847 on May 6 an enemy plane started a dive into the Seaplane group. Already at Battle Stations the Bering Strait opened fire. There was no time to lose, it was coming right at the ship.

"Get the bastard. For God's sake, get him." was the silent prayer in every mind. But he kept coming—then suddenly, he tipped on one wing and a cheer rose up as smoke and flame poured out of the plane and it veered away from the Bering Strait. Unfortunately, it crashed into USS St.George causing considerable damage.

Later that day, under another attack, two crewmen of the Bering Strait were injured. W. R. Hayes, S2c, sustained severe wounds of his right arm and abdomen and W. W. Covington, S3c was slightly wounded by shrapnel from friendly fire.

The next day, news of the surrender of Germany came in and once more excitement rose as hopes of seeing home and loved ones appeared imminent.

When mail arrived, letters from home told of the Victory Celebrations being planned to welcome the soldiers and sailors coming back from Europe.

"When are you coming back?" they asked. "You've been out there long enough. Ginny's husband coming home Tuesday and Mike and John Davis are coming next week, so their mother told me."

"I don't know about your folks, but mine write as if its my fault I'm still out here. They seem to think because the war's over in Europe, there's nothing going on over here." Sam said somewhat bitterly.

It was true, this stage of the war in the Pacific was not given the Press coverage that the Invasion of Europe was given. The tremendous losses of picket ships had been suppressed and when it was given out, it coincided with the death of President Roosevelt, so it was not even noticed.

The war had gone on too long. People wanted to see the end of it and were delighted at the chance to celebrate the great victory in Europe and forget that the war against Japan was still there.

Peace overtures had been rejected by Japan in spite of the fact that at a meeting of the Supreme War Council on June 22. the Emperor had stated that he wished the leaders of Japan to study ways to conclude the war. Now the Japanese were preparing for what seemed the inevitable invasion of their land.

Meanwhile the terrible land battles on Okinawa and the massed Kamikazi attacks on the ships continued. Among those hit was the carrier USS Bunker Hill. It was hit and set on fire by a Zeke followed by a Kamikazi . With 1,870,000 gallons of aviation fuel on board, fire engulfed her. 396 crewmen were dead and 264 injured.

The incredible bravery of the crew kept her afloat, but she was knocked out for the duration of the war.

Day after day rescue missions were flown from the Bering Strait and somehow, the crews kept the planes "up" in all kinds of weather. On May 12 Lt. Eddy rescued 13 survivors of 62V465 who had been in the water for 24 hours. The sea was rough with 12 foot swells, but he managed to land and take off with 25 men aboard and return safely to base. But the plane was badly damaged and had to be struck.

One morning, Innis was surprised to receive a visitor from a Royal Navy ship.

"Glad to see you again, sir, I had to bring my ship in for repairs. Got quite a bit of damage. Damn Japs. You were Air Plot Officer on the old Wasp when I saw you last. April 42, wasn't it?"

"Yes, that was a hell of a trip, so was the next one. Its good to see you. I often wondered what happened to your squadron when you took off."

"Well, as you see, I made it, but we lost quite a few. I heard the Wasp picked up the Ark Royal at Gib and escorted her back to port."

"Yeah, poor old girl. She could only make 19 knots, but we were anxious to get out of there. There were all kinds of subs stalking us. Somehow the Ark managed to get up to 22 knots but we could see her decks shaking with those reciprocating engines pushing like hell. Anyhow, we made it back all right. Come on down to my cabin for a bit. Things seem to be quiet for now, at least."

Later that day, in answer to a question from his Exec, Innis told him about the two trips the old carrier, USS Wasp, had made carrying Spitfires to the besieged island of Malta.

"Wasn't that when Churchill sent the message about a wasp stinging twice or something, Captain?"

"Yeah, the Royal Navy hadn't had much luck getting supplies to Malta and they were mighty grateful when the US Navy managed to get through twice. It was about the same time Doolittle and his raiders made the first hit on Japan."

"That was a busy month for the Navy ."

"It sure was. I remember Doug Fairbanks, Jr. was our Public Info at the time and he wrote something to that effect, if I remember rightly."

"I never knew he was a Navy man. Was he regular or reserve.?"

"He was Reserve."

"Did you spend much time with the Limeys, sir?"

" "Quite a bit. I was in the Neutrality Patrol and we had to put into Glasgow to load the Spitfires. Took me a while to get used to the language. One ship had a call name, 'Jehova' and the first time I heard this very English voice calling, ' This is JEHOVAH calling, OVAH.' I thought it was God." the skipper smiled at the memory, "The old Wasp was a good ship. Losing her was hard."

"She was sunk soon after she made the Malta trips, wasn't she?"

"Yeah, in September. She was in the battle of the eastern Solomons. I left the ship at the same time the skipper, Black Jack Reeves, made Rear Admiral and was relieved by Forest Sherman.".

May went slowly by and still the bitter fighting continued on Okinawa. Rescue missions were flown every day from the Bering Strait as the Kamikazis kept up their attacks. On May 24, six missions were flown and Lt. Kouns, Lt Commander Bonvillian and Lt. Dorton were sent to assist USS Braise ( DD-630) hit by two suicide planes. Ten men were rescued from the water and flown to Kerama Retto for urgent medical treatment.

All told, during May, there were 83 rescue missions, many under enemy fire, and 39 survivors picked up. The ship stood at General Quarters 63 times.

By now, men were wondering if they were going to be stuck out there forever. The Japanese showed no signs of giving up. The rainy season had started. Visibility was bad at sea and on Okinawa tanks, jeeps and ambulances were stuck in the mud. Sodden, weary troops slogged their way through. Then, on May 29th. a company of Marines captured what was left of Shuri Castle, the highest point and the most heavily defended on the island. Forced to retreat, the Japanese stubbornly fought on as General Ushijima prepared to make his last stand on a line across the Kiyama peninsula.

The air attacks on shipping continued. On one rescue mission, Lt. Kouns with 5 survivors on board taxied 150 miles back to base escorted by USS Schroeder. Three times during June, missions from the Bering Strait picked up survivors inside Kago Shima Bay in Kyushu, under enemy fire.

Spekhart recalls that on June 2. Lt. Dorton answered a distress call from a Coronado which was badly damaged as it attempted to land and rescue a ditched fighter plane's crew.

"They were right up inside Kago Shima Bay, Kyushu. I remember thinking, God we're in Japan. They'll get us for sure.

"Lt. Dorton was pilot and he was pretty good. But he didn't much like the stuff them Japs were firing at us. I didn't see as how we could get out alive what with the rough sea and the heavy fire.

"But we landed in a bit of smoother water and then taxied out to the survivors. Were they glad to see us! We had a hell of a job getting them all aboard and we did it just in time. That Coronado just turned over and sank like a stone. All aboard were wondering whether we could take off with all that weight, but we did and we got them all back to base in one piece."

The survivors were Ens. R. G. Koeller, VBF9 USS Yorktown; Lt. G. W. Head, Lt.jg H. S. Miller, Ens. R Straws; Bailey, E. R. AAMM2c, Brislow, H. A. Amm3; Cottell, C. R. ARM2c; Nurnberg, G. W. AOM3c; Williams, C. E. ARM1c; Johnson, R. F. AMM2c;

Myers, D. N. AMM2c; Collins, C. H. AOM2c; all of VPB13.

Later that day Lt. Watson landed in the same area and rescued Lt. M. Hershey, from USS Ticonderoga.

So it went on day after day. Officers and crew were all feeling the strain of broken rest and the ever present threat of death and destruction from so many directions. Even fueling a plane could be life threatening in a rough sea or if someone was careless.

Plane V-4 of VPB-21 was being towed clear of the Bering Strait by the ship's personnel boat after having just been refueled when the pilot shouted, "Hang on to the towline until I get one engine started." Then as soon as his engine started, without any warning, the pilot began taxiing with the towline still attached dragging the boat under. Immediately it capsized trapping one man underneath.

"Stop that damn plane." shouted the refueling officer knowing the trapped man must be rescued right away if his life was to be saved.

Already a rescue team was in the water but they could do nothing until the plane stopped.

"The SOB can't or won't hear. What the hell's the matter with him.?"

Finally, after what seemed a life time they got the pilot's attention and the man was extricated, but not a moment too soon.

"I thought I was done for." he gasped as they brought him up, "There was no way I could get from under that thing."

"Engine no good now salt water in it." Blanket remarked sadly, he liked the boat. He fantasized about taking the little boat and finding his way home. He knew it would never happen, but thinking about it helped to forget the war.

"Don't worry about the boat, Blanket. A good overhaul will put her right." Sam reassured him.

On June 21st Lt. Strayer was just returning to the ship after rescuing 1st Lt. John Dooley of the 333rd Army Fighter Squadron, when the Air Raid alert sounded.

The Bering Strait was already at General Quarters and to the cheers of all aboard, the ship splashed a Jake (Japanese float plane). But they didn't have long to rejoice.

"Two bogies to port, sir." CIC reported as two kamikazis flew low over the anchorage.

With a terrible explosion one suicided into USS Curtis causing her to burst into flames. Then the second plane circled over the Bering Strait ignoring her gunfire.

Even the skipper thought this was it. But the plane suddenly turned and made for the Kenneth Whiting. Just as it started its dive to suicide her, it nosed over, smoke came out of the cockpit and it fell just short of the port side of the ship.

"That was a close one." the skipper said. The gun crews sure earned their keep today."

Later they learned the Curtis had sustained considerable damage and had many casualties.

"Our luck can't hold much longer." Bat mourned, "We ought to get out before its too late."

"I'm all for it. Any suggestions, Bat." but before he could answer General Quarters sounded again. It was midnight before all was quiet, at least for a while.

By now Kerama Retto had a horrible smell of death and corruption hanging over it. The sea was filled with debris, oil slick and trash. The sight of heavily damaged ships everywhere added to the feeling expressed in the mess next morning.

"This place is getting on my nerves. It's nothing but a graveyard."

"Floating funeral home that's what it is. If we don't get out soon we'll all be corpses."

"When you look at all them ships that's been hit, its a wonder we're not corpses already."

"It's when they come in at half mast and then start singing Eternal Father — that's what gets to me."

"You get used to it. You have to. After you've lost a few shipmates, you get used to it. You just hope they go quick."

But they didn't have much time to think as General Quarters sounded five times that day and six rescue missions were flown.

So it went on day after day.

Meanwhile on Okinawa, the Japanese were being forced back in every direction. By 21st June General Ushijima realized that the end was near. Both General Ushijuma and General Cho were samurai. They could never surrender and so they went about their preparations for hari-kari.

As dawn was breaking on the 22nd June, the two Generals came out of their cave and seated themselves on a white cloth facing the rising sun. Each is disemboweled with a ceremonial knife and then decapitated.

So ended all organized fighting by the Japanese. However, there were pockets of resistance in caves and tunnels which required almost two more weeks of mopping up.

On June 30th. Air Sea Rescue was assumed by CTU 30.5.2 in USS Gardiners Bay and the Bering Strait ceased to act as coordinating control tender. However, she continued to support and maintain the aircraft and house part of the flight crews of Rescue Squadron Three. After going through so much together, it wasn't easy to part company.

In the wardroom and the enlisted mess there were some resounding send offs. The Commanding Officer of Rescue Squadron Three extended the congratulations and appreciation of the pilots and aircrewmen to the Aviation personnel of the Bering Strait.

"The teamwork, efficiency of all hands in the V division made it possible to maintain an operational availability of 81% of all planes. In addition, the aviation unit of the Bering Strait accomplished an exceptional amount of work on the water, none of which has ever been considered a routine operation." said Lt. Commander Bonvillian.

Later he sent an official communication to the skipper praising the work of the aviation crewmen and asked that a copy be put in each man's service record.

This appreciation and a Naval Dispatch to the Bering Strait from Admiral Halsey saying,

> CONGRATULATIONS TO YOUR DUMBO CREW WHO THUMBED THEIR NOSES AT THE EMPEROR BY MAKING A SUCCESSFUL RESCUE IN KAMASHIMA BAY X SUCH PERFORMANCE OF DUTY IS A LASTING INSPIRATION FOR ALL HANDS X WELL DONE X HALSEY XXX

raised everyone's spirits, but it was a great relief to all aboard when the ship received orders to leave Kerama Retto for Chimu Wan, Okinawa, on July 15th

Planes under the direction of the Bering Strait carried out 270 missions during the three months she was in Kerama Retto. 105 men were rescued representing 39 different squadrons - 26 Navy, 10 Marine Corps, 2 Army Air Force and 1 Royal Navy. During this period the Bering Strait stood at General Quarters 154 times.

# IN THE UNITED STATES OF AMERICA

## JULY 1945

By now the peace faction in Japan was urging Foreign Minister Togo to seek the help of the Soviet Union in making peace with the Allies. The Emperor had made the suggestion that Prince Konoye should lead a delegation to Moscow. However, the Soviet Foreign Ministry refused to receive such a delegation or to act in a peace making capacity. Stalin was not ready to help with the peace process at this time. He had his own plans for ensuring that Communism would take over the newly liberated countries of Europe now that the Americans were shifting their troops to the Pacific, also, he wanted to acquire southern Sakhalin and the Kurile Islands from the Japanese and had promised at the Yalta Conference to declare war on Japan in return for these acquisitions.

Although the Emperor of Japan and Prince Konoye were prepared to explore the possibility of making peace, the war lords of Japan were strongly against it.

Meanwhile, scientists in the United States were working night and day to have the two atomic bombs ready by the next Summit meeting. The tragically heavy losses in Okinawa had made it clear that the Japanese would fight with fanatical strength to protect their homeland and that an invasion would cause losses of over a million American lives. While aware of the risks of letting loose nuclear power on the world, the President's Interim Committee unanimously re commended that the atomic bomb should be used as soon as possible to bring an end to the war and save American lives.

Harry Hopkins had met with Stalin in Moscow and the Summit meeting was arranged to take place in July, starting on the 16th.

If the bomb tested successfully, it would be ready for use in August and this would provide what Secretary of War Stimpson called " a master card ," to play at the Summit.

Far out in the salt grass desert of New Mexico, a tall hundred foot tower has been built from which the explosion heralding the new age of nuclear power, will blast off. J. Robert Oppenheimer, the leader of the Manhattan Project, is scarcely able to eat or sleep. Excitement mingled with dread, is everywhere as the test date draws near.

Will the test be successful? Are the calculations regarding the effects correct? Will the deadly radiation extend farther than expected? These are the unanswered questions in everyone's mind.

The night of July 15-16 was rain soaked, but it cleared enough by early morning. Oppenheimer and General Thomas Farell waited in a bunker five miles south of the tower. At 5:29 a.m. the bomb dropped from the tower and exploded with an intensity of color and light never seen before. Then came the great shock wave and the a tremendous roar of sound which echoed and re echoed among the surrounding mountains. The test was successful! Suddenly, Oppenheimer exclaimed, " I am become Death, the destroyer of worlds."

One of the physicists standing near him shivered. Oppenheimer's words reminded him of the name given to the desert area by the conquistadors, Jornada del Muerto, Journey of Death. Was this morning the start of a Journey of Death for the whole world?

President Truman was already at the Summit Conference held in the beautiful Cecilienhof Palace in Potsdam, a suburb of Berlin when he received the "master card" sent by General Groves in a coded message confirming that the first atomic explosion had taken place successfully. With his confidence boosted by this amazing news, Truman was prepared to take a hard line with Stalin demanding that the countries liberated by the Russians must have democratic governments.

To Truman's surprise, Stalin received the announcement of the successful atomic explosion in silence. What the President did not know was that Russia had been getting information from their spy network about the Allies work on the bomb since 1941 and were using this information to make a 'super bomb' themselves.

\When Hitler invaded Russia, many intellectuals in the West thought it necessary to help the Russians in every way they could. In fact, it was Donald Mclean, a British diplomat and member of the Cambridge spy ring, who gave top secret information regarding the work proceeding in the British uranium factory, to his counterparts in Russia. Also, a spy known as 'Perseus' was actually placed by the Russians in Los Alamos to keep them informed. The wife of this man, Lona Cohen, acted as a courier between Los Alamos and the Russians intelligence in New York.

However, Stalin had not expected the United States to have the Bomb ready so soon. Always suspicious of the West, Stalin was afraid that the Bomb might eventually, be used against Russia and the Russian scientists were urged to hurry up their work on the project.

A 13 point appeal to end the war was agreed upon and broadcast to Japan calling for unconditional surrender, but, as there was no assurance about the future of the Emperor, the appeal was rejected. Was the possibility of an early peace lost? The appeal, which was to become known as the Potsdam Declaration, was initialed by the United States, Britain and China, but not by Russia.

Although Churchill attended the early meetings and signed the Potsdam Declaration, his place was taken by Clement Atlee the new British Prime Minister, for the remaining meetings. This meant that Stalin was the only one left of the leaders who had conducted the war from the beginning.

No one was sure why Churchill's party lost the election. Was it because the British people were fed up with the 'Blood, Sweat and Tears' of war and wanted a change? Churchill had lost many votes by taking away the little bit of extra pay the Royal Navy had always given sailors for 'destroyer' duty. When that happened, Churchill, who always referred to himself as a Naval Person, lost the support of the sailors who felt he had let them down.

The loss of both Roosevelt and Churchill left Stalin as the strongest player in the maneuvering for control of the liberated countries.

Meanwhile, the men in the ships, the planes and on the battle field were still fighting and dying.

## MIKATA'S JOURNEY

The Mikata's had a much closer relationship than the typical Japanese man and wife. In the 40's the Japanese husband treated his wife as an inferior and she expected to stay in the background.

When her husband brought male guests, the Japanese wife would serve the meal but she did not sit and eat with them.

While the Japanese wife was expected to stay quietly in the home with the children, the Japanese husband came and went when he liked. Yoshio Mikata was different. When he was ashore he liked to spend the time with his family. Although the Mikata marriage was arranged, they had quickly fallen deeply in love with each other.

Every time he came home from the sea, Joshio Mikata and his wife had another honeymoon.

The long separations and dangers that both were exposed to in the war, served to deepen their love even more. Mama Mikata did not let the children see the tears she shed or let them know how her heart ached with fear for their father's safety. She tried to keep a cheerful face though she knew, from whispered rumors, that things were going badly for the Imperial Navy. Sometimes she felt as if her heart was weeping tears of blood, draining her life away drop by drop.

Nothing official had been heard about Yoshio Mikata's ship for over a month and they knew this was bad. If all was going well the radio told what glorious deeds had been done over and over again, but when a ship was sunk, it was never mentioned openly.

"How will Papa san find us, Mama?" Ariko asked as they trudged along the road one morning.

"I wrote a letter to him telling him we are safe and on our way to your Grandmother in Kyoto."

"Do we have to walk much further? I'm so tired, Mama"

"It's a very long way to Kyoto, but we will rest a while and perhaps some kind lady will give us shelter for the night.

"I wish another man would come with a big cart and give us all a ride like that one did yesterday." Kiko said.

"Yes, yes, I wish for the same thing, but most people who are lucky enough to have a cart, only have room for their family and belongings." said Mama.

"Couldn't we buy a little cart, Mama and then we could take turns riding in it." Ariko asked hopefully.

"Carts cost a lot of money and we only have a few yen left which we must keep for food. Also, it is not possible to find a cart. Everyone with money is trying to buy one so they can escape with their property."

"If I could find some wheels and boards , Mama, I could make a cart." Kiko said eagerly. "I saw a bicycle near the side of the road. It was all broken, but it looked as if the wheels were all right."

"Where was it?"

"It was where that big house had burned down."

"That's about a kilometer back." said Mama, "I'm just too tired to walk back and it might not be of any use, someone might have taken it anyway."

"I'll go back and look while you and Ariko sit and rest.

"There's no need for us all to go." and without waiting for permission, he started back along the road.

Ariko squatted down beside her mother on the roadside. Their feet were sore and their clothing covered with dust.

"I'm thirsty, Mama."

"Yes, I know. As soon as Kiko comes back we will ask at the next house we see. They will surely give us water."

There were so many refugees begging for food and shelter, that no one offered anything anymore. They didn't have enough food for them selves, they had long since given away what they could spare but usually, they would give water and sometimes shelter for the night. The Mikatas hated to sleep out of doors now that the noise of American planes coming to bomb the cities, shattered the silence of every night. Indoors it was possible to shut out the sound.

Kiko hurried back along the road hoping that no one had taken the bicycle. It seemed a lot further than a kilometer. But he kept going, knowing that if he stopped to rest, it would be all the harder to get going again.

They had had no food since the previous night and all he could think about was a large bowl of steaming rice with some juicy pieces of fish or meat to go with it. Would he ever get a good meal again, he wondered? It seemed like years since his stomach was really filled. He'd been hungry so long that he was sure he would eat a mountain of rice if he ever got the chance.

People passed him also fleeing from the city, dragging their few belongings in a handcart. Some old people were lying by the roadside, too exhausted to move. Kiko no longer took much notice of them. After ten days on the road, he had seen so many dead and dying that they had become part of the nightmare of their journey - Hardly real.

In the distance he saw the burnt ruins of the house and he trotted faster, fearful that someone would take the bicycle before he could get there.

But he need not have worried, there in the middle of the charred beams and rubbish was the bicycle crushed beneath the debris of the outer wall. Carefully, he pulled it out and found that the frame was shattered but the two wheels were intact. Then he realized that he had no way of getting the wheels out of the twisted bicycle. He had been so excited at the thought of using the bicycle to make a handcart, that he hadn't stopped to think about needing tools. Then he noticed that the bars joining the two halves of the bicycle were badly cracked and bent. Could he break them through and then somehow drag the two halves along with him? Gathering all his strength he put his foot on the mangled bars and bent them in two until the two wheels rested on each other. But the bars did not break. Panting for breath he stood looking at the thing while tears of exhaustion and disappointment rolled down his face. He would have to go empty handed after all.

There would be no handcart.

It was beginning to get dark and he knew his Mother and Ariko would be sitting by the roadside waiting and they would be frightened and worried thinking something had happened to him if he didn't get back soon.

"What are you doing, boy?" a rough voice startled him and

Kiko turned quickly afraid it might be the owner of the bicycle.

Then he saw it was a policeman and he was even more afraid.

"I was going to take the wheels to make a handcart for my mother and sister to ride in, Sir. The bicycle is all broken." he answered timidly.

"I don't see your mother and sister. Where are they?" "They are waiting for me by the side of the road. We are trying to get to our family in Kyoto?

The policeman said nothing but he walked over to look at the bicycle. "Are the wheels in a good condition?" "Yes, sir." Kiko said eagerly. "But I can't get them out. I don't have any tools."

"Let's see." and the policeman rested his bicycle against the ruins and bent over the bike. He twisted the bent halves back and forth several times until they broke in two.

"Now, boy, you can take one piece in each hand and pull the wheels behind you. When you come across someone with tools, ask them to help you."

" Thank you, sir, thank you, I will start on my way now. My mother will be worried."

"If I see them, I'll tell them you are on your way." Kiko found it was easy to drag the wheels along and he was able to keep up a good pace. Getting the wheels renewed his strength and he got back to his mother and sister before it was dark. They were still sitting on the side of the road where he had left them.

"Look, Mama-san! I found the wheels!. I'll be able to make a cart. A policeman helped me and he said he would tell you I was coming. Did you see him?"

"Yes, he told us you were on your way and he gave us some bread. I saved a piece for you. He was very kind."

Kiko's eyes lit up as he took the little piece of bread, " I'm so hungry, Mama, I could eat a whale. I keep thinking of all the lovely rice and fish you used to cook for us."

"I keep thinking about it too." Ariko said. "When we had plenty, I never thought about it very much, only if I wanted something very special."

"When you're hungry it is natural to think of food, but it is better to think of other things if you can." Mama san said sadly. "Now we had better see if we can find somewhere to sleep before its too late."

“Do you think someone will let us sleep in their house.?”

“I hope so. We will ask.”

“There are no houses anywhere here.”

“Well, we will keep walking and find one or some kind of shelter. There are so many people ahead there won’t be any room left for us.” Kiko said.

“We will sleep under a tree if there is nowhere else.

Remember, my children, we must suffer everything for our Emperor and our country.”

"I know, Mama, but I’m so tired and hungry.”

“Food always tastes better when you are hungry. Let us go a little further before we give up.”

So they walked on and on, conscious only of putting one foot in front of the other. Then, suddenly, there was the most delicious smell of food cooking.

“Mama, I can smell fish cooking.”

“Yes, I can also.”

“Let’s go and see if they will give us some, Mama.” Kiko said.

“It is too dark to see if there is a house. There are no lights anywhere. Where can the smell be coming from.” Mama san began to wonder if hunger was turning their minds.

They stood still, sniffing the air like hunting dogs. The smell of food made their empty stomachs ache.

“I think its across the road. There’s fields over there, I think.” Kiko said.

“Lets go and see. There maybe some trees where we could shelter.”

They crossed the road and by the light of a faint moon they saw what had once been a cultivated field for growing vegetables.

But nothing was growing now. The smell of frying fish was getting stronger.

“There must be somebody there in those trees.”

As they got nearer they saw something or someone moving.

“Be careful, there’s someone there.” Mama said. “We had better not go any further.”

“Shall I go and ask if they’ will let us have some of their food?” Kiko asked.

"No, we will walk over together then they will see we mean no harm. If they will not share their food, they might let us sleep under the trees."

"I'm frightened." Ariko said clinging to her mother.

"Don't be frightened. Stay close to me."

Then the figure of a man came towards them and they saw, as he came close, that it was an old man..

"Go! Go away. This is my property." he shouted waving a stick at them.

"Could we sleep under your trees, sir. We are so tired and we won't disturb you." Mama asked bowing low.

The old man came closer and took a good look at them. The moon was brighter now and they could see he was very old.

"I suppose you could, but I don't want you here. Go away."

"Oh, please let us stay, sir. We have been walking all day." Mama said.

The old man grunted something they couldn't hear and then waved his stick to the last tree in the group and said, "You can stay there, but only until morning."

"Thank you, thank you sir." Mama said bowing and Ariko and Kiko murmured their thanks bowing even lower.

The walking over to the last tree, they thankfully sank onto the soft ground, their empty stomachs aggravated by the delicious smell of the fish.

"He must have a cooking stove." Ariko said.

"Yes, but I can't see anything, but he must have it hidden among the trees."

"I wish he would give us some."

"Do not think about it. Just try and sleep. Tomorrow we will be more fortunate, perhaps." Ariko crept up close to her mother and wondered how she could possibly go to sleep with that smell of fish so close. I don't want to suffer anymore for the Emperor or my country, she thought, I just want something to eat. Immediately she was ashamed of her thoughts and murmured an apology to the Emperor and her country, hoping that nothing terrible would happen to her for thinking such a thing and she crept even closer to her mother for comfort..

Then suddenly, out of the darkness, the old man appeared.

Mama sat up quickly and tried to stand, but the old man said, "Do not disturb yourselves I have brought a little of my food for you to share." and he put a small tray with two little piles, one of fish and one of rice, into Mama san's hands and bowed.

Tears came into Mama's eyes and rolled down her cheeks. For a moment she could say nothing. Then, placing the tray on the ground she knelt and kissed the old man's feet murmuring her thanks over and over again. Then, just as suddenly as he had appeared, he disappeared again.

"Our prayers are answered. Look! Real fish and Japanese rice! Eat slowly children." and Mama divided the food in three portions. Never had anything tasted so good.

After they had finished the meal, Mama Mikata said , "We must say our prayers of thanks."

"But there is no Shrine here, Mama."

"We will say the prayers without the Shrine tonight. The Emperor will forgive."

The Mikatas were of the Shinto religion and prayers were usually said in the Shinto Shrine. Every town and village has its own Shrine. The head of the Shinto religion is the Emperor and up to the end of World War II, the Emperor was considered Divine and Shinto prayers were always addressed to him.

After saying their prayers, the sleeping mat was unrolled and they lay down under the shelter of the friendly tree. Ariko and Kiko were asleep immediately, but Mama could not sleep. Too many questions and too many fears surged through her tired mind.

Sometimes she felt she could not bear it any longer and would have to kill the children and herself. Where was her husband? Why didn't he write? How would he know where to write? How could she tell him where they were? How could she find food for the children each day? How long could they stay alive with hardly any food, only a few yen and no place to sleep or bathe or wash their clothes? Supposing their relatives were gone when they finally reached Kyoto what would they do? Their house might have bombed. There was never any news of destruction given to the people, all they knew were rumors passed from one refugee to another.

By daylight, Mama was worn out from lack of sleep and worry, but she tried to put on a cheerful face for the children's sake.

They had slept peacefully throughout the night and woke up bright and full of energy.

"Do you think the gentleman will give us more food, Mama?"

"He said we must leave this morning so I don't think he will. We can drink some water from the stream and then go back to the road. We might find a house where they will give us something to eat."

Obediently Ariko and Kiko went to the stream and took turns drinking from the bowl Mama carried in a sack on her back. After they had all had a drink they washed their hands and faces.

"Today when we see a Shrine we will say the hundred prayer.

You will humbly ask for a little food and shelter and strength to continue our journey."

"Yes, Mama." and both bowed to their mother. They both knew the importance of the hundred prayer. Things must be very bad if it was necessary to do this. Usually they stopped at a Shrine several times day and said a short formal prayer to the Emperor, but the hundred prayer was different. It was a very solemn thing said only when something was desperately needed. The request had to be repeated over and over one hundred times. Mama san must be very hungry, they decided. What they didn't know was that Mama had a different request- She wanted her husband home, safe and sound. Even wounded and crippled will do, I will take care of him, she promised when they prostrated themselves at the Shrine.

"Do you think our prayers will be answered soon, Mama?" Ariko asked.

"We will say the hundred prayer every day and the Emperor will surely answer us."

That afternoon they came to a farmhouse occupied by an elderly woman. She said her husband and son were in the Imperial Army and her daughter was working in an arms factory in Yamamato.

She was alone and could not do all the work on the farm herself, so if they wanted to stay for a while she would feed and shelter them in return for work.

Mama thanked her with tears in her eyes. "We will work hard for you, my lady." then turning to the children she said, "You see, the Emperor answered our prayers. Thank the kind lady and then we will thank our Emperor."

Life on the farm made the time pass quickly. They worked hard doing whatever was needed both inside and out. The children began to look healthy again and they gained weight. While the food was plain, it was nourishing and they had the occasional egg from the fowls. Mrs. Sansara, the farm lady, had a little rice stored away and she brought some out every Feast Day It was cooked with the greatest care and respect. Not a grain was wasted.

Mama got some comfort from seeing the children happy and healthy again. But she got no answer to her prayer and the ache which never left her heart grew sharper.

Any spare time Kiko had after doing his share of farmwork he spent making his handcart. Mrs. Sansara, told him he could have some of the old pieces of wood that lay around the yard. Although this varied in length and width, Kiko was able to make a frame and nail the pieces on like a jigsaw puzzle. Then he found an old fence post and when he cut off the rotten end, there was enough good wood left for an axle. But he had no way of fixing on the wheels and for a while he had to give up.

One day Mrs. Sansara asked, ' How is your cart? I thought it would be finished by now."

"It's all finished except for the wheels. I don't know how to fix them on the axle."

"My cousin is coming next week. She might help you."

"She! Is she an engineer? I didn't know that a woman would know about such things."

"There are not so many, but some have been trained during the war to take the place of men."

Shugo san turned out to be a wizard with wheels. She had a box of second hand spare parts and soon she had the wheels firmly fixed on to the axle.

"You'll need shafts to pull it along."

"Yes, I will make them now the wheels are on. It is a good cart do you not think? "

"It's the best I've seen. There's some old paint cans in the shed. There might be some paint left in them. You could paint the cart, if you liked."

So, by the time they were ready to leave Mrs. Sansara, the cart was finished and painted a dark brown.

This time the Mikatas started their journey with mended shoes and clean clothes. Also they had some rice and vegetables and a little bag of tea which they packed into the handcart together with the sleeping mat, three rice bowls and a saucepan and there was still enough room for a person to ride.

"You shall have the first ride, Mama." Kiko said.

"Thank you, my son, but I am not tired yet. I will walk for a time and rest in the cart later. We still have a long way to go."

"How far is it, Mama ?"

"It will take us many days, but it will be easier now we have the cart."

It was the middle of July before they reached Kyoto. They were excited and worried at the same time. Would their grandmother be there? Would the house be there? Or had it been burned by the Americans? Mama Mikata was silently praying that there would be a letter or some news of Papa san. She had written telling him where they were while they were with Mrs. Sansara, but there had been no reply in spite of the fact that she had said the hundred prayer every day. Also she had written telling that they were making their way to Kyoto so maybe there was a letter waiting for her.

What shall I do if there is nothing— How can I live without him? Poor Mama san trudged on keeping her despair locked in her heart where it was slowly and remorselessly eating it away.

Kyoto is an ancient and beautiful city. It was once the capital city of Japan and the Imperial family lived there for eleven centuries until the capital was moved to Tokyo. There are many Shinto Shrines and some of the important Buddhist sects have their headquarters in Kyoto. The famous golden pavilion where the Shogun, Yoshimitsu lived, is now turned into a Buddhist temple.

As the Mikatas walked down the mountain road they could see the city in the distance. It looked undamaged. Their hopes rose, their Grandmother must be alive and well and her house safe. They began to hurry. The house was just outside the city and, at last, they saw it. Kiko and Ariko started to run, but their mother stopped them, "We must arrive politely. Comb your hair and straighten your kimonos. We will go to the house together. Remember to be respectful to your grandmother."

Grandmother Mikata was delighted to see them, "I have been expecting you every day. We heard rumors of Tokyo being very badly damaged by the American fires and bombs and we thought you would come to Kyoto for safety. You must stay until the Americans are all killed by our Emperor" Mama Mikata and the children thanked their grandmother with many bows and Mama said, "Thank you, many, many times, you are of the greatest kindness. We cannot repay you, but many blessings and long life will be yours because of your goodness."

Then tea and rice cakes were brought on a lacquer tray and they knew at last, they had a home once more.

Now Mama could ask the question she was almost afraid to utter, "Is there a letter or message for me?"

"Were you expecting a message, my daughter? I am sorry to tell you there is none."

Mama felt a terrible numbness, then a sharp pain cut through her heart. For a moment she thought she would die and go to her ancestors there and then. Then she felt the tears roll down her cheeks as she whispered,' "I am worried about Yoshio, my husband, I don't know where he is. There has been no letter or message from him all these months."

"But you know he is with our great Imperial Navy. He has the honor of serving the Emperor and our country. He has no time for letters, my daughter." grandmother spoke reprovingly.

"He used to send letters regularly."

"When he is able he will send a message you may be sure. He would be shamed to have you doubt him."

Mama bowed her head, her mother in law was probably right, but somehow it didn't take the ache from her heart.

## YOSHIO

Although the Imperial headquarters put out constant details of the successes of the Imperial Forces, Yoshio, like many other Japanese knew that there were terrible losses that were never revealed. When he learned that his ship with seven other destroyers was ordered to accompany the famous carrier, Yamato, to Okinawa, his first thought was of joy to have the honor of being in the Special Surface Task Force with this great ship. The biggest and most beautiful ship in the world was how she was described in Japan.

She had nineteen 18.1 inch guns and 150 antiaircraft and machine guns and although she was such a large ship, she had a top speed of 27 knots. Japan was resting its Fate on the Yamato as she set forth for Okinawa.

As he boarded his ship, Yoshio had a strange feeling he might never return, so before the task force left, he wrote letters to Mama san and to Kiko and Ariko, telling them many things a Japanese parent would not talk of normally.

Because he had been at sea so long, he had not received Mama san's letter telling him that they were leaving to go to Kyoto, so he addressed the letters to Tokyo but, by the time they arrived at the burnt down home, the family had gone.

The Task Force moved out of the Inland Sea on April 6. taking a route which it was hoped would avoid being spotted by enemy search planes. But Admiral Ito had not expected that two submarines, the USS Threadfin and the USS Hackleback would be in sonar contact with the Task Force and had already reported that they were leaving through the southern entrance of the Inland Sea.

With this information Admiral Mitscher was able to move three of his task groups close enough to fly searches in the early morning of April 7 At 0823 an Essex plane reported that the Yamato was moving west after passing through Van Diemen Strait. Without air cover the Yamato had little chance as the American planes attacked with bombs and torpedoes and at 1423 she had sunk to the bottom.

Meanwhile the other ships were being ferociously attacked and Yoshio ship was hit by nine bombs and three torpedoes.

With a horrible slow determination the bow of the ship began to settle in the water. Men were desperately trying to scramble up the steep angle of the deck to avoid being sucked down into the sea.

Guns were still firing, boats were being lowered, orders being given, then there was a flash of fire and it seemed the whole ship blew apart.

Yoshio found himself in the water. He looked around trying to locate a lifeboat but all he could see was debris and wreckage and the bodies of sailors thrown into the sea by the explosion.

There were enemy planes still overhead and he waited for the bullets to hit him. He was sure the Americans would strafe the survivors as the Japanese planes did, but nothing happened and he saw the planes were flying off.

Clutching at a piece of wood he swam as hard as he could to get away from the suction of the sinking ship. He tried to keep his head above the water, but it was impossible the waves were too high and he gagged as the oil and salt water got into his mouth and nose.

A wooden crate floated near him and he struggled to wards it thinking he could use it to keep afloat. It was covered in oil, but he managed to get hold of a piece of the wire which held it together. He knew it was his duty to stay alive and continue fighting for the Emperor. His life was not his own.

More planes flew overhead, but he could tell from the sound they were American. He tried to get under the crate so he wouldn't be seen as he was sure they had come back to kill any survivors they saw in the water. But nothing happened, they circled the sinking ship and flew off. For the moment he was safe.

Yoshio knew there wasn't much hope of being picked up, all planes and ships were needed to attack the enemy so the Emperor and the Homeland could be kept safe. He must try and reach one of the islands and find some way to get back and fight again.

Where was he? Which direction should he take? Then he realized he had no choice. He could barely keep afloat. He'd have to go where the winds and waves took him. A chill went through him. Would he ever see home again ? His wife, his children, Kiko and Ariko. He'd been away so long would they remember him? He had never felt fear in battle, but to be alone, drifting in the unforgiving sea filled him with horror. But his lifelong training made him pull himself together. If to suffer this with dignity was what was required of him, he would do so.

Where were the boats? Some must have been lowered. He looked around but there were no boats to be seen. Now he was away from much of the debris, he could see other men struggling to keep afloat. Some had life jackets, most had nothing. There seemed to be a lot less now. Many must have been injured in the explosion and they would not be able to stay afloat. He was lucky to be unhurt, but, he thought, it would be better to die quickly for the Emperor in the explosion, than to die bit by bit in the ocean. Then he was immediately ashamed of his thought.

Suddenly something clutched at his foot. A shark ! He kicked hard then, to his shame, he saw it was a sailor who was trying to get his help. The man's face was a mass of blood and oil. His features were almost obliterated. It was impossible for him to speak. Yoshio put an arm around the man and supported him until he was able to cling to the crate. There was nothing more he could do.

Neither of them had a life jacket.

They could hear the guns from the ships and planes as the battle continued and then after what seemed hours there was silence.

Not long after they sighted a ship coming towards them. By now Yoshio was too exhausted to recognize whether it was friend or foe.

The shock of the explosion and the battering of the waves had numbed his brain. He was also having to support the other man who was getting weaker and weaker. He could scarcely believe it when the ship hove to and a boat was lowered and came towards them.

In a moment a boathook jabbed into the crate and pulled them to the boat and they saw it was manned by Japanese.

Yoshio never forgot the relief of hearing his own language as a voice shouted, "Bring that one aboard." pointing to Yoshio.

Strong hands lifted him out of the water and brought him safely into the boat. Immediately, it sped away.

"Stop! There's another man there. You must go back. He's injured."

"We do not take the injured. They are not able to fight."

"You cannot leave him. He will die." Yoshio pleaded desperately.

"We have our orders. We continue on to battle. We take only those who can fight again."

Yoshio knew it was no use to say more, but he was never to forget the sight of the man's bloody face as he sank down into the ocean unable to hold on alone. Can this truly be the wish of our beloved Emperor, he wondered?.

The ship that rescued Yoshio fought on until she was badly damaged and then she was one of four who managed to limp back to Sasebo.

Yoshio hoped to be allowed to go to Tokyo to see his family.

He did not know that they had left for Kyoto. None of their letters had been forwarded to him and, as none of the crew were given leave, he wrote a letter and gave it to a friend to deliver for him.

Sadly, the friend never reached Tokyo. He was killed in an air raid on the outskirts of the city.

About a week later Yoshio died of pneumonia brought on by swallowing the oil and salt water which had gotten into his lungs when he was struggling in the sea after being blown from his ship.

Mama Mikata never learned what had happened to her husband, she lived on waiting and hoping that some day he would return.

Sometimes she would go to the Sento Palace Gardens where she and Yoshio had walked together on their honeymoon. There, in the peace of the 17th century garden and the memories it brought back, she would find a little solace.

Her favorite place was that part of the garden which once belonged to the wife of the Emperor Gomizuno-o who was forced to abdicate by the shoguns.

The whole scene reflected the love the Empress had for her husband. The Akose Pool, so named from 'Ako' the respectful term for 'husband' is bordered by the golden blossoms of wild roses.

This rose is the symbol of feminine love. Somehow she felt

Yoshio must know that she was there waiting and sending her love to him.

After a while she would walk up the Hill of Good Fortune and then on to the Hill of Calm. This was where she and Yoshio had watched the moon rise in those happy days gone by.

Those days before any thought of war had touched them. When the future stretched before them like the gleaming rays of the rising sun.

Will those days ever come again she wondered sadly, as she made her way from the garden.

## CHIMU WAN

### OKINAWA

It was while the Bering Strait was at Chimu Wan, Okinawa, that a strange thing happened. A man on a raft made of a couple of logs lashed together, was spotted paddling with his hands towards the ship.

"I can't tell what he is— doesn't look like a Jap. He's not in uniform." the skipper said as he sighted the man through his binoculars.

"Think he's an escaped PW, sir." the Exec asked.

"Hard to tell, but he isn't armed and seems very weak. He's not making much headway. Have a boat lowered and help him aboard. I'll take a look at him."

As soon as the man was aboard, Innis saw he was in very bad shape. He was almost too weak to stand and there was a horrible festering wound on the side of his head. He stared straight ahead and said nothing.

Without wasting time, the man was put in the care of the medics with instructions to do all they could for him. Later the medical officer reported to Innis that the man had been wounded by shrapnel and the wound was infected.

"We can take care of that and we can feed him up. He's evidently been without decent food for sometime. But there's something else wrong. I don't know if its the head wound or shock, but he doesn't know his name or anything else."

"What about dog tags?"

"Doesn't have any and he's only wearing some ragged swim trunks so there's no way of knowing what outfit he belongs to, if any. I think he's American, though."

"Is it the infection that makes him so weak.?"

"Could be. Lack of food could account for much of it, but there may be some brain damage and or shellshock. The 10,000 yard stare, you know."

"Yes, I know." Innis was aware of that stare. He'd seen the look on the faces of exhausted and shellshocked Marines after the battles on Iwo and Okinawa.

"Well, he's sleeping now and he's young, not more than 19 or 20. That's on his side. We cleaned him up and fed him and maybe he'll be a different man when he wakes up."

"I hope so for his sake and for his family. They've probably been told he's missing and going through hell waiting to hear. Let me know if there's any change."

"Yes, sir, I certainly will. In any case he should be transferred where there are more facilities. He needs some tests to make sure there's no brain damage. I've already made a few calls."

" Good, let me know if you meet with any difficulty or want any help from me."

"Yes, sir.

The man was flown out later that day, still as silent and numb as when he came aboard.

"Wonder who he is. Must be awful not knowing your own name.

Funny he had no dogtags or nothing." Sam said to Bat.

"He might not be in the military. But some who are throw their dogtags out when they go into battle so their folks will keep getting their allotment if they're killed."

"How does that work out?"

"Well, say you're killed and your body isn't identified you're listed as missing and the pay goes on."

"But then you're folks won't know what happened to you and keep on worrying. I don't think that's right."

Bat shrugged, "If you've got a wife and kids they need the money, I reckon."

"Yeah, it sure is hard on them. You know, Bat, I've sort of changed. I was all fired up to enlist in the Navy as soon as I was old enough and do my bit for my country and all that and I'm not sorry I did. But war's so awful on everything and everyone, civilians as well as military and animals and trees and crops and stuff and seeing all those ships shot up and sunk and all the casualties—

I don't know— war isn't what I thought it was."

"War's a cruel and terrible thing. I read somewheres that its a failure of the intellect."

"What's that mean?"

"I dunno, I suppose it means that people should think their way out, not fight it out."

"Well , what could we think about Pearl Harbor?"

"To my mind all we could do was fight back as hard as we could and that's what we're doing. Once you're stuck in a war it does no good to think too much - just get on with it the best you can. But don't you worry, son, you're doing just fine." Bat put his hand on Sam's shoulder, "Come on, let's get a cup of coffee."

Sam smiled gratefully, Bat wasn't so bad really.

A few days later, a Marine Lt. Colonel requested permission to come aboard to see the Skipper.

"I'm on my way back to the States, Captain, but I wanted to let you know that the man we transferred to the hospital ship is probably one of the Navy's Underwater Demolition Team. The trunks he was wearing are their issue. He's being checked out and fingerprints etc. are being compared with the MIA list."

"Good. How's he doing? Is he able to tell you anything?"
"Couldn't get a word out of him. Maybe he'll start talking when he's built up some strength, or it may be brain damage. Hard to say without the tests."

"What's the UDT doing around here?"

"They're long gone. They were here to do a job clearing the way for the landing. Hell of a job if you ask me. They were mapping the reef. Marking the coral heads, water depth and such.

"The mine sweepers had done a good job, but the damn Japs had rigged up hundreds of wooden stakes 4-8ft high linked with barbed wire with small explosives attached. Covered the whole reef with them.

The Navy unloaded over a 1000 swimmers and they got rid of the lot. Under fire too. This poor guy was probably hit and been wandering around trying to keep out of sight of the Japs ever since."

"It's amazing he's alive."

"Yeah, there's not much food to be had. The people there are all starving."

"Don't we have camps for them?"

"Yeah, we do, but they've been pretty much brainwashed by the Japs. They think we'll torture and kill them if they get anywhere near us, so they try and hide in what's left of the caves, though a good many have come in now. Well, I'd better be on my way, sir."

"It was good of you to come. All aboard will be glad to hear the news. Hope he does well and good luck and a safe trip to you, Colonel."

Most of the day was spent transferring all of Rescue Squadron 3 personnel who had not left earlier, to USS Pine Island (AV-12).

In response to CTG 30.5 the Bering Strait continued to maintain and support four aircraft of that squadron. If the Bering Strait crew thought life would be a bit easier now, they were soon to find out their mistake.

Shortly before midnight the Captain approached the Officer of the Deck and gave him the night orderbook, "When you've read and understood the night orders, let me know. I'll be in my cabin."

"Aye, Aye, sir."

The O.O.D had joined the ship on her commissioning. Before the war brought him into the service, he'd been a plain clothes policeman in Jersey City. In his middle twenties, he had a ready wit and a good sense of humor. He had a flare for looking into things and could be depended upon to follow through. In the wardroom his messmates called him 'Bird Dog.' Bird Dog was surprised to be given the night order book.

Usually the skipper only wrote up night orders for the O.O.D when the ship was underway at sea. Something must be up.

As he sipped a mug of hot coffee, he read, "Anchored in Chimu Wan Harbor, Okinawa in 72 feet of water with 45 fathoms of chain out to starboard anchor. No l. generator in use for auxiliary purposes. Ship is in standby condition for getting underway on four hours notice from Task Force Commander to ride out the approaching typhoon. Flight crews are on 2 hours notice to execute the evacuation plan."

Next came the weather conditions and orders to check weather readings every 15 minutes then continued, "Report to me hourly and oftener if the barometer drops more than four hundredth of an inch or if the wind veers 10 degrees or more."

"Plot in the ship's position on the chart in the pilot house every

15 minutes and check the anchor chain at regular intervals for signs of ship dragging anchor. Forecastle watch is asleep on deck."

"Maintain a close watch on the ship's boats secured to the booms at the port and starboard quarters. Boat crews are sleeping on deck with life jackets readily available. Man the boats only if there are signs of their carrying away."

"Deliver to me immediately any signals received from the Task Force Commander. Call me immediately in case of any unusual occurrence or if in doubt."

signed Innis.

Bird Dog initialed the night order book after reading it through carefully, passed it to the quartermaster of the watch to read and then informed the Captain that the night orders had been read and understood. Then he busied himself about the deck. He took note of the boat crews sleeping in cots on deck and checked to see there was a life jacket lying under each cot. Then he crossed to the port side and satisfied himself with the conditions there.

"The boat crews need all the sleep they can get" he thought to himself. "Once the order comes for the planes to evacuate, the crews will be as busy as a one-armed paperhanger."

Walking up to the forecastle he pulled the chinstrap of his cap under his jaw and rested one foot on the anchor chain. There was no vibration so he knew the anchor wasn't dragging across the ground. Next he took a good look at the white wind streaks on the water which showed up in the glow of the light from the jack-staff.

They were streaking past the ship from dead ahead so he knew the ship was not yawing.

Returning to the bridge, he took the bearings and plotted them on the chart.

"Bull's eye." he exclaimed as the fix on the chart turned out to be the ship's plotted position.

The rest of Bird Dog's watch was routine and as soon as he was relieved he turned in to get some sleep while he could.

At 0430 the communications watch officer knocked at the Captain's door, "An operational priority message from Task Force Commander, sir."

It read as Innis had expected. All planes to evacuate as soon as they could get off the water at first light. Ships to get underway at 0700 and stand out- all except the Bering Strait whose orders were to remain behind and tend planes until they all got off safely, then get underway and proceed independently.

Reveille sounded at 0430 for "all hands" as scheduled in the Plan of the Day. For the next three hours the seadrome was alive with activity. Boats crisscrossing back and forth between the tenders and the hulks of multi engine seaplanes riding at their mooring buoys.

As soon as it was light take off clearance came from the tower control of the flagship. Fortunately, the weather was above minimum conditions for visual take off. The wind was still not above thirty knots but they needed the Jato pots to take off in the heavy swells and one by one the seaplanes took off at two minute intervals.

Soon Chimu Wan was all but deserted but there were still seven planes on the water, all of them at their moorings. Their engines had not been started. The skipper sent for the aircraft maintenance officer.

"Lieutenant, all our planes got off. Give my congratulations to the maintenance crews. Now, I want you to take your leading chief and whatever you need and go out in a boat and see what the hold-up is. Give me a call over the voice radio on the seadrome control circuit and report the situation from each plane. The sooner we're out of here the better for all of us."

The winds were increasing and the barometer dropping. The surface of the bay was a rolling mass of swells and foam. One by one the reports came in from the aircraft maintenance officer. As he determined the mechanical troubles and gave a 'down check' for flight readiness, the skipper gave the orders to remove the flight crews, abandon the planes at their moorings and land all flight personnel ashore.

The boat officers and crews had a tough time. The winds chopped off the crests of the waves and blew streams of water through the air. The crews were pasted with spray and stinging pellets of salt as the boats pitched and wallowed.

At 1300 the skipper called his Exec.

"Make all preparations for getting underway." and shortly there came the sound of the boatswains pipe over the ships announcing system,

"Now hear diss. Secure all loose gear about the deck. Set conditions for heavy weather. Make all preparations for getting underway. Go to yer special stations all special sea detail."

While the Exec. was making a swing around the deck for a topside check up, all preparations were being made down below.

"Why we go out in that bad sea and wind, why not stay safe in harbor." Blanket asked plaintively as he struggled to right himself after being thrown against the bulkhead as the ship rolled heavily.

"We'll have more space to sink in out in the open." a passing voice shouted above the rising wind.

"We going to sink.?" Blanket looked resigned to the worst.

"We're not going to sink." Bat exclaimed. "We move out of the harbor so that we don't run the risk of running into other ships. Got to have room to maneuver."

Those who had been in a typhoon before were as anxious as the captain was to get out of the narrow and dangerous waters of the bay before the worst of the typhoon hit. Time was running out fast.

All they were waiting for was the report that all flight personnel had been landed safely on the beach.

By now the Captain had maneuvered the ship from its anchorage and headed the bow into the channel. All engines were stopped as they lay to waiting for the aircraft maintenance boat to return.

At last a boat was seen approaching through the spray and heavy rain. Four men were manning buckets, bailing out water to keep the boat afloat. Ordering the ship's engines kicked over the skipper swung the ship in a wide sweep to make a wake of smooth water and placed the ship between the beleaguered boat and the running sea.

As the boat swung into the slick and came up under the lee, the Exec. shouted through the megaphone, "Boat ahoy! Have all flight personnel been landed safely on the beach?"

"Yes, sir."

"Where are the rest of the ship's boats.?"

"All tied up to the pier, sir."

Next the Exec. gave the skipper's last minute instructions regarding the boats and personnel, then barked through the megaphone, "Shove off! Carry out your orders."

Then the Bering Strait stood out prepared for heavy weather.

She was just passing down the cleared channel when the helmsman suddenly shouted, "Steering lost on the bridge."

Both the helmsman and the quartermaster of the watch lunged for the emergency steering alarm at the same moment. Immediately a report came from the after steering station, "Steering aft has control."

"Steer zero eight zero degrees by steering compass."

shouted the quartermaster down the voice tube.

A minute later steering control was shifted back to the bridge. The skipper acknowledged the report with his usual " Very well." he showed none of the concern he felt about the accelerating speed of the approaching typhoon. When the Exec. who was acting as navigator reported the sea buoy was in sight one thousand yards ahead, the skipper replied,

"Mr. Jennings you may secure the special sea detail and set the normal steaming watch. Keep a rated quartermaster in the after steering station and use a quartermaster on the helm in the Pilot house. Post sentries at the exits to the weather decks to keep all personnel clear. Tell the engineer officer that I would like to see him."

As the engineer came in the Pilothouse the skipper smiled and asked how things were below in the engineering spaces. Then he said,

" Mr. Meisner, we will need steerageway at all times to ride out this thing. That means, of course, that the main engines and the steering motors must hold up. We shouldn't have any trouble if you can keep the water level down in the engine room bilges. Watch the blowers and keep me advised of how much water we're shipping.

"Keep your bilge pumps running and cut in as many as you need. It's going to get a lot rougher out there. With luck and the engines running, we'll make it okay."

"Aye, Aye, Captain, we'll do the best we can." replied Meisner. He lingered a moment on the bridge before going below. This was his only chance to see what things were like topside.

Looking ahead beyond the sea buoy, he was amazed to see the mountainous waves of the open sea. They looked like a great wall the ship would have to climb. On the starboard bow there was a huge area of yellowish white water, bubbling and churning like a giant fountain. At intervals columns of water shot up a hundred feet in the air accompanied by a thunderous pounding. Meisner had never experienced anything like it. Could any ship survive in this?

As the ship moved from the shelter of the bay the increasing intensity of the storm became more evident. The skipper set a course which put the wind on his port bow and the swells on the starboard bow. The ship was heeling over to starboard under the wind's blast of 45 knots, but the swells rolled the ship back to port and balanced the wind's effect.

It seemed as if the mast was lying on the sea as the ship heeled and rolled from one side to the other.

Now the power of Nature was the enemy, the Imperial Forces of Japan were as nothing compared to this. There is no way to overcome a typhoon, all man and ship can do is struggle to stay alive. At sea there is no hiding place, no shelter from the fury of the storm. It has to be endured. To survive it a ship has to be seaworthy, to be able to keep enough power to maneuver, the skipper must keep his head and know his ship and the ways of the storm.

Officers and crew are tested to the uttermost.

Big, heavy ships, carriers and battle ships, roll and pitch but they are not at the mercy of the storm in the same way as the smaller, lighter ships such as destroyers and seaplane tenders.

By 1530 the ship was about five miles east of the sea buoy. The wind had increased and the swells were rising higher and higher. The ship was seesawing up the swell and then down into the deep troughs.

It was only by using 15 degrees rudder that the helmsman was able to hold course against the yawing.

By his reckoning the skipper knew the storm center was likely to hit Okinawa no later than midnight. That left only eight hours, not enough for the ship to reach the China Sea and escape the storm which had been his original plan. If the typhoon continued on its course, heading directly towards Buckner's Bay, the ship would lie in the "danger semi-circle". As it was, the ship's position was 10 degrees on the danger side of the storm's track.

Their only hope was to try for the "navigable semi-circle" where the wind could be as much as 30 knots less, enough to spell the difference between the Bering Strait surviving or foundering.

"Have the Chief Quartermaster take the helm." the skipper yelled against the wind. "All engines ahead standard."

In a moment the engine room responded and the revolutions indicator was turned to 208 rpm.

As the ship accelerated the men down below wondered what was going on. Those topside could at least see what the storm was doing, down below all they could do was hope for the best as they were flung from deck to bulkhead and back again. The wallowing corkscrew motion of the ship as it pitched and rolled, increased with the increasing speed. They could sense in the sounds of the ship's struggles as the swell rolled aft along her length, that there was daylight under her keel as far aft as the bridge. They could hear the propellers churning the air as the stern rose on the crest and the bow was slammed down on the sea with a loud bang and a shudder that shook the whole ship.

Sam's stomach was giving him trouble, but he wasn't going to let on. This was worse than anything he had ever expected to experience, then he cheered up, if he lived to tell the tale, he'd sure have something to talk about when he got back to the States. Sure they'd get back, the 'old man' usually had something up his sleeve in every situation. He'd got them this far without a scratch. He knew what he was doing. And they all said this a was lucky ship.

In the Pilot House, the deafening roar and screeching of the wind had died down considerably and the ship was running almost down wind at 15 knots. The Chief, an old hand at the helm, was whirling the steering wheel now to port as the ship rose on a swell, now to starboard as it neared the crest, again to port as the bow dipped into the next trough. The men on the bridge were clinging to handgrips and to stringers in the structure, for it was easier to stand on the bulkheads than the deck after the ship rolled more than 45 degrees. The inclinometer indicated 52 degrees roll to starboard.

The ship was practically lying on her side. For a terrible moment she stayed there, then like a groggy fighter she rose up, water rushing from the deck carrying away one of the boats, only to roll over 52 degrees to port. Again she struggled back. How long can she keep it up? The skipper was intent on the radar bearings and ranges, mindful of staying away from the reefs. The swells on his port beam were bound to wash the ship towards them. There had not been enough time to run further to the east for the swells would soon be too great to risk the run down wind. It was touch and go.

It was two minutes past five when the skipper ceased running down wind. The swells had increased in height and the wind was now above 50 knots. At 18 hrs it was dark. The swells were setting the ship 30 degrees to the westward and she was holding her own against being set against the reefs. The skipper reckoned his position was 15 miles safer than when they passed the sea buoy. His hope was that the storm would veer to the right as it approached Okinawa and pass about 20 miles west of Buckner's Bay.

During the next five hours the barometer dropped and the winds rose and the seas grew more violent. Now all that could be done was ride it out.

By midnight it was still dropping and continued to drop until the typhoon passed 15 miles to the east. The lowest pressure recorded was 27.79 and highest wind velocity 100 knots. The highest waves estimated at 60-80 ft, but all aboard had their own estimates and they were decidedly higher.

"I bet they'll get higher and higher and the barometer will get lower and lower when we start telling about it back home." said Hukk.

The ship was lucky, damage was not as great as expected. All aboard were exhausted and most suffered bruises and a few had injuries from falls, but as Bat pointed out, they were lucky to be on the top and not at the bottom of the ocean.

Joe Ferris was commended at captain's mast for," diligence and efficient performance as coxswain of plane personnel boat during the typhoon at Chimu Wan, Okinawa."

Weather information had greatly improved during the past two years. The Navy had started using heavy landbased bombers of the 'Coronado' type as weather scouts a few months earlier. Their flight crews demonstrated what was regarded at that time as an amazing amount of guts by flying right into the typhoons, locating their center or 'eye' and tracking their paths. The weather readings they transmitted throughout their flights, enabled the Navy Weather Central in Guam, to plot conditions over the whole area and broadcast periodic weather synopses. This invaluable data was broadcast to the fleet and could be plotted by the aerological personnel who made the canned weather maps.

These Navy weather scouts later developed into Squadron WV Four, the "Hurricane Hunters" of the US Navy. This squadron, flying Super Constellations, regularly flew into the hurricanes threatening the coastline and shipping of the United States, to gather weather information. This information was radioed back to Weather Central Miami and disseminated around the world. Nowadays, this is done by satellites.

Up to a few years ago hurricanes and typhoons were given female names, but many women objected to their name being given to a violent storm and now mostly men's names are used.

To the relief of all aboard it was possible now to go ashore and have the couple of beers they'd been looking forward to for sometime.

The Okinawans welcomed them. By now they were over their fear of the Americans which the Japanese had tried to instill into them. Camps had been set up to house the homeless and food and supplies provided.

Many had been starving, their homes destroyed and their crops ruined and they were pathetically grateful for the help the Americans gave them.

The skipper and the crew always took candy and cookies for the children when they went ashore and the children very quickly picked up enough English to ask for "candee" and to say a few other words. There were still Japanese hiding out in caves so there was always the danger of being hit by a sniper, but a good lookout was kept all the time they were ashore. The Okinawans helped by pointing out where Japanese soldiers had been seen.

Bat was standing by the jeep watching the children line up for candy, when he felt something touch his hand. Looking down he saw it was a little boy about 3 years old who was holding on to him and smiling up at him. The child said something in Japanese which Bat couldn't understand, but he could tell from the boy's expression that it was something pleasant. He reached down and put his arm around him and the boy clasped his arms around Bat's leg.

"He thinks you're his Dad." one of the sailors joked.

Bat said nothing. My boy would be almost his age if it wasn't for this damn war, he thought bitterly, as the old heartache hit him again. Would he ever forget that awful day when he got the message that his wife and child had been killed? Then one of the older children pointed to the little boy and said, "He no have father. He dead - gun bang, bang."

God! Bat thought, he lost his father and I lost my son. Why did he pick on me? Could he tell? Gently he unclasped the boy's arms and gave him some candy, then said to the older child, "Take care of him." obediently the little boy took older one's hand and Bat watched as they joined the other children.

God help them, he thought sadly.

Another day an old woman beckoned to one of the men, "Japs I see. Come."

"Okay, wait I've got to get permission and some more men."

"I stay." the woman said sitting on the ground.

Then four Japanese soldiers appeared with their hands held high above their heads and surrendered.

When the skipper was informed by walkie talkie he said he would be right there.

"Be careful, you never know what they might be up to. Make sure its not a trap. There may be others lurking around. Have them escorted to the beach and we'll pick them up and take them back on board." Later they were handed over to the prison authorities.

It appeared that the soldiers had been hiding out in one of the burial caves but ,as they had no food or water, they decided to give themselves up.

While many of the Japanese hid out for months or even years, rather then surrender, some accepted the inevitable and gave up.

"I thought them Japs never give up."

"There's some that don't and some that do." Hukk answered, "There's a special lot, samurai they're called, who have to kill themselves. They're not allowed to surrender, if they do, they won't go to Heaven or where ever Japs go and their families are disgraced as well as them."

"Well, there's something to be said for it. If they do themselves in, it saves us the trouble. "said Bat.

"On Aug 6th the astonishing news that the "New Bomb" had been dropped on Hiroshima was broadcast. Aboard the ship there was much speculation on what kind of a bomb it was.

"I heard as its the biggest ever made." said Blanket.

"Well, being big don't mean it does the most damage. I heard as its the most powerful ever made."

"How do you two know anything about it, its been kept a big secret from everyone, even the top brass. "Bat pointed out.

"As long as it does them in I don't give a damn what is

Then the Air Raid Alert sounded putting a stop to the speculation for a while.

Two days later came the news that Russia had, at last, declared war on Japan. But still there was no word of surrender from Tokyo.

In spite of the fact that leaflets were dropped by the Allies telling that further destruction would follow if their terms were not agreed to, the Japanese, fearful of what would happen to the Emperor if they accepted unconditional surrender terms, fought on and, on the ninth of August the second bomb was dropped, devastating Nagasaki.

As the enormous extent of the damage and the horrendous suffering of the victims became known, even the most embittered hoped that this would be the last atomic bomb to be dropped anywhere. Ever.

Colonel Robert Ping, who was Air Inspector, General Division 313th Wing, remembers how well the secret of the A-Bomb was kept while the bombs were on Tinian Island. Colonel Tibbets, of the 509th Squadron, was in charge of the A-Bomb project and by now, was expert in giving misleading information.

As the 509th was the fifth group of the 313th, Colonel Ping was told by General Davies the CO, to go down to the 509th with the best people he could assemble and find out what Tibbets was up to.

Ping had had considerable experience as Wing Air Inspector in the States, so he felt he should be able to solve the puzzle very easily.

But Tibbets was well practised in giving evasive answers and Ping got nowhere. All he got from Tibbets and his people, was that they were dropping blockbusters on supposedly hardened targets as they had been ordered to do. Actually they were practising dropping simulated atom bombs from 30,000 feet with a circular error of approximately 200 feet.

When Tibbets received the order to load the bomb on Aug 5 th, in order to camouflage what was going on, Tibbets had a dummy airplane put out with guards around and men loading all kinds of stuff into it while the Bomb was being loaded into the Enola Gay at another place.

It wasn't until President Truman announced on the evening of the 6th that an atomic bomb had been dropped on Japan, that everyone knew what Tibbets and the 509th had really been up to.

It was ten days later on August 15th that news came over the radio that the war was over. No serviceman in the Pacific on that day, whether on land or sea, will ever forget it. Every ship sounded its whistle and it seemed that the whole Pacific was filled with music as those ships with a band played God Bless America and everyone aboard sang along with them.

The following Saturday, 18th, notice was given that on Sunday the Japanese were to fly to a little island not far from Okinawa, called Ie Shima and then proceed to Nicholas Field in Manila to sign the surrender terms. Orders were given to hold all fire.

The Japanese would fly in twin engine bombers marked with green crosses for easy recognition.

Even though the war was officially over, all precautions were still taken as no one wanted to take any chances at this stage and ships stood at General quarters night and morning as usual, but the atmosphere aboard was one of jubilation.

"When do we sail for the good old USA was the question everyone was asking."

It was just as well they didn't know it would take another four months before the Bering Strait set sail for home. Meanwhile the news that Admiral J. Perry would be aboard to make annual military inspection on September lst. kept all hands busy sprucing up the ship.

"Maybe, after the Admiral has looked us over, he'll give us the order to shove off for home." Mug said hopefully.

"They say he's a terror and likes a real tight ship, so you'd better start getting squared away. " Hukk answered.

"I like see Admiral. He is great Chief?" Blanket inquired.

"He's not only a great chief, he's like God, that's what. His barge brings him over and makes a great sweep around the ship to let us know he's arrived, then he's piped aboard with all the ceremony you'll ever see, and he brings his staff with him. Soo — you'd better watch your step when he's around."

"Maybe, I not like see Admiral, I stay in bunk."

"You won't get a chance. If you're absent for muster on that day, you'll be stuck in the brig for ever."

Punctually on Sept. lst. Commander Fleet Air Wing One, Admiral J. Perry came aboard at 0955 and left the ship at 1122. At 1122 the ship was secured from inspection.

"Thank God, that's over and, whatever he says, that Admiral won't find a ship as good as this one anywhere." remarked Bat as they waited in the chow line.

The Admiral must have almost agreed as word was passed down that he said, "the Bering Strait most nearly approached the standards he desired to find in the ships of his wing."

The following day, Sept. 2. the formal signing of the instruments of surrender took place aboard the USS Missouri in Tokyo Bay.

The Foreign Minister of Japan who had been quietly working for peace for some months, signed first, then Japanese General Umezu.

General McArthur signed for the Allied Nations and Admiral Nimitz signed for the United States. Then the representatives for each nation that had been at war with Japan signed and General McArthur closed the ceremony saying,

"Let us pray that peace be now restored to the world and that God will preserve it always."

All ships received the following statement released by Admiral Nimitz and it was broadcast throughout the Pacific and the United States.

"On board all naval vessels at sea and in port, and at our many bases in the Pacific, there is rejoicing and thanksgiving. The long bitter struggle is at an end."

"Today all freedom loving peoples of the world rejoice in the victory and feel pride in the accomplishments of our combined forces."

"We also pay tribute to those who defended our freedom at the cost of their lives."

"On Guam is a military cemetery in a green valley not far from my headquarters. The ordered rows of white crosses stand as reminders of the heavy cost we paid for victory. On these crosses are the names of Sweeney, Bromberg, Depew, Melloy, Ponziani-names that are a cross section of democracy. They fought together as brothers in arms; they died together and now they sleep side by side. To them we have a solemn obligation- the obligation to ensure that their sacrifice will make this a better world in which to live."

"Now we turn to the great tasks of reconstruction and restoration. I am confident that we will be able to apply the same skill, resourcefulness and deep thinking to these problems as were applied to the problems of winning the victory."

But the war was not over for the prisoners of war and their anxious families. Many long days were to pass before all were located and rescued.

The rejoicing over the surrender turned into a bad let-down.

Expecting to go home in a few weeks, if not immediately, service men were disgruntled when this didn't happen.

Crews envied the ships and planes engaged in the rescue and return of PWs, feeling that they were doing something useful, not just hanging around. As descriptions of the sufferings of the prisoners at the hands of the Japanese spread around, the bitterness against Japan increased.

A letter to his other Bill LeBaron, Store Keeper, 2c. of the USS Witchita (CA45) which was bringing PWs from Nagasaki, tells the story.

*September 16, 1945*

*Dear Mom and Dad,*

*I just got back from the beach. I was on a reception committee for these war prisoners. It was an interesting assignment and a happier bunch of fellows you'll never see. Not loud about it but you can really see that it means the world and all to be free again altho most of them are walking in a dream. So little means so much to those fellows that it's hard to believe how happy they are. Just talking to them makes them very happy. These guys that were in this morning were from a camp about a hundred miles up the river from here. We are handling about twelve thousand in all. Thirteen hundred of them today. A comparatively few Americans. Chinese, Dutch, Australians, English, slaves and just about every kind of people. They are all very thin and not at all sure-footed when they step around. Most of them are wearing shoes for the first time in from three years to four. Most of these guys have been in these camps since the first part of the war. I was talking to one Chinese soldier this morning that was captured December 8, 1941. Some of these guys are off the old HOUSTON and then there are a few of them from Bataan and Corregidor. All of them admit that the Americans were treated much worse than any of the rest of the prisoners. This is very easy to see of course. Out of a hundred and thirty-four Americans that came down yesterday all of them were stretcher cases, These guys aren't just in the stretcher because one limb is fouled up, their whole body is marked. It would be impossible for them to walk if they wanted to. It is truly a sad sight to see these guys in this shape but I use everything in the books that I knew to cheer them up and I do think it worked pretty good. As much as I've seen guys bumped up it is still hard for me to talk the way I ought to to them.*

*I was talking to one English doctor that was taken when Singapore fell and he had been in five different camps all told. He said that this one was far better than any of the others that he had been in and if you could see these guys you'd wonder how any of the rest of them are still living.*

*I was working with the Red Cross outfit over here passing out these kits made up especially for P.W.s and believe me, if only one in a thousand of those things ever got through you can bet your sweet life that it was worth the money and effort that was put into them.*

*The English doctor said that in all the camps that he had been in he hadn't seen any Red Cross or other outfits like that that were working for the prisoners. They did however get some of these boxes that were sent to them. They didn't give it to them with the package it came in or they didn't give all the stuff that was in them to the prisoners but I hardly believe that anyone was expecting that. He made mention of the fact that what they did get was with their daily rations and it took the place of them in most cases but to these prisoners eating some food from their home countries that was prepared for them meant more to them than the actual food value did. That is why I say that although most of that stuff did not get through to them it was well worth the effort put in to sending it.*

*A lot of these prisoners are carrying swords and knives that they have taken from the guys that have been carrying and using on them and their fellow prisoners. These guys killed some of the guards that have been mean to them just before they got on the train to come down to the dock. One was telling me about this* other guy and himself who only yesterday took a Jap car and made the rounds of the camp and collected everything they figured they wanted or that any of their buddies wanted. He said that when they got back they had the whole glove compartment full of watches. He showed me a coffee can full of them that he had saved for himself and some of them were very nice watches. These guys will give you anything they have up to and including the shirt off their backs but I hope they can get home with their stuff before too many fast-talking guys get their things.

These guys weathered Hell with all that it has to offer and yet come back out in a surprisingly good sense of humor. It makes me feel small to think that I will bitch.

As Ever, Bill

# CHILDREN OF THE OCCUPATION

On Friday 28th September 1945 the Bering Strait became part of the United States occupation of Japan. With the Captain at the conn and the navigator on the bridge, she steamed into the mine swept channel leading to Sasebo Harbor, Kyushu, and joined the U.S. and Allied ships which filled the whole bay. Crews were hoping for liberty ashore. But they were not sure what sort of welcome they would get from the Japanese. After all they had not only brought them to their knees and demanded unconditional surrender, but had devastated their cities and dropped the 'New Bomb' killing thousands of people.

"They asked for it and they got it. They started it with Pearl Harbor and they've got to take the consequences." said Bat.

"You're damn right. When you think of the way they've treated our P.W.s I think we've been too good to them."

"Well, thank God the war's over. All I want is to get back home. I've had it with the goddamn Pacific." C. K. muttered.

"Same here. I thought we'd be back in the States long before this." Joe replied. ' Anyhow, I'm going to have a good look round while I'm here."

"They say the Jap women do everything men tell them. No arguing. They know who's master and wait on you hand and foot." a young sailor said wistfully, conjuring up unspeakable delights as he gazed at the shore.

"Don't get your hopes up, sailor, you can't speak the lingo so how can you tell them what you want?"

"I'll make signs. They'll get it."

Language was a barrier, but the Bering Strait crew was lucky. Standing on the dock at a respectful distance from the ship was a group of young boys. They had come to see what the Americans looked like. They had been told how terrible and cruel the conquerors were and that they would probably kill them if they went too close. Women and girls had been told to hide themselves lest they be attacked and raped. But the boys were curious, especially as they had heard that some of the Americans were black. Not only did they have black faces, but they were black all over. Most Japanese had never seen a black person, male or female, and they found it hard to believe that there were such people, so the boys had decided to go and see for themselves.

To the crew of the Bering Strait the boys looked a pathetic, ragged bunch. They were all very thin. Some wore shirts made out of rice sacks and some had outgrown kimonos patched with odd bits of material. One boy stood out from the rest. He was a little taller and wore a black kimono, mended but clean and neat. His name was Shiguru Ebihara and he had come with the group, not only out of curiosity, but in hopes of earning some money. He had been working in an arms factory until it was bombed and now there was no work anywhere.

Shiguru Ebihara was the sole support of his mother, his little sister Yuko and his grandmother since his journalist father had been killed in an 'accident' after he had written an article supporting the rumors that the Emperor and the Crown Prince considered the war was lost and Japan should seek peace. A number of Japanese who spoke out for peace had died in similar 'accidents'.

The young Ebihara hoped the Americans would want a translator or a guide to show them around the city. Now the war was over and the Emperor had said it was necessary to pave the way for peace, he thought it was important to get to know the conquerors and to show that some Japanese were ready to obey the Emperor. He spoke English fairly well and knew the city thoroughly since his ancestors had lived in Kyushu for generations.

The family had lived in Tokyo until their house was destroyed in the bombing. Then they came to live with old grandmother Ebihara who had stayed in the ancestral home not far from Sasebo.

Once the family had been wealthy, but their land had been confiscated and all they had left was a small rice patch and the house.

Shiguru and his sister had been brought up according to the three important duties of every Japanese person, child or adult which are: To be absolutely loyal to the Emperor.

To respect ones parents and elders.

To give all to the country.

They had shared the belief of all Japanese, that their land was specially protected by the Heavens and would never be invaded.

Hadn't the Heavens sent the Divine Wind, the kamikazi , to destroy the ships of Kublai Khan when he was about to invade Japan back in the 13th century? And since that time no invader had dared set foot on their land. But when they heard the rumors of the terrible losses the Allies had inflicted on the Imperial Navy, and realized that the enemy was as close as Okinawa, they feared the Heavens had deserted them.

The family would never forget the day when they sat together waiting to hear the message from the Emperor. They had been told that the Emperor himself was going to speak to the country. They could hardly believe it. No ordinary person and very few of the most illustrious, had ever heard the Voice of the Crane, as the Emperor's voice was called.

"I am fearful. Something of the greatest importance must have happened." and grandmother Ebihara shivered as she pulled her old kimono closer around her bony shoulders.

"Perhaps the war is won. Our great Armies and Navies are at last victorious."

But before anyone could answer, the voice of Chokugan Wada, Japan's greatest radio announcer, said," Will all listeners please rise. His Majesty will now read the Imperial rescript to the people of Japan. We respectfully transmit his voice."

Then the National Anthem was played and speaking in the ancient Imperial language, the Emperor addressed his "Good and Loyal Subjects."

Although she was standing rigidly upright, young Ebihara could see his grandmother's shoulders shaking with sobs as the Emperor told the people that, "We have resolved to pave the way for a grand peace for all generations to come by enduring the unendurable and suffering the insufferable——" When the Emperor's quiet voice ended Yuko, who had been clinging to her mother, cried.

"What does it mean, mama? What will happen now?"

"There will be peace, no more fighting and bombing and maybe we will have food to eat and clothes to wear again."

"But we have lost all honor. The Emperor said the Empire has accepted the provision of our enemy's Joint Declaration. Does that not mean surrender?"

"The Emperor did not mention surrender, grandmother, it is a resolution to pursue peace and that is good. That is what my father said should be done a long time ago." Ebihara said." We must obey our Emperor."

And in obedience to the Emperor's resolve the boy made his plan to be a kind of goodwill ambassador to the ships in Sasebo Bay.

But many Japanese people felt differently . In spite of the fact that all men and women were expected to fight to the death should Japan be invaded and even the children had their part to play, (they would become 'Sherman Carpets' by having explosives attached to their body and made to throw themselves under the American tanks,) they felt so dishonored by the surrender that hundreds committed suicide.

They felt they could never hold up their head again. Even as the Emperor was speaking, the Palace gates were stormed by a group of War Lords who tried to stop the broadcast and continue the war. But they were driven back and now the Emperor had spoken and the war was over.

It was about six weeks after this that Ebihara and his friends went to the harbor to see the American sailors and their ships. The boys stood watching for a while hoping that some of the Americans would come ashore so they could get a closer look.

When this didn't happen Ebihara said he was going to go up to the gangway and try and talk to the man standing at the top.

"He's got a gun. You will be shot."

"You might make them angry and then they'll kill us too."

"If you stay here while I go to the ship you can run away very fast if anything bad happens .." and Ebihara started towards the Bering Strait. He hadn't gone very far when he saw three officers coming ashore. They looked very big and tall and very important in their uniforms. His courage began to fail. They won't trouble themselves with someone like me, he thought. They will have very important people to translate and guide them. Then he thought of his family. They had food only for one more day and gathering his strength, he walked towards them and bowing low, he said, "Honorable sirs, I come full of help for you. I can translate, I can guide you through the city. I can do many things."

The three officers stopped surprised, then one of them who happened to be the Bering Strait's captain said, after looking him over, "Come back tomorrow morning and I'll talk with you. I'm not making any promises, mind you." and turning to one of the officers, the skipper said, "Take his name and address will you and check it out before tomorrow if you can."

"Right away, sir."

"Be here tomorrow at 10:30 in the morning and don't be late." the skipper said turning to Ebihara.

Thank you, honorable sir, I will be the right time" and bowing again lower than ever, Ebihara turned to join the boys who were cautiously watching from a distance.

So began the friendship between the Ebihara family and the USS Bering Strait and her skipper. Although they did not know it at the time, this friendship was to have strange and unexpected consequences which would last until the present day.

Because Shigaru Ebihara wasn't the easiest name to pronounce the crew nicknamed him 'Abie' which is the way the first syllable of Ebihara is pronounced. They also told him about Abe Lincoln when he confided that he hoped to become a lawyer one day.

The boys who had come with him were invited aboard the ship and shown around and given a good meal. Whatever they might think of the Japanese, the sailors didn't hold it against the children.

"I wish my kids were as well behaved as these little Jap kids. I'd like to have mine bow and scrape to me for a change."

Barny Barnes announced.

"Do you think they're like that all the time or just when they're with handsome, important guys like us?'

"We'll soon find out. I asked Ebi if there was any chance of visiting with a Jap family and he said he'd fix it up."

" I'd rather go to one of them geisha places and get to know a Jap woman or two."

"It's off limits. You'd better watch your step."

"The skipper's afraid you'll catch something. He's trying to get some movie they showed when he was at Annapolis called,

'One night with Venus and a lifetime with Mercury.' It's guaranteed to put you off sex for a lifetime."

"Christ in the foothills! Does he think the Jap women have the clap or something.?"

"The medical name is syphilis and they say mercury doesn't always cure it."

"Well, I'm willing to take a chance."

Ebi was good at his word. He invited the skipper and three of the crew to come to his home for tea. Knowing of the shortage of food, they took a few supplies with them.

The Ebihara home was a typical middle class, eight tatami (room) house. The roof was of mud and tile. Two sides of the house were walled and there were sliding glass doors and full length windows to the north and south.

The Americans were formally greeted by Mama san and Grandmother Ebihara and with many gestures invited to sit on the low cushions before a lacquered table. Then Ebi's sister Yuko appeared with a tray and very shyly handed tea in paper thin china cups. Ebi sat with the men while the women offered some tiny rice cakes and some small sweet cakes, and refilled their teacups.

Later Ebi showed the house. The sleeping quarters with the rush mats, the bathing place, the household shrine and finally the little garden and rice patch. To the Americans who had been away from home and loved ones for over a year it felt wonderful to be with a family again. But at the same time it made them feel the separation from their own family all the more.

"God! I can't wait to get back to the good old USA.

Seeing that little Jap kid and her mother made me homesick."

"We can't all get back at the same time. Someone's got to stick it out here." the skipper said.

"Yeah, but I'd rather it wasn't me." C. K. said bitterly.

Now the war was over life on board was flat and routine.

Life had been at fever pitch for so long that it felt strange to be able to sleep without being wakened by an air raid alert or call to General quarters. When planes flew over they no longer had to count them and wait for their return. They weren't their problem any more. Though the crew was kept busy re fuelling and tending ships and planes, the excitement and momentum were gone. They envied the pilots of the Navy anti submarine planes who were now flying out prisoners of war from the Japanese camps, they were doing something useful.

When are we going home was the question in everyone's mind.

On October 2. the crew watched enviously as ten men of the US Navy Reserve Fleet left the ship for the US.

The Navy had worked out a system for the return of regular Navy to the States. It was a system based on points. So many for every month overseas, so many for each medal and so many for each dependent. Men worked on their numbers calculating who went when.

Meanwhile life went on.

Ebi knew all the places to get anything from delicate and beautiful antiques to 'no go's' (wooden platform shoes) and paper fans and, as he spoke English, many of the other ships were glad of his help.

The Japanese were glad to sell their treasures for a fraction of their value to buy food. A black market in such things, aimed at the Americans started up almost immediately and while some of the things were priceless antiques, some were cheap copies. Ebi kept the crew from falling into that trap after Sam came back with what he considered a valuable ivory statue of the Goddess Quon Yen.

"Sadly, it is not ivory." Ebi said, "it is what you call fake"

"But I paid ———" Sam objected.

"You were cheated. I am sorry, but I will go with you and we will find some real ivory."

"I'm going back to that bastard who sold me this damn thing. I'll make him give me my money back."

"I will go with you. It is possible we will get real ivory statue, if he won't give back money."

"O.K. Let's go. I'll let him know he can't make a fool out of me and get away with it."

"It is better I do the speaking, sir. You smile."

"Smile! for God's sake! I'll throw him in the harbor."

"It will not be successful way to get your money , sir."

"O.K. I'll leave it to you.

Sam was a good-hearted sailor who fell for most rackets. Everyone liked him and he was always ready to help anyone. Being tall and lean with muscles like iron, he'd always been a favorite with the girls and their mothers, but Annie was the girl back home whose picture he carried round with him. She was tall and blond like Sam and had the healthy look of someone who spent her life out of doors. Annie was waiting for him and counting the days to his return.

One day when Sam and his shipmate Mug, were going ashore they noticed an old man standing by a rickety handcart with a large birdcage on top of it. Inside was a bright , yellow bird.

The old man was thin, he looked as if the wind would blow him away. His wispy gray beard was neatly trimmed, but his kimono had seen better days.

"Lets see what the old guy is up to."

"O.K."

The old man bowed as they approached him and said something in Japanese. He quickly realized that the sailors didn't understand and brought out a piece of paper with BIRD TELL FORTUNE. printed on it in English.

"It's a gag, but lets have a go. Maybe he'll tell us when we get to go home."

"How much?" Sam asked the old man holding out a handful of yen.

The old man took about five cents worth and, with many bows, he spoke a few words to the bird who hopped obediently to a little box at the back of the cage and returned with a scrap of paper in its beak.

The old man took it from the bird and handed it to Sam.

It was in English, obviously the old man had prepared for his new customers. Sam read it aloud," Now hear this, Mug,"

"Beautiful girl awaits you." How about that?"

"Does it say where?" "As long as she awaits, I'll find her. Now let's see what you get."

Mug held out some yen and again the old man took what he wanted and spoke to the bird who dutifully produced another scrap of paper.

Mug's face lit up, "Get a load of this, Sam, 'Great riches will be yours.' How about that?"

"Does it say when?"

"As long as I get rich I don't mind waiting a bit."

"That bird's a living fortune cookie. How does the old guy get him to bring the paper?"

"God knows. If he spoke English we could ask him."

"Wonder what kind of a bird it is? It's a bit like that bird that came aboard on the shakedown cruise. Remember? It sure shook me up that night when it flew against my face."

"Yeah, I remember. This one's the same color. I'd like to know what it is."

"It's called Magic Bird." a voice said behind them. It was Ebi and he was laughing. "Magic Bird knows everything about you-he gives special message."

"You have a go, Ebi. Let's see what the bird knows about you. Come on. It's your turn."

But Ebi was reluctant. He didn't want to spend his hard earned money on the Magic Bird if he could help it.

"Come on, Ebi, be a sport and help the old guy." So, seeing there was no escape, Ebi gave the old man money and received his paper.

"Read it, Ebi. What does it say?"

"It is good, sirs. It says, Many wish you well." and turning to the old man he bowed and said a few words of thanks.

"How does he get the bird to pick up the paper?" Sam asked Ebi as they went towards the city.

"It's magic."

"O.K. but what kind of magic? What words does he say?"

"Abracadabra, for sure." Mug said laughing, "you sound as if you want to get into the act Sam."

"I'm just curious, that's all. I hope the poor, old guy gets plenty of customers. He looks as if he could do with a good meal. Do you know him, Ebi?"

"No, but I have seen Magic Birds before. Most Japanese cities have one."

"Do you believe in them?"

"It depends, sirs. Some better than others. This one is good, I think."

"How do you know?"

"He gives good messages."

Soon the old man and his bird became a fixture on the harbor and he had more customers than he could manage.

Oct. 10th brought more action than anyone wanted. Another typhoon was blowing up. Winds of over 100 knots were expected.

At 1345 special sea detail was set and the Bering Strait was underway to avoid collision with other ships anchored in the Bay.

"The barometer is still falling. Looks as if we're in for a bad one this time.." the skipper said to his Exec.

"We rode out the last one without too much damage, so maybe we'll be just as lucky this time."

"We weren't in such close quarters last time. We'll have to ........" his words were lost in the roar of the wind as a gust tossed the ship as if it were a rowboat and sea poured over the deck as the full force of the typhoon hit them. Before the ship could recover, another enormous swell hit taking the port anchor with it. From then on it was nothing but a desperate battle to keep afloat and prevent colliding with other ships. The wind was so strong that both engines had to be used to hold position against it. By 1620 the wind was still rising. At times it seemed as if the ship was standing on her bow and would never right herself. At other times she sank down into a trough with walls of water far above the bridge. Miraculously no one was swept overboard as the torrents of water hit and exploded on the deck like a kamikazi.

By 1700 she was still afloat and underway to keep the starboard anchor from dragging. The roaring of the wind was like an express train and the torrents of rain fell with such violence that it sounded like bullets hitting the deck. The noise was so great that although the skipper and the navigator were close together on the bridge, they could only hear each other by shouting at the top of their voice.. Then, amidst it all, there came another sound. High above the roaring of the storm came the piercing shriek of the ship's whistle. Now the force of the wind was such that it caused the whistle to blow. Nothing would stop it. Like a banshee or the voice of an avenging angel, it rose and fell and rose again, each time a bit higher causing more apprehension among the crew than the storm itself.

All through that night they fought the storm maneuvering to keep their position against the typhoon. By morning on Friday 11th to the blessed relief of officers and crew, the whistle was silent.

By 0250 all engines were stopped as the winds died down and by 1033 the ship was back in her assigned berth.

The Bering Strait was lucky. Although several ships had been badly damaged and two sunk, apart from losing the port anchor the

Bering Strait had not suffered any damage. There were only three injured crew men who needed medical treatment, but most had bruises from being thrown against the bulkhead as storm waves hit the ship.

"We're going to have a good time when we get back to the States. There's not too many who can say they survived this goddamned Pacific war and a couple of typhoons." Joe said.

"For a while there I wondered if we'd make it, but its a good ship. Always has been. She's a tough one all right."

"That goddamned whistle got to me . I was all right until that thing started blowing. It put the fear of God into me." Mug said.

" Well, the skipper always says there's no atheists at sea. Once you've been in a typhoon if you haven't believed there's a God before, you sure enough want one after that."

"Have you heard that one about the Bishop aboard a ship in a typhoon?" Bat asked.

"No."

"Well, there's this ship at sea and a great storm comes up and the ship's tossed around and everyone's afraid they'll sink and the Bishop goes to the Captain and he says, "How bad is it, Captain?" and the Captain says, "Well, we've done all we can. All we can do now is to pray." and the Bishop looks at him terrified and says, "You mean its as bad as all that ?"

"Bat, when are you going to stop telling these no-soaps and get a good one for a change?"

"When you start telling some good ones yourself." Bat answered goodnaturedly.

October is rice harvest time in Japan and this particular year rice was more precious than gold. Gohan, which means boiled rice, is the heart of every meal. For over eighteen centuries rice has been the staple meal of the Japanese family high and low, but with so many men called from the fields to serve in the Imperial Forces, production had dwindled. While some rice had been imported from China, it was not considered nearly as good as the home product, but food of any kind was so scarce that women would offer a precious jewel in exchange for a bowl of rice to feed their children.

Farmers had some food for themselves, but they did not have enough to sell. In 1945 six people per day starved to death in Tokyo and three per day in Yokohama.

General McArthur had set up Army kitchens to help feed the starving people and had asked Washington for 3,000,000 tons of food. The harvest of 1945 would be the seed of the future and was cherished accordingly.

Japanese rice is the result of careful crossbreeding and endless loving care. Sasanishiki is considered the very best kind and it is the most expensive. Seedlings, which have been raised in a protected nursery or the farmhouse bath tub, are transplanted in late June. The drenching rains of monsoons and typhoons and the humid summer make the rice heavy with grain by October when each kind is carefully harvested by hand.

Knowing how precious the rice was, the skipper was very touched when towards the end of October, Ebi invited him to his home to a harvest meal.

"Honorable sir, my mother invites you to come and share our special rice."

"Please tell her I will be most honored."

The rice was served in small, black lacquered bowls covered with a matching lid. One for each person was placed to the left of the plate which held a small serving of delicate white fish.

Following the example of Ebi, the skipper first tasted a mouthful of rice. It was delicious, different from any he had tasted before.

"It's so much better than any I have ever had. Is it because you grow it yourselves?"

"We like to think so, but it is Sasanishiki which is the best of Japan rice."

"It's the cooking that makes the difference." said Ebi.

"It is of no good to have best rice and cook it badly."

"How do you cook it?."

"My mother and grandmother cook it. Tell how you cook, Mama."

"First the grains are washed in cold water. Then soaked for half an hour. After, it is put in pot of iron. Water then is put in pot to cover rice. We measure how much by the first crease in index finger. Then pot with lid on, is put on brazier with charcoal burning under and made to boil. Then lid is opened small bit, and left ten more minutes. After this, close lid and take off fire and wait quarter hour. Then eat." she smiled, "It tastes very good."

This was the last meal the skipper was to have with the

Ebihara's. He had orders to report to Corpus Christi, Texas and take command of the Naval Air Station there. On November 19th he would be relieved by Commander F T. Corbin, 61131, USN, who would be the Bering Strait's new skipper.

Though neither Innis or the Ebiharas knew it at the time, they were fated to meet again and again.

Christmas 1945 the first Christmas with the world at peace, was celebrated by the Bering Strait in Sasebo Harbor, Japan, anchored in Berth 46. By now, many of the original crew had been transferred back to the States and those still with the ship couldn't help feeling they'd had a raw deal. But, as Hukk pointed out, "Thank God, next year we'll all be home for Christmas, and, when you think about it, we're among the lucky ones. There's some who'll never go home."

On the 26th C. K. was reported missing.

"He's the one who's been complaining the loudest about being stuck out here. Why the hell would he go AWOL now?"

"God knows. I don't."

"Maybe he went ashore and got drunk."

"Wasn't he spending time with some Jap girl? Do you think that's where he is?"

"All I know is he's the one who was fed up with the war and the Pacific and kept talking about it, til we was all fedup with him."

"I betcha he'll be back before night." Mug said, he won't want to miss the boat home. He knows were due to sail for Pearl on the 29th."

But the next day a typhoon blew up and C. K. was forgotten for awhile. In spite of the fact that the winds were high it was not as bad as the October storm. Although the ship took a beating, no one was hurt.

On the 29th. Bat and Sam and Mug went ashore to shop for some gifts to take home, and as C. K. was still missing, they decided to take a look around for him at the same time.

"They say that a couple of sailors got drunk and some Japs who hate Americans took them and locked them up in a shed with a bunch of pigs and it was a week before a shore patrol found them. Do ya think that's what's happened to C. K.?"

"I heard that tale, but I don't know if its true. But there's no harm looking around. Where was that place he used to go? A bathing place or something, wasn't it.? Bat had no great liking for C.

K. but he didn't want to see him get into any more trouble.

"I went with him one time. The whole lot, everyone, men and women take a bath together naked. Its better than skinny dipping and they had rooms where you could go with a girl if you wanted." Mug replied relishing the memory.

"Well, what are we waiting for? lead on, sailor."

But when they got there no one knew anything of C. K. and obviously all the proprietress, known to the Americans as 'Mama san' and to the Japanese as 'Lady in Between', wanted, was more American patrons, so she wasn't likely to harm a sailor.

"It is possible he went to a lady's house." she said.

"Which lady? Where is the house?" Bat asked.

Without hesitation, the Lady in Between gave directions and they started on their way.

It was a small house in a poor neighborhood and a young girl came out when Bat knocked on the rickety door post.

"No one here. Only me." she said nervously in answer to Bat's questions. "I no see him."

While Bat was talking to the girl, Sam and Mug looked around the back of the house and saw a small shed. It was bigger than the usual outhouse so they tried to open the door to see what was inside. But the door was jammed so tight they couldn't move it.

"Lets tell Bat there's a shed back here. Maybe the girl's a cover for some damn Jap."

"Hey, Bat, Come back here." Mug called going round to the front.

"O.K. What is it?"

"There's a shed back here."

But before Bat could move the girl shouted, "No, no you must not go there. It is my house. Go away quickly." and she ran and stood in front of the shed door with a terrified look on her face.

"What are you afraid of." Bat asked quietly." We're not going to hurt you. We're just looking for our friend."

"Go away. No friend of you here."

"If you'll just open the door and let us take a look we'll go right away."

"No, no. Go. You no right to look. Go."

By now the three men were sure C. K. must be inside.

After all the Lady in Between had mentioned the possibility of him being here with the girl.

"C. K. are you in there. Answer us for God's sake." Bat shouted.

"He not answer. Go."

This was enough for Bat, and with a shove of his strong shoulder he pushed the door in. The girl was crying hopelessly as they crowded inside. For a moment they could see nothing.

There was only light from a tiny window at the back, then a terrible sight rose from the dirt floor. Something so grotesque could only come from a nightmare, it couldn't be human. Its face had lost all humanity. Great folds of empty skin hung from the forehead to its chest and from every part of its body empty skin hung like folds of drapery and dragged along the floor.

Sobbing, the girl flung her arms around the apparition." I couldn't stop them, my uncle. Forgive me."

Over the girl's head the man looked at the sailors with such tragic eyes that they seemed to bore straight into their soul.

"Oh, my God ! Forgive us!" Bat whispered as they turned to go.

"Wait, I must speak to you." the girl said following them and pulling the door shut, she said," You must tell no one what you have seen."

"Can we help him? Can anything be done? Why does he stay in that place?"

"He is dishonored. He does not wish any to know he is still alive. You must not tell what you saw. He was ozeki before war. But family all burned in Tokyo bombing and he lost spirit. He tried to kill himself but too fat and knife not long enough. He did not die. I to ok him with me, he my uncle. All I have left. He grow very thin like you see and because of dishonor he has no spirit. I beg you will not say to anyone."

"We'll forget we've been here. We're very sorry we frightened you, but we thought it might be our shipmate in there.

"Take this for mending the door." Bat said giving the girl a handful of money.

"What a godawful sight. What did she say her uncle was?" Mug asked as they hurried away anxious to get back to the ship .

"Ozeki. A famous wrestler."

"You mean one of those that look like mountains?"

"Yes, that's why he's got that skin hanging down all over him. When he lost all that fat the skin had nothing to hold it up."

"His eyes looked dreadful. So awful sad. I could hardly keep from crying like the girl." Sam said.

"Why does he think he's dishonored. Just because he can't wrestle any more doesn't matter that much, does it?'

"I don't know. They have some funny ideas of honor. I suppose its because he didn't commit hari kari properly. Say, we'd better put a move on or we'll be AWOL ourselves. C. K. might be back on board by now."

But C. K. was still AWOL and on the 31st Dec. the Bering Strait was en route to Pearl Harbor without him.

By Jan. 7th the Bering Strait crossed the dateline and all clocks were set back 23 1/2 hours.

"Hell! this means we have two January 7ths. That makes the trip a day longer." Barnes exclaimed.

"Don't worry we lose half an hour when we get to Hawaii."

someone shouted.

On Thursday Jan. 10th, amid cheers from all, the pilot, Lt.

Commander Harris came aboard and by afternoon they were moored alongside Berth Fox. 1. Ford Island, Pearl Harbor, Oahu.

The next day the watch was startled to see a familiar figure come up to the ship to report in. It was C. K.! What's he been up to? Where's he been? How did he get here? There were a host of questions, but they had to wait for the Captain to hold Mast before they learned anything and then it wasn't much. C. K. wasn't talking.

The charges were 1. Making Official communication to superior authority other than commanding officer without sending via commanding officer, 2. False representations (1 specification) 3. Absent without authority. 4. False representation (1. specification) 5. Disobedience of written orders.

He was awarded a Summary Court Martial and later, back in the States, he was found guilty of specification 1. and sentenced to loss of $50 off his pay for 2 months. Later, loss of pay was remitted by higher authority.

Bat, Mug and Sam never told C. K. how they went looking for him and to their disappointment he kept a close mouth about what he'd been up during the 15 days he'd been AWOL.

At 1415 after taking on fresh water and provisions, with the Captain at the conn and the Executive Officer and navigator on the bridge, the Bering Strait was underway from Pearl Harbor to San Francisco, California, in accordance with ComAirPac dispatch #110330.

The days across passed too slowly. One man grew tired of looking at the sea and was found "Laying in bunk with his shoes on." The Captain held mast and he was given a warning.

Then , at last, on January 17th at 0753 the Bering Strait, her battle honors streamer 200 feet long, passed under the Golden Gate Bridge with the south tower abeam to port.

Even the toughest man aboard had a lump in his throat when it first came into view. For a while, all had wondered if they would ever see it again.

At 0816 the Bering Strait passed under the Bay Bridge rendering honors to C-80 at 0819. At 0821 she rendered honors to USS Nashville and at 0830 honors to USS Bon Homme Richard.

By 0842 she was moored to Pier no l, Berth 4. Alameda Naval Air Station amid the cheers of welcome from well wishers, friends and families who were impatiently waiting for them.

To all aboard and especially to those who had been with the ship since she left for the Pacific in July 1944 it seemed a lifetime away. They were home, but they would never be the same.

Too much had happened. They had seen death, despair, destruction in too many shapes and guises. But they had also seen courage and compassion and experienced comradeship of the highest kind. The Bering Strait had been their home, their security through it all. She had seen them through the worst that warring nations could inflict on each other, through Nature's storms and tempests and finally, she had brought them safely home to those nearest and dearest to them. Even though they had longed for this day, it would be a wrench to leave her and she wouldn't be forgotten..

They need not have worried about her, she was too good a ship to be idle for long. The Bering Strait was to have three more careers.

But that's another story.

Meanwhile work on the "Bridge Across the Seas" started by the Bering Strait in Sasebo, was to be continued by a much larger ship, the aircraft carrier, USS Philippine Sea, CV 47.

# KOREA 1950

## USS PHILIPPINE SEA

In June 1950 the Bering Strait, now painted white, was on station in the Pacific as a Weather ship for the Coast Guard when the news came that South Korea had been invaded by Communists from the North. Shortly after, her old skipper, Walter Innis, then on the staff of the Naval War College in Newport, Rhode Island, received orders to report to the fast carrier, USS Philippine Sea, CV 47, as Executive Officer. This ship was to be the Flag ship of Task Force 77.

For the first time in history US Forces were to fight under the United Nations Flag.

This came about when the United Nations Security Council passed a resolution to assist the Republic of Korea in defending herself and recommending that all members make assistance available to a Unified Command under the United States. The forces of the Unified Command were authorized to fly the UN flag concurrently with the flags of the nations participating in the Command, at its discretion, while operating against the North Koreans. Seven countries voted for the resolution. These were the United States, the United Kingdom, France, China, Cuba, Ecuador and Norway. India, Egypt and Yugoslavia abstained and the Soviet Union was absent. Thus the Korean War set the precedent for the Unified Command of the UN Forces in the Gulf War of 1990. There was another similarity between the two wars. Both Secretary Dulles and later President Eisenhower said that the Korean War started because the United States failed to make clear to the Communists that it would support the Republic of Korea if it were attacked. In the Gulf War, it was also conceded that the failure of the United States to make clear to Saddam Hussein that it would support Kuwait if it were attacked, led to his attacking that country. But there was one great difference between the two wars - when the United States went into the Gulf War, the Armed Services were well equipped. There was a sufficiency of ships, planes, submarines, missiles, ammunition and advanced technical aids. Most important of all, there was sufficient well trained personnel. This war was over in six weeks. The Korean War was unexpected and the United States went into it unprepared and ill equipped.

This war lasted three years. At the end of World War II, it was believed that Russia was the only threat to peace and, as the United States was the only country with the atomic bomb, it was thought that this would not only ensure the safety of the country, but also world peace. It was not known at this time that Stalin's spies in Los Alamos had already provided him with many of the secrets of the bombs that were dropped on Japan and Russia was well on the way to building its own nuclear bombs.

So, much of the America's great Fleet was mothballed, the Army was cut back to 590,000 men and the Marine Corps was also substantially reduced. This meant that in order to send troops to Korea, Reserves, National Guardsmen and draftees were hastily called up to fill the shortage even though many had little training, no wartime experience and much of their equipment was ineffective against the fully equipped North Koreans. Their 2.36 inch bazookas could not stop the enemy tanks neither could the US light tanks.

The North Korean Army was well trained by the Russians and was organized and experienced from the war with China. Also, the North Korean troops were well equipped with tanks and guns. However, they had a very small Navy and little air power. The South Koreans had no tanks and no anti tank guns and their army was small and ill trained.

By the time the Philippine Sea arrived, in August 1950, the Communists had over run three-quarters of South Korea. They had captured Seoul, the capital city, and driven the South Korean and Allied Forces back to the Pusan perimeter. "Pity the country was ever divided up, I thought it was supposed to be independent after World War II." the Skipper, Captain Goodney, said to Innis as they studied the maps of the area.

"That was the agreement. Trouble was that Japanese Forces south of the 38th parallel, were directed to surrender to the United

States Commander and those north of the parallel to the Russians. The division was only for surrender purposes, but the Russians took over and sealed off the north from the south."

"But wasn't there an agreement not too long ago, between Russia and the US to withdraw troops?"

"There was after the elections in May '48, but the North Koreans were not allowed to vote and they formed their own government with the blessings of the Russians. They want to get the whole country under the communists."

"Now the Russians have the atomic bomb, God only knows what they'll try."

"Washington's afraid of getting into a war with Russia, that's why they call this a 'police action'. They don't want to give the Russians any excuse to attack. No one wants to risk war with Russia for fear it leads to an atomic bomb on the White House."

What wasn't realized until later, was that while President Truman was distrustful of Stalin's motives, Stalin was equally suspicious of the intentions of the 'Western Imperialists' and was anxious to avoid a Third World War and the possibility of Moscow being hit with a nuclear bomb. George Kennan in his memoirs mentions Stalin's warnings to the Italians about American Imperialism.

In spite of these fears, for several reasons, one of which was the fact that the US had withdrawn occupation troops from Korea as well as the Marines from the Shantung Peninsula, Stalin did not expect American opposition to the communist attack on South Korea.

On August 5th, in the wardroom of the Philippine Sea, Rear Admiral Edward Ewen, ComCar Div. 1. and Commander Raymond Vogel, CAG 11, gave the briefing to the pilots before the first launch. In spite of the fact that the ship was suddenly ordered to Korea on July 5th, being originally scheduled to relieve the Valley Forge in October, its air group was ready and raring to go. Intensive training in Hawaii and en route to Korea enabled the jet squadrons to familiarize themselves with the new planes. In his book, SEA WAR IN KOREA, Malcolm Cagle says "It is a high complement to both ship and air group that despite these handicaps, their performance in Korea was outstanding."

VF-111 was the first off, led by Lt. Commander William Amen. They swept the enemy held airfields at Kwangje, Mokpo and

Kunsan.

VF-112 Panthers followed to hit targets in the same area and VF 114 was successful in knocking out two dams, a bridge and some warehouses, south of Iri. From then on, planes were kept in the air 24 hours a day and there was little rest for anyone. Lt.jg Frank Pearce, who, in World War II, had command of an LCT in the Normandy Landing, said when describing his time aboard the Philippine Sea.

"There was no time to worry about anything but keeping the planes in the air. In a way I was glad to be so busy, it kept me from worrying too much about my wife and son. My son was born with club feet and had to have a serious operation. We had been preparing to take him to a very good doctor in Atlanta - Dr. Kite, his name was. He'd been successful operating on cases like my son. But when I had to report back early, Evelyn, my wife, had to take him on her own.

"She had to find a place to live while our son was in hospital and I hated to have her do it all by herself. Anyhow, she managed. She got a little apartment and took a job in a bank to help out. I was real proud of her."

As the situation on the ground grew worse, all air efforts were concentrated on close air support and interdiction. General McArthur was afraid that the 8th Army would be overwhelmed and so Vice Admiral Strubel put the Fleet Operation on such an intensive schedule that there was a constant never-ending pressure on the North Korean armies.

Led by Lt. Commander Vogel planes from the Philippine Sea bombed targets in and around Seoul and Inchon doing considerable damage. On the 9th August Vogel led a VF 114 strike against Pyongyang the North Korean capital.

"We'll show 'em." he promised. And show 'em they did. They hit the Riken Metal Co. with 500 lb bombs and rockets and that same day VF 114 and VA 115 together, blasted the marshalling yards and the Standard Oil warehouses in Seoul while Corsairs of VF 113 hit a factory in Inchon. So the days went by with no rest for anyone. Then, on the 19th Vogel led another strike against targets near Seoul. After hitting the span of a bridge, Vogel's plane was hit by enemy anti aircraft fire and burst into flames.

Realizing he had to jump, Vogel bailed out to the great relief of the other pilots who were afraid he'd been killed. They watched his chute stream, anxiously waiting for it to open, but it stayed tightly closed.

"Open up, damn you." Vogel's wingman shouted to the empty air. Then watched helplessly as Vogel's body hurtled down and smashed into the ground. Vogel's death saddened all who know him and the loss of such a leader was a hard blow to the ship, but the strikes continued with Commander Weymouth temporarily becoming CAG -11.

The ship's planes continued demolishing targets in North Korea and, when called upon, conducting CAS in defense of the Pusan Perimeter. Then came the breakthrough. General McArthur conceived a plan to make an amphibious assault on Inchon, recapture the city of Seoul and cut the enemy's supply lines. In spite of the reluctance of the military leaders and the Chairman of the Joint Chiefs of Staff, General McArthur was confident that the Navy would make the Inchon plan a success even though he admitted that it was a gamble with odds of 5000-to-one.

The landing was planned for 15th September which left little time for planning or for gathering intelligence. Vice Admiral Struble was in command of the invasion and Rear Admiral Ewen in charge of the fast carrier force. "Well, the Navy will have its work cut out pulling this one off. Take a look at that chart. Inchon's a hell of a place to make a landing. Its got to take place at high tide and that's at 1730 and with those high sea walls—"Goodney's voice trailed off as he studied the charts.

"Yeah, everything's against it, but McArthur's decided it can be done - you're right, though, Captain. The Marines will have a hell of a job climbing those walls and it'll be dark before they can settle in for the night." Innis replied.

"Well, we've got the ships, the ammo and the know-how to soften up the place for them and enough air support to keep the skies clear, that'll help."

"Is there much info on what we'll be up against, Captain? I heard there's a man been near Inchon for a couple of weeks scouting around."

"Yes, a man named Clark, used to be a chief yeoman. He made Lieutenant and did a good job commanding the USS Errol. He's been up around Inchon with two South Koreans sending back intelligence to HQ."

Later the whole story of Lt. Eugene Clark's contribution to the success of the Inchon landing was told when he received the Navy Cross for bravery. Clark was perched on the island of Yong-hong-do about 13 miles from Inchon. He captured several North Koreans who sneaked over at low tide hoping to capture him and sunk a number of their sampans.

He, and the South Koreans assisting him, measured the height of the sea walls on the landing beaches and charted observation posts and gun emplacements and provided information on the seabed and mud flats. Clark also discovered that one of the main navigation lights in the dangerous Flying Fish Canal, had not been completely destroyed. When he informed HQ of this, he was instructed to try and get the light going by midnight on the 14th Sept. With incredible bravery Clark risked his life sneaking up to the light in enemy territory. Managing to get it alight at midnight as instructed, he enabled the Invasion Fleet to make a safer, easier and quicker passage through the dangerous waters in the early hours of invasion day.

From the 12th September on the Philippine Sea's planes launched attacks on the Inchon - Seoul area and provided air cover for the invasion forces. With their accustomed bravery and skill the Marines of the First Division surmounted the difficulties of tides, sea walls and lack of surprise and captured Inchon with few casualties.

By the 17th, they had secured the Kimpo airfield. Later the Marines together with the US 7th Infantry Division, captured Seoul and the enemy supply lines were severed. McArthur's 5000-to-one gamble had paid off!

The North Koreans fled. The South Koreans and the Americans burst out of the Pusan Perimeter, and by late September, the UN Forces now well supplied with heavy tanks and guns, had driven the enemy back beyond the 38th parallel.

On one of the attacks on Seoul, Ensign Edward Jackson, flying a F9F2, was on a low level run strafing an area south of Seoul, when he hit some high tension cables strung over the Han river. The plane shuddered and began to drop. Somehow he managed to keep it in the air, but, to his horror he realized he couldn't see the instruments - in fact he couldn't see anything at all! God! I'm blind! Then a voice came over the radio,

"Hi, there Eddy. Are you all right?" it was his wingman , Ensign Daryl Crow who had seen the plane hit. "I can't see, God! I can't see a thing- I—"

"Hang in there, buddy. Just listen to me. I'll talk you in. We'll make it together." Back aboard the Philippine Sea the message had been received that a blinded pilot and damaged plane was about to make an emergency landing. Immediately the flight deck was a mass of men moving planes and gear and bringing up firefighting and rescue equipment readying for the worst.

AO2 Jerry Dirodus, who had also served in World War II, tells of the scene,

"I'll never forget it. As soon as it was broadcast that one of our pilots was in trouble and was being talked in, everyone on board who could was out there watching and pulling for him. It's no easy job landing on a carrier when everything's going for you, but when your plane's damaged and you can't see what the hell you're doing, you sure need a lot of luck."

"God! I remember how quiet we was when we saw those two approaching- would they make it? Could his wingman get him into the groove? We knew if he could get into the groove, that is get lined up right for landing, then the LSO would take over and talk him down to the deck.

"For a moment there we thought he was a goner- he was too low - then he pulled up and made right for the ship — but he was too fast. We all knew he was too fast. "Cut it. Cut it." we shouted.

"He went through the first wire, they're what catches the plane, then he missed the second and the third. I was holding my breath hard as he went through the fourth, then, thank God, the fifth wire got him.

"You should have heard the cheers as the firefighters charged over and the 'hot poppas', that's the men in asbestos suits who get to pull you out of the fire , got him out."

"His face was covered with blood and they had to carry him, but he was all in one piece, thank God. Any time it comes to mind, I hear those cheers as those planes made it safe back."

"She was a good ship." Dirodus added. "One of the best. Good officers and good men. Show Boat they called her. Mind you I was one of the oldest on board. I was 38. Most were in their late teens or early twenties. Sometimes we'd get together in the fire room and I'd tell them tales about World War II and they'd tell me what was on their minds."

In October the Philippine Sea was back on the east coast resuming its strikes on North Korea and supporting preparations for the landing of troops in Wonsan. General McArthur was anxious to make an amphibious landing there. Although few supported the plan, there was no opposition as the great success of Inchon was still uppermost in everyone's mind. The General had been right then and they hadn't so now they were silent.

Unfortunately, Wonsan turned out to be a big mistake. The harbor had been heavily mined with mines supplied by Russia and, when the Korean War began, due to budget cuts, the US had only four 180 ft. steel hull fleet minesweepers and six wooden auxiliary minesweepers in the Far Eastern waters, so it was decided to try to clear the mine field with an aerial strike by Task Force 77.

Early in the morning of the 12th October aircraft from the Philippine Sea and the Leyte, mainly Corsairs and Skyraiders lined up in two lines 500 ft. apart and dropped their thousand pound general purpose bombs. Unfortunately, it was not possible to assess the value of this operation. As Admiral Struble had had experience in World War II of aerial counter strikes which were not successful, he refused to allow any further air strikes on the mine fields, considering it impractical. Captain Richard Spoffard who commanded Mine Squadron Three, stated that the accuracy required for success meant that the bombs had to explode within thirty feet of a mine and that was too much to expect. Minesweepers were the best method of clearing the way.

So the gallant little Mine Squadron Three continued the effort to clear the 3,000 mines in the approach to Wonsan. When the three steel hulled ships were out of action, two sunk and one badly damaged, the little wooden ships took over aided by some small boats under the supervision of LTCD DeForest.

Good progress was being made until a small boat of the South Koreans was blown to pieces and it was realized that there were also magnetic mines ahead. With tremendous courage DeForest went ashore and was successful in contacting a North Korean who showed him a new search coil for their mines. This Soviet manufactured coil held the secret of the magnetic mine.

DeForest was also successful in getting information about the laying of the mines so that, at last, by the 25th October, the channel to the Wonsan beach was cleared.

By the end of October word got around that General McArthur had said that things were going so well that the troops would be home for Christmas. The North Korean Army was beaten. Thousands of their troops had surrendered and the UN Forces were moving rapidly ahead towards the Manchurian Border. When they heard this welcome news, the Philippine Sea was in Sasebo Harbor, Japan for replenishment and the crew were enjoying some well-earned R and R.

A bunch of sailors engrossed in a serious game of poker, suspended play in order to discuss the possibilities. "Maybe we won't be needed back in Korea and they'll send us back home from here." Spit said hopefully. Spit was an ever cheerful black man, so named because he provided a service of incalculable value to his shipmates. He had a dress shoe polishing service guaranteed to pass the closest inspection for a fee far below the value of his incomparable spittle.

"I hope to God its true. I'm goddamn sick of war. The good old USA looks better to me every day." his partner answered. "I heard as them Reds in China is sending troops to help out the North Koreans."

"That's only talk, the Peking radio said they weren't sending anything officially, there's only a few volunteers helping."

"Well, I thinks that McArthur knows what he's talking about and if he says we'll be home for Christmas, that's good enough for me." Spit said as they resumed the game.

Unfortunately, the skeptics were right. Huge numbers of Chinese Communist troops marched south to aid the North Koreans and the Philippine Sea was ordered to set sail on Nov. 6th. On the 9th she rejoined Task Force 77 and her planes were bombing the bridges of the Yalu river where the Chinese were streaming across.

By now, the weather was bitterly cold. Snow covered most of the ground area. The sky was dark and gloomy and visibility was poor. The decks of the Philippine Sea had to be constantly cleared of ice.

Pilots from the Philippine Sea encountered a new threat - the Chinese Air Force were now flying Mig-15 jet planes.

One, its guns blazing, came straight at Lt.C Amen who was flying a VF112 Panther. But Amen was ready for him. With deadly accuracy his guns raked the MiG and it went down in flames. Amen became the first Navy airman to shoot down one of these planes. He received a vociferous welcome on returning to the ship. Other pilots reported sighting MiGs but trouble with their guns due to the bitter cold which caused them to jam up, prevented them from duplicating Amen's success.

On land the Marines were pushing their way north towards Chosin with the intention of linking up with the Eighth Army. Weather conditions were worsening. Troops were slogging through snow and ice in mountainous terrain. Each night held the possibility of ambush. Many woke up with frostbite. Every drop of water had to be thawed out. Hot showers were just a dream. The dead lay in frozen piles until loaded up and carried down the mountains. Helicopters flew out the wounded after corpsmen or buddies had managed to get them to a place where the copters could get to them.

So far neither the Marines or the Eighth Army had met with heavy resistance and by the 21st Nov. the 17th Regimental Combat team of the Seventh Army had reached Hyesanin on the Manchurian Border. Then, suddenly, the Chinese struck with massed attacks splitting apart the Eighth Army and the Tenth Corps. The story of the fierce fighting as the Allied troops pulled back will always be remembered and honored.

Planes from the Leyte and Philippine Sea rendered close support to the Eighth Army and the Tenth Corps throughout. Then in answer to Major General Harris' urgent request, the Navy and Marine aircraft made their main effort in support of the First Marine Division which was in a critical situation in Chosin encircled by Chinese troops.

On Dec 4. four Corsairs from the Leyte were making an armed reconnaissance five miles behind the Chinese lines at Chosin, when the plane of section leader Ensign Jesse Brown, the Navy's first black pilot, was hit by enemy fire. Completely out of control, the plane crashed and broke up. At first his wingman, Ltjg Thomas Hudner, thought Brown was killed.

"I felt sure that the force that broke up the plane would surely have killed the pilot." Hudner said, "but then I saw the canopy open and Brown waved. Immediately the flight leader radioed for a rescue helicopter to pick him up. Then I saw smoke coming out of the plane and I thought for God's sake get out, man, get out. Then, I realized he must be too badly injured to move. There was no time to be lost. The plane could go up in flames any moment, so I got rid of my bombs and rockets and made a forced landing near Brown's plane.

"It was already getting dark so I piled up a whole lot of snow on the wreckage to stop the smoke going up in flames, and then tried to extricate Brown. By now he was barely conscious and unable to move.

"Thank God ,it wasn't long before a Marine rescue helicopter landed and the pilot joined me trying to get Brown out. We were working as fast as we could knowing the Chinese could attack any minute and with night coming on we were anxious to get him out of there. But we couldn't get him free and he died quite quietly while we were working."

"Well, as it was nearly dark we flew off in the helicopter and a few days later, planes from Brown's squadron flew over the site of the wreckage and to keep the body from possible desecration, we sprayed the area with napalm." Thomas Hudner received the Medal of Honor for his great courage and bravery.

As the First, Fifth and Seventh Marines fought their way back to Hagaru and then to Hungnam for evacuation and redeployment, planes of the Philippine Sea and the Leyte kept up their close support. Throughout the long march, air support bombed, strafed and napalmed the Chinese troops. Air Force planes dropped supplies of all kinds and flew out the badly injured by helicopter. Hopes of being home for Christmas had long since gone.

Christmas is always lonely away from home. Its a time when families are gathering together and everyone longs to be there with them. Its especially lonely in war time when Peace and Goodwill seem nothing but an impossible dream. Every year, as Christmas drew near, everyone aboard the Philippine Sea contributed to a fund for some worthy cause. One Christmas it was an old folks home, another an orphanage in Rhode Island. Old Showboat ,as the Philippine Sea was known in the service, was the most generous of all when it came to giving.

Even now, in the bitterest fighting, the men still thought of others, but somehow, no one came up with just the right cause. The Welfare Committee usually came up with a whole bunch of ideas, but out in the freezing winds, thousands of miles from home, none of their suggestions seemed much good.

"Let's ask the Chaplains, they might come up with something." Bosuns Mate James Clancy said.

"O.K., why don't you tell them what we have in mind and ask if they can come up with something real good. Something different." the committee agreed. So Clancy talked with the Protestant Chaplain, Dick Barnes and with the Catholic Padre Harold Meade, and both said they'd give it some thought. Then Chaplain Barnes said, "How about putting up a notice asking for suggestions from the whole crew. You ought to get something good that way."

That night in the fire room, some of the crew were sitting around with Jerry Didorus when he asked, "Seen the notice about the Christmas Fund?"

"Yeah, how much money in it this year?"

"About $ 3,000 take or leave a dollar or two."

The men whistled, "That's pretty damn good."

"Well, there's over 3,000 of us on board, so that's just around a dollar each. Say, Spit, how much did you cough up? You ought to give up some of that profit you make out of us."

"What you talking about? I don't make no profit. It takes like a gallon of spit to clean your shoes. When you thinks of what it costs me in extry coffee and lemonade to make up that spit, I don't make no profit, I'm out of pocket." Spit protested indignantly. "It's Icey what's makes the profit. You oughta go after him."

Icey laughed. "I'll give twice what you gives, Spit. You ain't got half the racket I worked up. I'm what you call a real business man, that's what." Icey was a ship's service man who was involved in the gedunk stand. Sailors loved ice cream and bought huge amounts of it for 10 cents a dixie cup. The ice cream mix they used was meant to make 100 full cups per gallon. However, Icey and his friends discovered that if enough air was added and it was frozen quickly, they could double the amount produced and make a nice profit for themselves. Nobody complained as it tasted just as good.

"You want to know what I think?" a fresh faced 18 year old piped up, "I think we should do something for one of those outfits that's for Peace and Goodwill. That's what Christmas is all about. I've had it with war."

For a moment there was silence, then several spoke up together, "I'm for that. Lets tell the Welfare lot what we want." So the suggestions piled up and the majority turned out to be for something that would promote world understanding and peace.

"It sounds fine and I'm all for it, but no one seems to know of any outfit that works for world understanding." Clancy said doubtfully.

Then they talked with the Exec. Innis was sympathetic, he knew how much importance the men put on finding the right cause. "I'll get back to you later. Sorry I can't come up with anything right now." He found it hard to put his mind to Christmas and peace and goodwill in the midst of all the fighting while so many were suffering and dying in the fall back from North Korea.

That night, when things were a bit quieter, he remembered the young Japanese who had been so friendly and helpful to the US ships including his ship, the Bering Strait, when they had put into Sasebo after VJ Day in World War II. What was his name? Ebihara, that was it. They called him Ebi. He'd come up to the ships offering his services as a guide or an interpreter. A good many of the oldtimers on the Philippine Sea knew him from those days.

Innis recalled how Ebi had told him that after his journalist father had been killed for writing against the war, he had decided he was going to do what he could for world peace and intended to go to college and become a good lawyer. Ebi might be the answer. They could use the money to send him to school. Later he discussed it with the Chaplains to see what they thought.

"Well, its not what we usually do, but its a real good idea and its in the true Christmas spirit." said Barnes.

"I'll go for it." agreed Meade. "I'll clear it with the Captain and then we can take it to the men and see if its what they want."

Captain Goodney knew nothing about Ebi and his work with the US ships in 1945, so he was skeptical. But after Innis told him the story, he said, "If the men are for it, its O.K. by me. But, if they do, try and steer him to my old school."

"That was Michigan wasn't it?"

"Yeah, the University of Michigan has one of the best Law Schools in the world."

The final decision was up to the crew. Officers can only advise, the crew has the final say. There were some who were doubtful, but the oldtimers who remembered Ebi were so enthusiastic that they were soon convinced. Also, as the Philippine Sea had been putting into Sasebo at intervals for replenishment, during the Korean War, many had made friends with the Japanese. So, it was decided that Ebi should be the recipient of the Fund and it was given its official title: the USS Philippine Sea Burse for the education of S. Ebihara.

Innis was given the job of contacting Ebi. It was over five years since Innis had last seen him and Ebi had left the old address. However, by enlisting the aid of the 'shore' Navy, he was located in Nagano City about a hundred miles from Tokyo. Ebi had not been idle. He had worked his way through Tokyo University and now had a job in small district court. He probably wouldn't want to give up his job and go back to school. When Innis passed this down to the crew, they were very disappointed. They had thought everything was all arranged and now they were right back where they started from.

Realizing their disappointment, Innis suggested that it seemed Ebi's job paid barely enough to support him, his mother and sister, if he was given the opportunity of further education, he would probably do a lot better. He had done so much on his own without help from anyone that it was obvious he was a hard worker. Why not go ahead?

When this suggestion was put to the crew, they thought it was pretty good and the Enlisted Men's Welfare and Recreation Committee which was made up of representatives from each Division of the ship, voted unanimously in favor of further education for Ebi.

By now the Fund had reached $4,000. Everyone from Task Force 77's Admiral Eddie Ewen to apprentice seamen had contributed.

Ebi knew nothing of what was going on and it was decided not to tell him until preparations were complete. It was possible that the University of Michigan would not accept him and it was now Dec. 21st. Not much time left. Fortunately, the TF operations officer, Commander Robert F. Jones, of Duluth, was a close friend of Professor Charles Davis who was on the staff of Michigan U.

"I know Charlie Davis, he was a demolition man in World War II. He's a fine guy, he knows how to get things done." Innis. said, "Lets get a message drafted and sent out right away."

"O.K. sir, my brother Steve, he's a Michigan graduate, he's Captain in the Navy now, but he's a friend of Davis, too. Might be good to get him to contact Davis also."

"Good, the more help we get the better." So the cable message was sent out with the urgent plea - "Rush this as a Christmas Gift to the brave men of a gallant ship."

On Christmas Eve as the last ships were leaving Wonsan after evacuating 105,000 American and South Korean military personnel, 91,00 refugees, 350 tons of cargo and 17,500 vehicles, the message came from Professor Davis that he was doing his best.

Both Innis and Jones knew that this was as good as a confirmation, so after speaking to the crew, Innis sent a message to Ebi telling him to report to the Philippine Sea on the 26th when she put in to Sasebo for replenishment.

Christmas Day at sea was freezing cold and windy. Snow and ice had to be cleared from the flight deck and planes tied down due to the wind. But the band kept spirits up by playing Carols and Christmas music and everyone knew Christmas mail would be waiting for the ship in Sasebo the following day. The Welfare Committee had decorated the crew's mess and plans were all made for presentation of the gift to Ebi.

"Pity we couldn't have done it today." Radioman Bob Craig said.

"Yeah, we could have put it under the Christmas Tree. I've never seen $4,000 all in one lump and I bet he hasn't either."

"Well, tomorrow's what the Limeys call Boxing Day. That's the day they give their gifts. They go to Church on Christmas, or that's what they say."

Back in Nagano City, Ebi was wondering why the American Officer who must be very important by now, wanted him to come aboard the Philippine Sea, which he had discovered was a great, big ship. He showed the message to his mother, "What do you think it means, Mamasan?"

"Perhaps he desires just to see you again. He was a very kind man to us. It is necessary that you go."

So on December 26th 1950 Ebihara arrived in Sasebo Harbor

where the Philippine Sea was riding at anchor. Innis met him at the gangway and took him immediately to the crew's mess without telling him anything and Ebi didn't like to ask. He was overwhelmed when he saw all the men and the decorations.

The chairman of the Welfare Committee, James Clancy stepped forward and said to Ebi, "Welcome aboard the Philippine Sea, Big Showboat, We have a gift for you. We want you to go college in the United States for two years." and he handed Ebi the package of money.

Ebi couldn't understand, "I-I — Why would you do this for me?"

"You will go to the University of Michigan, the best Law School in the States." Captain Goodney smiled.

Then a chorus of voices shouted, "Merry Christmas, Ebi, help us bring some Christmas Peace and goodwill to the world." then he understood.

All through the hardships of war, his father's death and his struggles to support the family, in true Japanese fashion, Ebi had never shed a tear. But this unexpected kindness from these men, most of whom did not even know him, made tears come to his eyes.

"How can I ever thank you?" he said his voice breaking with emotion.

"Do good in school, Ebi and work for peace, that's what it's all about."

When Ebi got back home his mother couldn't believe it. "It is a wonderful thing. More kindness than I thought in all the world."

It was a few weeks later when the President of Michigan U, Alexander Ruthven, and the Dean of the Law School, Edwin Stason, and Professor R. Smith worked out the details of the scholarship.

"I would never have thought that the crew of a warship would be interested in helping someone get a formal education. Much less a Japanese." remarked the Dean.

"Perhaps we should learn something from them. There they are out in that war zone in terrible conditions not knowing when it will end and yet they are thinking of something like this and hoping it will help with world understanding." answered Smith. "You're right and I think we should do all we can to help."

Ruthven agreed. Ebi managed to get leave from his job and the Chief of Naval Operations, Admiral William Fechteler, gave the okay for Ebi to travel by air to the States.

In the Fall of 1951, Ebi entered Michigan Law School. At that time no one dreamt of the far reaching effects this Christmas Gift would have.

# KOREA

## 1951

By January 8th 1951 the Philippine Sea had rejoined Task Force 77 and was supporting UN operations and attacking enemy supply lines around the 38th parallel.

In 1951 with the North Koreans defeated, the war was now between the Chinese Communists and the Allies with the North Koreans infiltrating South Korea and doing what damage they could there. The Chinese possessed the whole North Korean coastline which meant they could re-mine the harbors and put the coastal guns in place.

While Admiral Joy believed that the Navy was more effective supplying close air support, he was overruled and the Navy was back flying interdiction sorties striking at East Coast bridges and rail systems.

The Chinese, aided by North Korean laborers , were expert at bridge repairing. A bridge could be knocked out one day and almost overnight the Communists had it back in service.

The railways had a system of tunnels which protected parts of the lines but returning planes reported considerable damage from their strikes. However, the Chinese and North Koreans used man power for bringing up much of their supplies. Men wearing the A-frame, a kind of yoke, could carry mortar rounds and other types of ammunition and food supplies. This method of transportation was slow but it was cheap and reliable and much more difficult for the planes to interrupt.

During the months of January and February the Philippine Sea continued operating off the east coast of Korea. The weather was still bitterly cold and crews were working 24 hours a day keeping the flight deck clear of snow and ice.

The gun heaters on some of the planes didn't work causing the guns to freeze up and often the pilots hands were so cold they had trouble landing.

One of the things both pilots and flight deck crews complained of was the constant fatigue. They found they couldn't sleep much at night although they were hard at it all day. They found themselves dreaming of a comfortable bed at home in peace and quiet where they could sleep for a week on end.

Like most of the married men, Jerry Dirodus missed his wife Eleanor, and their two children. One day, remembering that Eleanor's birthday was coming up soon, he got in touch with a disk jockey in Cleveland, Ohio named Joe Mulverhill. Joe played the old tunes from the 30's and 40's that Eleanor loved. Giving Joe his wife's name and the date of her birthday, he asked him to play a particular song for her.

When he was asked the name of the song forty years later, Didorus was silent for a moment, then he said,

"Hell, I've forgotten what it was, but I'll ask her." and calling to his wife he said,

"What was that song I got Joe Mulverhill to play for you that time.?"

Without any hesitation she answered, "It was 'Try a Little Tenderness'. I'll never forget how wonderful it was to hear my name and the message from Jerry when they played the song on the radio. It was the most beautiful thing that ever happened to me. I'll never forget it. I know I'm a very lucky woman. I've been married to a good man for 53 years and we've got four sons all doing well. I tell them, 'You treat your wife like your Dad treats me and you won't have any trouble.'"

While it was suspected that the Russians were aiding the North Koreans with manpower as well as arms, there was no proof of this. Then, one day, planes from the Philippine Sea spotted a couple of MiGs coming at them out of the blue.

Yelling "Let's get 'em, guys." the planes went after them with all they'd got.

One plane was shot down and, when a body was rescued from the sea, he was wearing a Russian uniform! Here was the proof at last! As the Russian had no identification on him, he was given the name, Ivan Ivanovitch and handed over to the medics. After embalming him, it was decided to put him in cold storage for safe keeping until he could be handed over to the authorities when the ship put in to port

Unfortunately, no one thought of telling the ship's cooks what was going on, and when they went in to get meat for the day and saw Ivan, they couldn't believe their eyes. After the first shock, they spread the tale around the ship that the Marines now ate Russians for breakfast.

The Marine detachment on board took it well. They liked to keep up their incredible image.'

"But," warned one burly Marine when he heard it, "You'd better watch your step, sailor, and treat us right, or you'll find yourself on my breakfast plate of a morning.

"Ben Thompson, SKI, who later became Chief of Police in New Hampshire, remembers Ivan,

"I was the one who had the job of delivering him to the authorities when we put in to Sasebo. I recall one of the medics saying Ivan had some stainless steel teeth which they'd never come across before."

On February 25th, Rear Admiral Ewen transferred his flag at sea to USS Valley Forge and Captain Goodney was relieved by Captain Ira Hobbs. Then on the 4th April, Vice Admiral Harold "Beauty" Martin, Com7th Fleet, arrived on board the Philippine Sea and on the 8th they sailed for Formosa which was being threatened by the Red Chinese. But after a short show of force over the north of Formosa and off the coast of China, the Philippine Sea was back off the coast of Korea giving support to the hard pressed UN ground forces, by the 15th of April.

On the 3rd of May the ship sailed to Japan where Vice Admiral Martin transferred his flag to the USS New Jersey.

While in port the ship invited Ebi and his sister aboard and were delighted to find that while Ebi was rather quiet and reserved, Yuko was a very friendly little girl who loved ice cream. She had never tasted it before and much to Icey's delight, she said she could eat all he could make.

"You won't get no ice cream as good as this any place else.

It's special to this here ship, I mostly makes it myself." Icey pointed out. Members of the Welfare Committee visited the Ebihara family home and were served tea by Mama Ebihara who with many bows and smiles thanked them for their kindness to her family. "We say many prayers to keep you safe and for you to have goodness done to you as you have done to my family.". she said. The sailors were touched by the gentle sweetness of the Japanese woman.

"She made me think of my grandmother, she was like her, sort of like flowers or something special. She wouldn't want to hurt anyone."

They took photographs which were later put up in the enlisted men's mess so they could see Ebi's family for themselves.

On the l6th of May the Communists made another strong attack. Hampered by thick fog and heavy rain, the Allied Ground Forces called for close air support from Task Force 77 and the Philippine Sea was back on the old 24 hour schedule again. In spite of the bad weather, the Allies successfully counter attacked in the West on May 19th and again in the central sector on May 21st. These counter attacks drove the Chinese back and caused them the loss of some 40,000 troops.

Then, amid much rejoicing on board, the Philippine Sea detached from Task Force 77 on the 30th May and set sail for home.

Beating the record set by the USS Boxer by three hours, and trailing her 3,200 foot pennant, the Philippine Sea moored at the Alameda Naval Air Station on June 9th met by a tremendous welcome.

After an overhaul in Hunter Point the ship was back with Task Force 77 on Feb 3 1952.

Meanwhile, Ebi had entered Michigan Law School in the Fall of 1951. Professor Davis and Innis who was now Assistant Inspector General, Shore Establishments Surveys, arranged for Ebi to live in the Lawyer's Club attached to the University.

Studying Comparative Law was Ebi's choice, but it was not easy. Although his English was fairly good, there were many words and phrases he had never heard before. Words he thought he understood of quite well, were used in an entirely different context. But he had a determination formed by long practice and although it meant studying late into the night, he somehow kept up with the rest.

Then there was the food. Ebi was used to a very frugal diet of mainly rice and a little fish and it was some time before he could adjust to the different diet. Meals in Michigan seemed richly lavish and enormous in size compared with those Ebi had in Japan. He watched the other students hungrily devouring mounds of red meat, vegetables, bread and cake washed down by quantities of liquids and wondered how there was enough room inside to hold it all.

In order to get some pocket money, Ebi and another student worked at odd jobs in the town on weekends, so he didn't have much time left for pleasure.

He told Innis later that what kept him going was the thought of the goodness of the Philippine Sea sailors - he just couldn't let them down.

They were proud of being responsible for sending him there. Ebi replied to every letter and also made three broadcasts back to Japan telling of the interest and kindness shown him by Americans.

By the time Ebi had completed his two years at the University and returned to his government job in Novaro City, the war in Korea was over and the Philippine Sea was back in the United States.

By now, many of the crew had gone on to other things. But Ebi never forgot them. He wrote to Innis,

"There is no way I can ever thank you and the men of the Philippine Sea for sending me to the American Law School. Maybe I can help build a bridge of understanding between Japan and the United States by telling of their help and goodness to me."

Later he was to find another way to keep the bridge under construction.

Back in Japan Ebi continued to study International Law and in 1961 he wrote to Innis telling him that he was working for IBM Japan, as house counsel. Ebi said he was anxious to spend some time in the United States studying International problems, foreign trade and investment. One paragraph in his letter has proved prophetic.

"Increased interest in investments in Japan has been evidenced by American investors." he wrote, "and economical ties between US and Japan will be much closer year after year. For the future of our economy, Japanese attorneys must prepare themselves for all legal work confronting them."

It appeared that Ebi was so well respected by the Japanese Bar Association that he was appointed as their representative to the General Meeting of the International Bar Association to be held in Scotland in July 1962. Ebi intended to come to the United States in March of that year to visit Innis and spend some time studying in Chicago and New York.

Innis encouraged him and made some arrangements for Ebi with several companies. However, as Innis was out of the country when Ebi was on the East coast, they did not meet at that time. Later, back in Japan, Ebi wrote and said he had gathered much information and had met with some old friends from his days at the Law School in Michigan.

The Korean War ended in 1953, now at last, approval has been given to the erection of a memorial to the 54, 246 members of the Armed Services who gave their lives in the Korean War.

The dedication ceremony is scheduled for July 27 1995, forty two years after the war ended.

# VIETNAM

## COAST GUARD

Since 1948 when the USS Bering Strait now WHEC-382, had been made available to the Coast Guard, she was engaged in Air Sea Rescue and Weather reporting on station Victor in the Pacific. Then in early 1967 the Bering Strait took part in a study of the Kuroshio Current, sometimes known as the Japan Current.

This current is the northwestern Pacific's counterpart of the Gulf Stream. Flowing past Formosa and the islands of Japan, the Kuroshio Current brings warmth and rain to Washington State, Oregon and British Columbia just as the Gulf Stream brings the same to the coasts of the British Isles and parts of northern Europe.

The study of ocean currents has been going on since Benjamin Franklin made the first scientific study of what he called the "great river of the Sea." Franklin made a chart showing the "great river of the Atlantic Ocean" and wrote the name Gulf Stream at the bottom of the drawing.

The chart showed sailors how they could save two whole weeks sailing westward by going with the Gulf Stream.

Since then, the "great rivers of the sea" have been studied with great intensity. Not only because they are of importance to all mariners, but because they can be used for military purposes.

The Oceans of the world are never still. They are forever moving, kept in motion by the rotation of the earth, the winds, the warmth of the sun, the interchange of warm equatorial water with the frigid Polar water and the deflection of the Coriolis effect.

Cold water sinks and moves more slowly than warm water. In an ocean current there is the top layer of warm surface water and under this another layer of cold water. This cold water layer could be moving in an entirely different direction and at a much different speed. For instance, in the International Geophysical Year 1957-58, a large current was discovered underneath the Gulf Stream. It was flowing in the opposite direction between 6,000 and 9,800 feet below the surface.

Temperature differences in water can bend sonic beams and it has been found that sonar detection failed to detect submarines in deep, cold water, that were known to be below.

While much is known about the movements of surface water, there is still much more to learn about the deep currents.

It was while the Bering Strait was engaged in this study that the decision was made in Washington, to send her to Vietnam to take part in Market Time.

As part of Coast Guard Squadron Three, the Bering Strait served two stints in Vietnam. First from May 1967 to February 1968, with Theodore Roberge as her skipper, and from the 17th of May to the 31st December 1970 with Paul Henneberry as her captain. The ship was mainly engaged in preventing the smuggling of arms, ammunitions and supplies to the Viet Cong, (communist guerrillas) and guarding against the infiltration of guerrillas from the North into South Vietnam. The ship also provided gun support when called upon and some maintenance and gun support for the Navy River Craft and for the small Coast Guard boats.

The Bering Strait looked different from when she was a fighting ship in World War II. Now she was painted white, she had one five inch gun forward and a 50 caliber machine gun on her port side. But no planes assigned to her and no airmen on board.

In the early years of this country, the Coast Guard was under the Department of the Treasury in time of peace, then President Johnson placed it under the Department of Transportation in 1967.

However, in time of war, the Coast Guard is always under the Department of the Navy.

The Vietnam War which started out with the United States giving technical and economic advice and later supplying military advisors to South Vietnam in 1954, turned out to be the longest and most divisive war in U.S. history. By 1964 it had escalated into a major conflict and, by the end of 1964, there were 184,000 troops involved.

By the time the Bering Strait reached the war zone, there were over 480,000 troops in Vietnam with 16,000 killed in action.

Public opinion in the United States against the war was rising daily. 100,000 people rallied to protest in New York in April 1967 and 50,000 protesters marched on the Pentagon in October that year.

Many of draft age left the country rather than serve in the Armed Forces. The lack of support from home and the accounts in the Press of the terrible effects of the war on Vietnamese civilians , especially women and children, made the hardships of those serving in Vietnam even more difficult. South Vietnam was saturated with Viet Cong, so it was almost impossible to tell friend from foe.

Added to this was the fact that the Vietnamese were very distrustful of the United States and many looked upon the U.S. troops as their enemies.

It was hard for the Vietnamese villagers to understand when their pitiful little rice fields and thatched huts were destroyed by U.S. troops fighting the Viet Cong, that it was for their good in the long run. All that most of the villagers wanted was to be left in peace to tend their rice, their pigs or buffaloes.

There had been fighting over their land for so many years, that they lived in constant fear of being forced from their home, tortured, shot or imprisoned . Few knew what the fighting was about.

They rarely took sides, but obeyed whoever was in power at the time, hoping they would move on and leave them to patch up their broken lives undisturbed by politics and war.

If the Viet Cong took over their village, the people did what they told them. When the South Vietnamese soldiers came looking for Viet Cong, they followed their orders. Now, they were told, the Americans had come to help them so they should follow their orders, but things were no better, in fact some thought things were worse.

This distrust was fanned by Russian propaganda aimed at discrediting the United States' efforts. An example of Russian propaganda at that time was a letter supposedly written by Gordon Goldstein of the Office of Naval Research. This forged letter claimed to reveal that the Americans were using germ warfare in Vietnam.

Although, this was proved to be absolutely false, it caused much distrust as it was published in several newspapers, even appearing in the London Times of March 7 1968.

While much has been written about the harrowing experiences of service men and women, of civilians and of the incredible bravery and endurance of some prisoners of war, there is little about the men and women of the Navy, the Coast Guard or the Merchant Marine.

The Navy was responsible for the successful blockade of the 1,200 mile coastline of Vietnam. The seventh Fleet's guns gave coastal support wherever needed and its long range planes made strikes against ports, oil installations and other targets, throughout the war. In addition, most supplies of all kinds, were brought in by sea.

The Coast Guard's cutters, destroyer escorts and mine sweepers patrolled midway approximately 30-40 miles off shore, between the Fleet and the small Patrol Craft Fast, (PCFs) which darted in and out of the inlets and bays close in.

In addition were the 28 foot fiber glass boats known as the "Riverines" which operated in the tributaries, outlets and bayous of the Mekong Delta where the Viet Cong hid out protecting a communication line to and from the North through the supposedly neutral countries of Laos and Cambodia.

While the crews of the "Riverines" led a dangerous and extremely hazardous existence, they were actively engaged against the enemy and their morale was high. Life on board the carriers was busy with regular missions flown every day, but for the Coast Guard cutters there were many days of monotonous patrolling, inspecting junks and fishing boats suspected of carrying arms and avoiding the fishing nets of the sampans. Many of the alerts turned out to be harmless, but all had to be inspected.

Shortly after arriving on Market Time, a message was received asking that a large freighter be boarded as there was a strong possibility that she was carrying war materials.

Captain Roberge, himself took the con to maneuver close to the ship as the water was shallow and there was not much leeway.

However, the freighter turned out to be the Pacific Mariner out of Panama and Hong Kong, loaded with vehicles.

During the month of May alone between twenty and thirty sampans and junks were boarded and inspected.

Three miles north of Song Ong Doc, 2 MiGS were sighted.

General Quarters was sounded and as the crew raced to their battle stations, the gun crews shouted "We've gotten our chance at last."

As the MiGs roared overhead the old five inch gun responded mightily and cheers echoed around the ship as hit was scored on one of them. But to the disappointment of all, not enough damage was done to splash it and both planes continued on their way.

"Must be looking for bigger game." the Exec muttered thankful that the planes did not turn to attack the ship.

A few days, later orders were received to provide gun support for a ground attack on a Viet Cong stronghold and supply area. Again the five inch responded well. 56 rounds of ammunition were expended resulting in 18 structures badly damaged.

While the Bering Strait's main mission was military, her crew, like that of other ships, also engaged in works of mercy.

Chief Hospital Corpsman Joseph White tells of how he and two of his shipmates, Chief Warrant Officer Rodney Strelau and Corpsman 2nd class Le Quang Dung of the South Vietnamese Navy, set up a Medical Assistance Project in the Mekong Delta.

"Civilians there were in a bad way." said White, "they had no medical care of any kind. So we had the job of setting up a MEDCAP about 15 miles up the Song Ong Doc river. It wasn't much of a place- just a thatched tin hut with a mud floor, but, boy, were they glad to see us.

"They called us the "American Healers" and were real grateful that we'd come to help them. A good many had come as far as twenty or thirty miles on foot through the rice paddies in pouring rain.

"We only had the basic equipment with us, but we were able to help most of them. Those with more serious problems we sent up the river by water taxi to the Ca Mau hospital. I remember there was one old man with severe cataracts. We sent him up there.

"It helped having a Vietnamese working with us. They'd listen to him. Petty Officer Dung was good at translating and he also treated a lot of the patients by himself. He'd been trained in US service schools so we worked together pretty well.

"We all felt good being able to help these people out and to get them to trust us for a change."

The little village of Xom Chay also has some good memories

of the visit of the MEDCAP team from the Bering Strait. While Chief Jow White and Corpsman Le Quang Dung were there treating some of the villagers who were sick, they noticed that there were no recreational facilities at the village school or in the village where the children could play. So, they promised that they would see to it that some playground material would be there before too long.

The crew were so generous that the ship was able to buy six pieces of equipment for the playground when they docked in Singapore, the first Coast Guard Cutter to put in to this port since World War II.

This playground material was installed later by Commander Troutman with seven enlisted men and five Vietnamese from the ship, when they were next in the area. While ashore the civic action team from the ship dug a well for a nearby military outpost which had no satisfactory water supply fit for drinking.

The MEDCAPS set up in various parts of Vietnam, were valuable in counteracting the Communist propaganda and helping to dispel some of the distrust of the villagers. At least in the areas around the projects. But elsewhere mutual distrust was growing daily.

On September 7th the Bering Strait was moored in the US Navy Base in Sasebo, Japan, for replenishment. Sasebo was now a flourishing port, looking very different from when the Bering Strait had spent so much time there in the Occupation just after the end of World War II. All the damage had been repaired and it looked what it was— a prosperous, growing area. The crew were glad to get some shore leave and a chance to walk on dry land.

Ebi had long since left the area and was now a judge in Tokyo. His mother and grandmother had died earlier and Ebi was now married and had a son and daughter.

Because of his training and experience in the United States,.and the fact that he specialized in International Law, Ebi was often called on to preside over cases of International Trade disputes. In a letter to Innis, Ebi wrote, "you exemplified for me the Golden Rule and I intend to follow your example in all my dealings with the United States."

Back on Market Time the rest of the year passed slowly for the crew of the Bering Strait. They were kept on the alert guarding against infiltration of arms and supplies to enemy groups and providing "hotel accommodations" for crews of the swift boat crews of the Navy.

These little boats change crews normally, every 24 hours and sometimes the spare crew would stay aboard for some R and R before going back to their next risky patrol. The boats of the south Vietnamese also would come alongside for supplies of all kinds.

In December en route to Hong Kong, news came that they had just one more patrol and then en route to Honolulu.

Monday, Jan 1st. 1968, found the Bering Strait leaving Hong Kong. LT JG S E. Burgin had the watch and, living up to the time honored ritual of writing the log in verse on New Year's Day, Lt. Burgin wrote the following-

000-0400.

Underway steaming south we are steaming alone,
The straits rides swiftly with hardly a groan.
Now standard's the bell on the engine room's order
On the South China sea with the wind on our quarter.
In Market Time waters we are soon to arrive,
We're the last RONTHREE cutter of the original five.
From Hong Kong we've come - our wallets are thin,
We've just spent three weeks as SOPA ADMIN,
But we've had all our fun, our men are just beat
As we stay under the OPCON of that old COM seventh Fleet;
With an ADMIN assist from home district one four,
He's been our leader this whole WESTPAC tour.
But soon we'll arrive in Nines muddy waters
And watch oer the junks as per one one five's orders.
All the gear is working, Yoke Bravo is set.
It's just about as quiet as a night watch can get.
There are few of us up keeping watch by the night
But only the lookout knows the lights are burning bright.
Yet there's Combat, Radio and engine men down below
And maybe the baker's is mixing up dough.
It was a grand new Year's Eve, but there seemed no enjoyment
There's a mighty long time in a ten month deployment.
But there's cheers for us all as this New year comes round,
Cause there's one more Patrol and homeward we're bound.

No one is sure when writing the Log in verse on New year's Day became a ritual and not all sailors are poets, but some of the New Year's logs, like this one, show a great deal of skill.

After serving ten months on Market Time during which the Bering Strait detected over 5,000 vessels and inspected 1,000 of them and provided gun support causing much structural damage, the Bering Strait arrived in Honolulu Coast Guard base on Feb. 25th 1968.

After a short time for repairs, the Bering Strait was back on Ocean Station Victor patrol, until called back to Market Time in Vietnam in 1970.

# MEKONG DELTA

## 1969

Thuy Ha was 14 years old when the planes came over and took all the leaves off the trees and made everything die. Her father had been killed by Communists when she was five since then, she and her mother lived alone on their little piece of land in the Mekong Delta.

"Why did they kill him, Mama?" she had asked through her tears and, though many years had passed, she remembered her mother's answer as clearly as if it were only yesterday.

"Because they saw him talking with the Americans."

"Are the Americans bad people?"

"I don't know," her mother had answered shaking her head."

It's hard to tell good from bad any more. The Americans came when the French went away. It is said they come to tell us how to fight."

"But Papa wasn't fighting, he was feeding the pig."

"I know. But some Americans had come to ask questions and someone must have told the Communists. It is better to talk to no one."

So, Thuy Ha and her mother kept to themselves working in their little rice paddy and feeding their pig. From time to time they would go to the market to sell rice if they had any to spare, or to sell the piglets when the sow had a litter. Then they would visit grandmother and hear what news there was about the fighting.

Such visits were the highlight of Thuy Ha's life. Although she was only a child she worked side by side with her mother. It was the only way for them to survive. Thuy Ha did not know how to play. They lived too far from the village for her to meet with other children or go to school. The only company they had was when Thuy Ha's grandmother came from the village to visit them. Then in 1968 the terrible thing happened - Viet Cong guerrillas burned the village and tortured and killed everyone in it. Even the children.

After that Thuy Ha's mother changed. She was afraid of everything. Even a bird screeching would make her tremble with terror. She hardly slept, afraid that the house would be set on fire during the night. She was afraid to let Thuy Ha out of her sight.

With the village gone there was no place to sell or buy anything so they lived mostly on rice and roots and wild berries.

"It is good the trees hide us. We will let everything grow tall so none can see us."

"When will the fighting be finished, Mama? Why don't they stop so we are not afraid and can work and be happy?"

Her mother laughed harshly, "Happy! All happiness is gone from the world. There is no more happiness, only killing."

."Can't we go far away? Somewhere where there is no fighting? Then you would feel better, mama. I can work for us. I could learn to do a lot of things."

"I know of no place to go. We have no money. All we have is here. If we leave this place and go out where they can see us, we will be killed also. Worse things could happen. To be killed is not bad. But they do terrible things you know nothing of. These men - men are bad to women when they are fighting ." and she told Thuy Ha things that the girl remembered whenever she saw a man afterwards.

It was a sunny day, a week after Thuy Ha's fourteenth birthday, when the American planes came and the leaves went away.

The noise was the first thing. Thuy Ha looked out and saw the planes flying low overhead with a kind of mist coming out of them.

"Come, come, child, we must hide they will kill us." Mama shouted shaking with fear.

"They are up in the sky, mama."

" They have guns they will shoot if they see you."

" They are Americans. They are to help us, yes."

" They burn villages and they shoot just like all the others."

" Look! they go, mama, do not be afraid." Thuy Ha said as the noise of the planes died away and all was quiet again..

But they came back the next day and the next day and then Thuy Ha noticed that the leaves of the trees and the bushes were all slowly fading and dying. Her mother was beside herself.

"What can we do? The trees are dying. We will have nothing to hide us."

"The leaves will come back, maybe the weather is not right for them."

"It is not time for leaves to die. They were all young and strong. Some other bad thing has come upon us." and the poor woman began wail aloud.

Thuy Ha was trying to comfort her when they heard footsteps outside and a man in uniform came in.

Terrified, the two stood up expecting the worst. Then the man said, "Don't be afraid. I'm, not going to hurt you. We're Americans looking for Viet Cong. Have you seen any around?"

As he spoke in English neither Thuy Ha or her mother knew what he was saying.

"He's American fighter." mama whispered to Thuy Ha. Do not be afraid, I will kill him before he harms you."

Seeing that he was not being understood, the American turned and went out to call in one of his men who could speak Vietnamese.

Then, before she could stop her, Thuy Ha's mother leapt through the door after him, grabbing the heavy ax she used to cut wood.

Unhinged by all her fears and sufferings, with maniacal fury, mama brought the ax down on the back of the Captain's neck only to fall to the ground with him as a shot from one of his men went through her heart.

"Mama," shrieked Thuy Ha, struggling to get to her mother.

But she was held back by the soldiers who were trying to staunch the blood flowing from their Captain's neck.

"It's no good, guys. He's gone." one of them said grimly.

"Better radio for a chopper ."

Thuy Ha was never able to recall the rest of that day clearly.

They carried her mother in and laid her on the matting that served as her bed and covered her face. The interpreter told Thuy Ha, that her mother had died immediately without any pain. They were gentle with her and asked if she wanted a message given to any relatives or friends. But there was no one. Then the helicopter came and they all were gone, leaving her alone beside the body of her mother.

After a while she rose up, and taking a shovel, she began to dig a hole in the ground to bury her mother. With each shovel of earth she vowed to revenge her. She hated the war, the Americans, the Viet Cong - all of those fighting to destroy her life and the life of her country. They had taken everything from her. Everything she had.

Even the leaves from the trees which used to protect her. They had killed them all. She was as naked and desolate as the land around her.

She dug solidly for what seemed many hours and then she wrapped her mother's body in the matting which had served as her bed, and laid her in the hole.

After she had shoveled the earth back over her, Thuy Ha realized she had no way to mark the grave. Not even a flower was left to place there. They were all gone with the leaves. Her father had been buried in a real grave in a holy place, her mother had told her so. And there was a marker of stone made by a man from the village, so all would know where he lay. But the village was gone like everything else and there was none to care whether her mother lived or died and Thuy Ha, exhausted by shock and exhaustion, lay on the earth above her mother, and wept.

How long she lay there, she didn't know. It was the squeals of the pig demanding food, that made her get up.

Mechanically, she fed the animal and ate some of the rice that had been cooked the day before, hardly noticing the planes flying over, still going about their deadly business. Like most Vietnamese peasants, Thuy Ha had no way of understanding that the use of Agent Orange to defoliate the vegetation was an effort on the part of the US to root out the Viet Cong who were hiding among the jungle foliage to ambush Navy Patrol boats who were trying to prevent supplies from Cambodia reaching the Communist guerrillas.

Losses to Navy Patrol Boat personnel , nicknamed the Brown water Navy, had been escalating, yet the interception of the sampans filled with enemy arms was absolutely necessary. So, the somewhat controversial use of Agent Orange was ordered by Admiral Zumwalt, commander of the Navy Patrol Boats.

Even if she had known, Thuy Ha would have thought - they only make more fighting, why don't they all go away and leave us alone.

Alone in the house Thuy Ha continued feeding the pig with what little food was left. The vegetables in the garden which she and her mother had tended so carefully, had died with the leaves. But Thuy Ha pulled them up and planted more, hoping that the death would not come to them also. There was rice left from the past year's harvest, but there was barely enough for her to eat and for planting. She did not want to kill and eat the pig, she was the only friend Thuy Ha had left to talk to.

Thankfully, no soldiers had come near the house, but if there was any unusual sound, Thuy Ha would hide in the little cellar at the back where the roots were kept after harvest. She was constantly afraid of the fighting men coming and doing to her the things her mother had told her about. The Americans had not harmed her, but that might have been because they had shot her mother. Next time they might shoot or torture her.

By November, even though the pig had been allowed to go free and forage for herself, she was getting very thin and Thuy Ha knew she would have to kill her soon or she would starve to death. But she kept putting it off. For one thing, she wasn't sure she could do it by herself. She had seen her mother kill little piglets for eating, but the sow was so much bigger.

Then the decision was taken out of her hands. In early December, Thuy Ha was getting up from her sleeping mat, when she thought she heard a voices in the distance. Gathering up the mat she crept into the cellar and huddled against the wall behind some old baskets used for gathering the rice.

Trembling with fear she waited scarcely able to breathe. Then the worst happened. The feet came nearer and nearer and finally they were inside the house. Thuy Ha could hear them talking together in Vietnamese and she knew they must be Viet Cong.

"No one in this house. No womans for us."

"Bad place. No womans here. Maybe in field."

She heard them go outside then heard them laughing and talking and the pig squealing. Then with a horrible gurgling sound the squeals died away and Thuy Ha knew the pig was dead.

It was a long time before she dared venture out. All was silent.

They had taken the few bags of rice that she had been hoarding in the little cupboard and her precious jar of honey lay smashed on the floor.

Fearfully she went outside. The ground was all torn up where the pig had struggled before they killed her and blood was all over the place. With her tears mingling with the earth, Thuy Ha smoothed it over the blood, trying to hide it. She couldn't bear to think of the Viet Cong feasting on the animal.

Now she knew she must leave the place. There was nothing left. Her mother would understand that she had to leave her to sleep in the earth, alone. One day, maybe , the fighting stops and I return with beautiful flowers and marker for your grave, mama. Now, I must go. She tied up her few pieces of clothing in her blanket. There was nothing else worth carrying away except a long knife her mother used for cutting up the meat when the little pigs were killed. She intended to use it on any who attacked her or to turn it on herself if she were captured.

She set out with no idea of where she was going or what she would do. There was a trail which led to the old village but where it went after that she didn't know because she had never been beyond it.

On and on she walked, putting off eating her one and only rice cake as long as she could. But at last, she was so exhausted that she was forced to stop and rest. She ate the rice cake slowly trying to make it last. She was very thirsty , but there was nothing to drink. Surely there will be a well somewhere or a stream, she thought. Suddenly, she heard a baby crying. Could it really be a baby? There was no house in sight. Then she saw a man walking along the trail carrying a baby in his arms. As he came closer she saw he was Vietnamese.

Thuy Ha didn't know what to do. He couldn't harm her with the baby in his arms, she thought, and he wasn't dressed like a soldier.

All the same, she felt in the blanket for the knife. The man looked as exhausted as she felt. The baby had its arms around his neck. As she watched the man came up and sat down beside her still holding the child.

"I am On Quai and this my son."

"He is beautiful." said Thuy Ha, stroking his little face." I am

Thuy Ha, I have no one any more."

"Then you are more sad than me, for I still have my son."

"Where is your son's mother?"

"She killed. Communists come while I working in fields and they rape her many times and she die." On Quai 's voice broke, but he quickly recovered. "They did not harm my son, so I take him and we go to my mother not far away now. Where you go? You live close here?"

" I have no place anymore and no one left. This morning they killed even my pig." and Thuy Ha broke down and sobbed out her pathetic story. The relief of having someone to talk to helped with her grief.

" That is very bad. It is bad for everyone now with all the fighting. For this night would you like to come to my mother? Maybe she knows some place for you to go. Can you work?"

" Yes, I work hard. I am well used to work all my life."

" We go then." and so they started down the trail and after a while, On led the way through some bushes to a narrow path which took them to his mother's house.

" Will she be angry to see me?" Thuy Ha asked anxiously.

" She very kind." On assured her.

It was true. On's mother said Thuy Ha could stay and help her look after the baby and work in the fields. She was alone because her husband and other son were in the South Viet Army and she needed some help.

On stayed overnight and then went back to his own house. So began for Thuy Ha a better life than she had since her mother died and her only fear was that On would want to have his son back in his house when he was older and his mother would not need her any more. But the baby was only five months old, so she knew she didn't have to worry just yet. In any case, the war might be finished and then she could go and work somewhere else if she had to.

But Fate was to interfere with her plans once again. It was May and the planting was nearly done and Thuy Ha had blossomed on regular food and the kindness of On's mother and the affection of baby On.

"You are becoming beautiful." On said to her one day. "Soon you will leave us for a husband."

" Oh no! I do not wish to leave. I know no thought of a husband."

" There is plenty of time." said his mother. "Husbands are not always the best things in the world. We don't want to lose you yet. I couldn't do the work all myself."

"Do not worry, I will not leave you. I will stay all the time you want me." answered Thuy Ha as she went out to the field.

Just then, she heard some planes in the distance and before she realized the danger, they had passed overhead dropping two bombs near the little house.

One fell in the field, and one exploded so close to the house that it blew away the walls and the house burst into flames.

The force of the explosion threw Thuy Ha to the ground some distance from the flaming house. When she came to her senses it seemed as if the whole place was burning. The heat was intense. She tried to move but the pain in her arm and ribs was excruciating. She shouted desperately wondering what had happened to the family. But there was no answer.

For a while she lay quietly, hoping the pain would ease. It was so bad that she couldn't bear to shout again.

After a while she tried to move and, in spite of the pain, she managed to sit up. Her right arm was useless and she knew it must be broken. It hurt her so much to breathe that she wondered if she was dying. She called out again, but there was no reply and she feared all the family were burned up in the flames.

Tears rolled down her cheeks. She was alone again. She would die with no one to care. Pain and weakness forced her to lie back on the ground. The heat from the burning house was intense.

Mercifully, she drifted into unconsciousness again and when she came to the fire was almost out. She thought she saw someone standing near the ruins and tried to shout, thinking it might be On.

But when the figure came nearer, she saw he was in uniform. A soldier! Well, he couldn't hurt her any more. She was dying anyway.

What she didn't know was that two friends of On had seen the bombs drop and realized that they were near his mother's little farm. As soon as they could they came to see what had happened.

One of them heard Thuy Ha call out and came over to look.

"Here's one." he shouted, bending over the girl. "Looks bad."

"Is she alive?"

"She's breathing and I heard her shout."

"Must be that girl On's mother took in to help when his wife was killed."

"Better get her to the hospital." and he lifted her up in his arms. Thuy Ha screamed with pain as her broken bones grated through the flesh, then, mercifully, she fainted from the pain.

The two men took turns carrying her several miles along the trail to the little Vietnamese hospital. The one and only doctor took one look at her and said, "There is nothing we can do. We have no medicines left and no antibiotics. She needs to go to the big American doctors. They have everything."

"But she needs the care now. She is very bad."

"I know, I sorry, but all I can do here is bandage her wounds and let her die in peace."

"Can you not get medicines from the Americans, they send them other times?"

"They have sent, but the medicines did not come here." the doctor looked grim. "The messengers took them to sell in Cambodia. They give them much money. There is no way we can stop them."

The men shrugged. They had done what they could. They had seen so much death and dying that one more or less made little difference."

The little doctor's shoulders drooped with fatigue as he examined Thuy Ha. He had only two nurses to help him take care of forty beds and an endless stream of out patients. Like a great many of the other supplies provided by the United States, only a very small portion reached its proper destination. The black market was so strong.

"She's so young." he thought, "it is sad for her to die when she has seen so few years, but maybe, it is better, she will not have to suffer more."

So Thuy Ha was given what little attention the doctor was able to provide and put into a cot in a room full of sick and wounded.

But Thuy Ha did not die. Her hard life and work outdoors had given her a very strong constitution. In a few days she was fully conscious and although in much pain, she was able to ask where she was and whether On and his mother and son had been found.

"Two men carried you here." one of the nurses told her.

"They said they were friends of a man called On Quai . They said his house was all burnt up and only the bones of the family were left in the ashes.."

At first Thuy Ha couldn't believe it. To lose the baby she had carried so lovingly and On Quai and his mother who had given her new life and hope for the future, was too much to bear.

She looked blankly at the nurse, then she cried, "No! No! it cannot be. No, I won't believe it." and she began to sob so bitterly that the nurse begged the doctor to come and quiet her.

"Let her weep. It is necessary and I have nothing to ease her pain." the doctor sighed. "I think in a day we will send her out in a sampan and maybe the Americans will find her and take care of her. They have many doctors and medicines in their ships."

Putting the old, the sick and the wounded in a sampan had become a regular practice since the black market had so increased the shortage of drugs and equipment in the Viet hospitals.

If they were lucky, the sampan would be checked out by the US Coast Guard or the US Navy river patrol boats to make sure it was not bringing in supplies for the Viet Cong. They would take off the sick and get them to a hospital or the sickbay of a US ship.

The unlucky ones who did not meet up with the US boats, would be put ashore by the sampan owner if they could walk , if not, they were often pushed overboard.

So, one day later, Thuy Ha was carried down to the river and put aboard a sampan owned by a Vietnamese fisherman, just a few days after the Bering Strait arrived back on duty. Though she didn't know it then, her whole life would be changed and she would be become Little Star.

## MARKET TIME 1970

## VIETNAMIZATION 1971

By the time the Bering Strait was ordered back to Vietnam for her second tour of duty, there were 543,000 US troops in Vietnam.

Protests against the war were increasing daily and the casualty lists grew longer. President Nixon, who had promised a plan to end the war, announced that 25,000 troops would be withdrawn under a system of Vietnamization.

The Commander of the US Naval Forces, Vietnam, had sent a request that JCS authorization be sought for the turnover of two Coast Guard Cutters, specifically, CGC YAKUTAT and CGC BERING STRAIT, to the Vietnamese Navy.

It was pointed out that "with the addition of these two ships the Vietnamese Navy would provide a more satisfactory all- weather detection and intercept capability in the outer Market Time patrol areas, enhance the Naval Gunfire Support capability of the Vietnamese Navy and permit the release of additional US ships and men for other duty."

In September, the CNO formally requested the transfer of the two WHEC's to the US Navy for further transfer to the Vietnamese Navy. This was done in November 1969.

The revelation this same month of the terrible massacre of women and children in the little village of Mylai by a platoon of US troops led by Lt. L. Calley, Jr., caused further anti war protests in America. Many draftees, hoping to avoid being sent to a war they could not support, joined the Coast Guard, thinking they would not be sent overseas. What they did not know was that 10% of all Coast Guard personnel served in Vietnam. A greater percentage than that of any other Armed Service.

Unfortunately, this led to a loss of morale on the part of these men when they found they were being sent to Vietnam and there were cases of insubordination aboard the ships.

In order to facilitate the transfer of the YAKATAT and the BERING STRAIT to the Vietnamese, an increase in Vietnamese personnel was authorized for training aboard.

So, when the Bering Strait left Honolulu in 1970, she had only a small crew. This was supplemented by some US trained Vietnamese, including Lt. Vu Xuan An, who later became skipper when the ship was transferred to the Vietnamese Navy.

Captain Paul Henneberry and his Exec. Commander, later Captain, Troutman, had the task of integrating the crew and getting things working well before the ship was back on Market Time.

On June 5th. 1970, the Bering Strait was moored in Subic Bay prior to returning to Vietnam. On that day twenty enlisted Vietnamese and six officers came aboard. Some did not have much English.

They were scarcely back on station in the South China Sea, when a message was received regarding suspicious craft in the Delta.

Maneuvering alongside, the Bering Strait put a small boarding party aboard the sampan, to check her out.

It didn't take long for the party to see that there were no arms, ammunition or drugs aboard, but there was an injured Vietnamese girl.

"She looks pretty bad, sir." one of the Viet sailors said.

"Ask the old man if he knows who she is and why she's on his boat." the boarding officer answered.

"He say the hospital had nothing for her so they say he take her so Americans can make her better."

And that's how Thuy Ha arrived aboard the Bering Strait and was placed in the sick bay.

The ship's doctor quickly realized that she needed considerable surgery to straighten the fractures of her arm and leg which had never been properly set. While antibiotics would stop the infection spreading, gangrene had set into the wounds in her foot.

"She needs more than we can give her here." the ship's doctor told the skipper. "in order to have the surgery that's necessary and the constant care she needs, she ought to be in the hospital in

Saigon."

So arrangements were made and Thuy Ha, was transferred by helicopter two days later.

There were American doctors and nurses in the hospital and Thuy Ha was soon examined and put in a comfortable bed to await surgery. The surgeon, who could speak Vietnamese, told her that he would set her arm and leg so that she could use them properly, but he would have to remove three of her toes which were gangrenous.

Thuy Ha simply nodded her head... she had lost so much that three toes didn't seem to matter.

She was still too weak to think clearly and all the emotion she felt, was the horrible emptiness of utter despair. Everything she had was gone. She had no home and there was no one left to care what became of her. Her mother had been right when she said, "There is no happiness left in the world," and Thuy Ha turned her head and wept silently into her pillow.

For most of the month of June, the Bering Strait was patrolling the South China Sea. While the majority of the Viet officers were competent and could speak English quite well, the enlisted men needed considerable training.

Also, the Vietnamese never got used to the US Mess system. They made all kinds of little eating places all over the ship, but, on the whole, the crew worked together well.

The Coast Guard and Navy Patrols had been so successful in preventing the influx of arms and supplies to the Viet Cong by boat, that the Ho Chi Minh Trail was now the main support route.

This meant more calls for gun support but less for boarding parties.

From, time to time the ship was called on to give support to the Special Forces Groups which were living off the land in the Delta. One group near Song On Doc was always short of supplies.

Chief Damage Control man Robert Brisebois said, "They got short changed up there. They're off the track of the regular supply runs and they were glad to have anything we could give them such as old oil drums, nails, packing crates, soap."

I built them a barbecue grill one time and a stand for their .50 machine gun. What they really like though, was to come aboard for a real, good meal."

Somehow, the North Vietnamese got wind of the Special Forces Camp and attacked with napalm.

"It was a bad business." Captain Troutman recalls, "It was one of the worst things I've seen. They got the village as well.

Seeing those poor folks, women and children too, with burns all over their bodies hit us hard. They had nowhere to go. The whole place was burned out. Some were just standing there with their clothes burnt off them- in agony from their wounds. Doc Dumin and the corpsmen did what they could and we took some a board, but their burns were pretty bad."

The Vietnamese Corpsman put the feelings of many, both Vietnamese and American, into words when he said, "This war no good. This village hurt no one. No soldiers here. No guns. People work hard and now all gone."

Thuy Ha was still in the hospital in Saigon. Most of the time she lay there silent. Her arm and leg remained in a cast but her foot had healed up well.

"It's a good thing you've still got your big toe. You'll be able to walk very well with a little practice. " the nurse said cheerfully. "We'll get you up in a few days and teach you how to use the crutches. You'll like that, won't you?"

Thuy Ha nodded obediently. She had seen others walking around with what they called crutches and it seemed like hard work. But if that's what they wanted, she would do it. The doctor was worried about her apathy.

"Try to get her talking, nurse. She's too young to go into a depression."

"We've tried, but she doesn't respond. She does what she's told and doesn't complain or ask for anything."

"Perhaps she'll brighten up when we get her on her feet." and the doctor hurried away to another patient.

"I think it good if I take you in wheelchair to 'Holy Service.' You like that?" One of the Vietnamese nurses asked Thuy Ha.

Again Thuy Ha simply nodded her head. She had no idea what "Holy Service" meant but when she found herself in the back of the hospital chapel as the organ began to play, it sounded so beautiful to her that she actually smiled. The only music she had ever heard was the temple bell in the village shrine and once when she was visiting her grandmother, a friend came and played songs on his Tieu. He said he had made the little flute himself out of bamboo and Thuy Ha decided she would try and make one for herself one day.

It was one of the happiest things that Thuy Ha remembered, but now, it only brought back the terrible sadness of knowing that it was all gone.

Then the people in the chapel began to sing with the organ and the smile came back to Thuy Ha's face. She felt surrounded by something beautiful once again. Something that would protect and not hurt her. "It is good." she said to the nurse.

Surprised to hear her patient speak and seeing her smile, the nurse couldn't wait to tell the doctor, and after this, Thuy Ha was taken to the chapel for ' Holy Service' whenever anyone could spare the time. It wasn't long before she managed to wheel herself to the chapel. The music touched something that gave her hope again.

Although Thuy Ha never met David Priddy, the young organist, who, when he was there the previous year had composed the music she particularly liked, she thought he must be wonderful to be able to make such music.

David Priddy had been drafted from engineering school and sent to the Medical Corps ending up in charge of admissions and dispositions in the 91st Evacuation Hospital in Tuy Hoa. This hospital received some of the most horribly wounded service men and civilians. A grueling experience for an eighteen year old from Ohio. Priddy still avoids speaking of the tragic sight of the broken, bleeding bodies that were brought there for admission.

When the 91st arrived in Tuy Hoa, the hospital consisted of a series of tents in a vast desert of sand. But they quickly put up Quonset huts and improved the facility.

In addition to his medical duties Priddy played the rickety pedal organ in the chapel and worked with Chaplain Dick on the welfare problems that arose from time to time.

Then Priddy was given a promotion and ordered to the 44th Medical Brigade in Saigon. There he was put to work making maps for the USARV. At the same time, the Saigon Hospital was in need of an organist, so he was asked to play the organ in the chapel there.

To his delight, he found this organ far superior to the rickety instrument in Tuy Hoa which had been badly damaged by the climate.

"So you like this organ do you?" the Chaplain asked Priddy, when he noticed that the young man spent a good deal of his off duty time practicing. "I must say, I've heard better myself."

"This is wonderful compared with the one in the 91st chapel. That thing was in a terrible state. The chaplain was hoping to get a better one, but organs are the last thing the Army has in mind."

"I think there's a spare one around here somewhere. If I find out where it is, I'll let you know. You might be able to get it sent up there. Don't count on it, though. I can't promise anything. It could be gone by now."

But the organ was still there in a closet, and Priddy managed to get permission to take it up to the 91st by helicopter.

"I don't believe it." Chaplain Dick exclaimed when Priddy called and told him he was bringing a new organ. " I won't believe it until I see it."

Priddy says taking the organ up to the 91st chapel and receiving the gratitude of all concerned is one of the best of the few good memories he has of Vietnam.

One day a new patient was brought into the bed next to Thuy Ha. It was a very old lady who turned out to be as silent as Thuy Ha was. Then, that evening, a young girl came with some things which she put in the locker by the old lady's bed.

"Here's something to keep you looking beautiful, granny. "

she said. "A new comb and some soap. And don't start asking where I got them because I'm not going to tell you."

"You're a good girl to me." the old lady answered, "I'd be dead without you."

"You're going to last a long time. I like having you around to scold at me." the girl laughed with a happiness that made Thuy Ha look at her with surprise. She couldn't remember ever hearing anyone happy like that. The girl was very pretty too and had such beautiful clothes that Thuy Ha thought she must be a princess. But she was puzzled. How could even a princess be happy in these times? She listened to the grandmother and the girl talking together. They were Vietnamese so she could understand what they were saying. But seeing them made her feel all the more lonely. If only she had someone left to come and say they liked having her around. Suddenly all her misery welled up again and she couldn't help giving a loud sob as the tears rolled down her face.

Immediately the girl turned to her, " You hurt? Shall I find the nurse?"

" No, I'm all right." Thuy Ha sobbed.

The girl came over and said, " What makes you cry? Perhaps we help you. I'm Pretty Flower and this is my granny."

"I am Thuy Ha."

"Do you live in Saigon?"

"No."

"Where is your home."

"I have no home any more. All is gone."

"Aaee, "the old lady cried. "It is the fighting. It is very bad."

"Now granny, I told you. Do not complain. it is not good. I promised I'll look after you" she patted the old lady's hand then, turning to Thuy Ha, she asked, "Where is your family? "

" All are killed. I have no one now."

" That is bad, but you will work and find a man to make a home for you."

" It is not possible."

" Why not? You are not very sick are you? Just your leg and arm to mend by the look, I see."

" I have only worked with the pig and the vegetables and I am not a Pretty Flower, like you."

The girl laughed. "I wasn't always Pretty Flower, that's what they called me when I started work. Now I always Pretty Flower." and she twirled around and looked over her shoulder at Thuy Ha with a knowing look in her eye.

" What kind of work do you do? "

Pretty Flower smiled secretively, "I tell you another time. Now I go." and giving her granny another pat, she was gone.

"She is very beautiful and good, isn't she?" Thuy Ha said to the old lady.

"Aah, she cared for me when my own son left me to die alone. She is kind, maybe she help you too. I sleep now." and the old lady turned on her side.

Again Thuy Ha felt a little hope rise in her heart. The doctor had said she would walk properly when her leg was out of the cast.

If Pretty Flower would really tell her how to get some work, maybe she could get money and find a place to live. Also, she could save up and go back and place her mother's bones with those of her ancestors and make a marker for her mother so she could sleep in peace.. and she smiled at the nurse who came to show her how to use the crutches.

It seemed to Thuy Ha that the whole place lit up when Pretty Flower arrived and she watched for her anxiously. Pretty Flower had become the center of her hope. She did not come every day.

"I come when I can, but I do not forget you." she told her grandmother and Thuy Ha.

The doctor and the nurses noticed the difference in Thuy Ha's attitude. She had begun to talk after hearing the music in the chapel and now she smiled and constantly asked when the cast would come off so she could leave and find some work.

"You mustn't be in too much of a hurry, dear, But it shouldn't be too long now." the nurse said. " Do you have any work to go to?"

"No, but I have someone who said she'd help me find some."

but when Thuy Ha told her it was Pretty Flower, the nurse said, "I wouldn't depend on her, if I were you. Don't you have any family who could help you?"

"They are all killed, I have no one." Thuy Ha said. She didn't dare ask the nurse why she wouldn't depend on Pretty Flower, but her remark frightened Thuy Ha. Then she decided the nurses were jealous because Pretty Flower had lovely clothes and was beautiful and happy. She wondered what work Pretty Flower did. It must be something very important for her to spend so much on clothes and jewels and to be so happy.

Still on Market Time the guns of the Bering Strait were kept busy during August supporting the shore operations of the riverines.

One morning they escaped a bad accident on board when a shell stuck in the gun barrel. It was red hot and the danger of a bad explosion sent the Viet gun crew running to safety. Through the quick action of the gunnery officer and several of the sailors, buckets of water thrown down the barrel cooled it off and averted the danger.

Someone with a sense of humor, took a picture of water being poured into the gun barrel and labeled it, "New methods of fighting on Market Time."

In September, the ship was ordered to the Philippines for a paint job prior to being transferred to the Vietnamese Navy.

"Well, its official now. It'll seem strange to see the ship painted gray." the Skipper remarked to the Exec.

"It sure will, sir. Do we have a date for the ceremony yet.

They're taken their time making the change."

"Yeah, it was way back in '69 when we heard about it first, I thought the turnover would have taken place before this, but I expect it to take place soon after the paint job's finished."

"Well, its allowed more time for training the Nam crew. "

"That's true."

When the ship docked in the Subic Bay Ship Facility in the Philippines, a big surprise awaited them. The man in charge of the paint job was none other then William Osgood, the same one who had painted the Bering Strait white when she was transferred to the Coast Guard in 1948. At that time Osgood had been working at the San Francisco Naval Shipyard.

"I don't believe it." Troutman exclaimed when he saw Osgood.

"How did you get here?"

"Ordered out here in '68. Must have known the old girl was coming. She seems to be holding up pretty good."

"Yeah, she's a good ship. I hope she'll be taken good care of when she's handed over. Any idea when the Turnover will take place?"

"No, but orders are for the Bering Strait and the Yakutat to be painted gray, but to keep the red,, white and blue slashes and "Coast Guard" in capital letters, on either side of their hull, until they are formally transferred, so I don't think its expected right away."

Because most of the U.S. servicemen on board held orders for transfer back to the States when the Turnover was made, they were anxious to find out when it would take place, but shore leave during the paint job was a luxury they enjoyed in the meantime.

Too soon, the ship was back in the China Sea on Market Time again and the intensive training of the Vietnamese crew continued.

At long last , information was received that the Turnover of the Bering Strait and the Yakutat would take place on New Year's Day 1971, in Saigon Harbor.

"That was some New Year's Eve." White remembered. "The

Vietnamese were making the most of it. Fire crackers all over the ship. It was really wild. Guards were put on the guns, in case they tried to fire them to add to the excitement."

But on New Year's Day, the excitement was gone. Moored to pier Echo in Saigon River, the ship awaited the Turnover Ceremony.

At 0800 the U.S. Colors were raised for the last time.

By 1000 all guests and dignitaries, including the Chief of Naval Operations of the Vietnamese Navy and the Commander of U.S. Forces, Vietnam, had arrived. After the Invocation short speeches were made by Captain R.E. Hoover, Commander Coast Guard Squadron Three and Captain J. W. Moreau, Commander Coast Guard District 14 Representative.

Then Vice Admiral J. H. King, Jr., Commander of the U.S. Naval Forces Vietnam spoke and the Turnover Documents were signed.

In spite of the fact that the Coast Guard crew knew they would soon be on their way home, they felt a deep sadness as the Colors were lowered and the Star Spangled Banner echoed over the ship for the last time.

As soon as the U.S. crew debarked, the Vietnamese crew came on board and the colors of the Republic of Vietnam were hoisted to the strains of the Vietnam National Anthem and Commander Vu Xuan An, RVN, took command.

The last entry in the Log reads, "Friday 1.1.71.

0000-1200 Moored starboard to Pier Echo in Saigon River of Republic of Vietnam, with doubled lines, receiving freshwater-power from shore ties.

This vessel is under the OPCON and ADMINCON of COMGARDRON Three, 0624 held sunrise secured all deck lights brightly.

0800 held morning colors. 1000 held turnover ceremony.

1001. This vessel is under the OPCON and ADMINCON of the Vietnam Navy"

The Bering Strait now became Tran Quang Khai ( Dragon 2) and her four year career with the Vietnamese Navy began.

# LITTLE STAR

## IS BORN

By the time Thuy Ha was ready to be discharged, she and Pretty Flower had become real friends. Although granny had gone home earlier, Pretty Flower came to visit Thuy Ha now and again.

"You now my friend and you can stay in my house with granny until you have your own place.

Thuy Ha did not know how to thank her, "I will work hard and pay back to you." she said fervently.

"For this week you stay with granny and help her, so you get strong and next I help you about work."

To Thuy Ha's surprise, the house where Pretty Flower took her was a miserable little hooch. It seemed to have been made of odd pieces of timber dangerously held together with a few nails. Its tin roof was rusted and drooping. Inside it was dark and dirty.

It was so different from what Thuy Ha had imagined that she could have wept. How could Pretty Flower live in such a place and be so happy? Her own home in the Delta had been only a small hut- like structure but her mother had always kept it clean and cheerful with mats she wove herself on the floor and painted doors on the cupboards. And, until all the leaves went away, there was always the garden with flowers and vegetables, to walk in. Here, there was no garden, just a whole lot of temporary shelters almost on top of one another, some of them made out of flattened tin cans.

They had passed through some of the great buildings of Saigon to get here and this made it seem even worse. Thuy Ha made up her mind she must find a better place of her own as soon as she found some work.

As they went inside Pretty Flower said, "We used to live out in the countryside north of the city, but our house was bombed by the Americans and my mother and sisters were killed."

"Was your father killed too." Thuy Ha asked sadly.

"My father was fighting with the Viet Cong and we have never seen him since that day. I was on my way to visit granny so I wasn't hurt. I could hear the planes and the bombs bursting but I didn't think it was near my home.

"I started to run because I could see smoke over where granny lived. Her house was burning and she was lying outside with her head bleeding. I thought she was dead. I didn't know what to do. I didn't want to leave her there alone. It was very bad, but granny doesn't like me to talk about it. It makes us too sad."

Thuy Ha was startled when Pretty Flower said her father was Viet Cong. They were the enemy. They had killed her father. Yet Pretty Flower was so kind to her. Was she of the Viet Cong too? But she couldn't very well ask such a thing. If Pretty Flower was living with an American she couldn't be Viet Cong. Then the old lady appeared from around the side of the house.

"Aah, you have come." she said. "I was washing."

Later Thuy Ha found the only washing place was a kind of communal well at the back of the hooches.

"Thuy Ha will stay with you, granny. I will help her find some work very soon. Now I must go. I will come again in two or three days "

"Pretty Flower lives with her man. He is very good to her.

She gives me money for food or I die without." said the old lady as Pretty Flower left.

"Is Pretty Flower married?"

"She not married. Her man is American. She take good care of him. Make him happy. It good. Better than some who take many men. That no good. You take care. Find one good man."

"I will find some work. I not looking for men."

The old lady shrugged her shoulders, "I tired, I rest myself." and she went inside and lay down on an old mat on the floor.

Thuy Ha lingered outside not anxious to go into the dark , smelly room. She was shocked and disappointed. She had expected to find a beautiful house filled with carved furniture presided over by Pretty Flower. Then she pulled herself together. If Pretty Flower had not brought her here, she would have had nowhere to go.

She would do what she could to clean the place and tell Pretty Flower she wanted to start working right away. She still limped and had some pain in her leg, but she felt her strength coming back all the time.

The next days seemed like weeks to Thuy Ha. She cleaned the floor with a brush borrowed from the woman next door, she washed the ragged pieces of cloth the old lady used to cover herself at night and walked among the people hoping to find someone who could tell her about getting work.

" There is nothing. " one young girl told her. " If you read and use the writing machine, the Americans might want you."

" I cannot read and I do not know the writing machine. I used to work with the pig and the rice field."

"That no good here." they told her. "Perhaps you get luck like Pretty Flower."

Pretty Flower came at the end of the week. She had a new dress and some golden bangles on her arms.

"Look how they shine. They are all gold." she said waving her delicate arms in the air.

" You bring food?" her granny said to Pretty Flower scarcely noticing the bangles.

"You greedy thing. Yes, I bring you something. Look, all these good things ." and she brought out from a basket bags of rice, tea, and some tins.

"What the tins for?" granny asked.

" They filled with special American food. See this one says Beef, that meat from cow. This one says Beans, that beans.

"Why it in tin?"

"In tin it not go bad. It is good for long time."

"I like eat not keep." granny said picking up one of the tins.

"I show how to open tin when you ready to eat." said Pretty Flower.

" When you learn to read the tins?" asked Thuy Ha.

" My man tells me and I remember. He reads and writes a lot."

" I cannot read or use the writing machine. Is there work I can do without it?"

"Yes, I tell you, but you need to be strong."

"I am strong now. Tell me about work."

Pretty Flower looked at her and saw that Thuy Ha was anxiously waiting for her to reply, but she hesitated. Then she said, "Come, we will sit on the stone at the bottom of the road and talk."

As they walked Thuy Ha said told Pretty Flower how anxious she was to make enough money to go back and bury her mother next to her ancestors and then rebuild her house.

"That will take much money."

"I will work very hard.. You must make much money to have such beautiful things and to be so happy."

"I was not always like this. After our house was gone and granny's house was burned, I had nothing and she had nothing and she was sick. I had no work. So I did what all the girls do here if they are poor. I went to the lady who keeps the house of" The Ladies who make Men Happy". Do you know what that is?"

"No, I have not heard of such a house.

"Well, you know what makes men happy, don't you?"

Suddenly Pretty Flower's life became clear and Thuy Ha was terrified. She remembered the awful things her mother had told her that men do to women in wartime.

"But you are so happy." she exclaimed. "How can you be happy when they do bad things to you?

"Bad things? They don't do bad things. Did something bad happen to you from a man?"

"No, I never be with a man, but my mother told me ——."

Then Pretty Flower told her more about the House of Ladies who make Men Happy.

"It's the only way you will get money and if you are lucky you will meet a good man- perhaps a rich American like my man, and he will take you to live with him in a nice house and give you clothes like mine."

"You get married?"

"No, they have wife in America and they go back to her, but perhaps not if they grow to love you more. But it is the only work you will find in Saigon now, unless you can read and use the writing machine or something like that."

"If that is the only way. I will do it. Perhaps I will get money very fast and then I go."

And so Thuy Ha went to stay in the "House of Young Ladies who make Men Happy" and was known as Little Star.

## WITH THE VIETNAM NAVY

### 1971-1975

Under the command of Commander Vu Xuan An, RVN, the Bering Strait, now Tran Quang Khai, continued to supply gun support and to inspect ships for arms much as the Coast Guard had done on Market Time. A small group of American Advisors remained on board to assist with training.

By the end of 1971 American troop strength in Vietnam was down to 140,000 and it was hoped that a cease fire would shortly be declared. But in spite of the peace keeping efforts of Henry Kissinger, the fighting continued and it wasn't until after President Nixon ordered heavy bombing raids on Hanoi and Haiphong, that a Cease-fire agreement was formally signed in Paris in January 1973.

On January 27th 1973, Secretary of Defense, Melvin Laird, declared that the draft in the United States had ended and by March 29th, all American troops were out of Vietnam.

After the American advisors left the Tran Quang Quai, the ship appears to have spent considerable time moored in the Saigon River.

Attempts to obtain the Logs through the Vietnam Representative at the United Nations, have not been successful. Although the request was forwarded to Hanoi with the promise that replies would be forthcoming, nothing has been received so far.

Then, with the help of Admiral Yost, USCG, Rtd., and Captain Bui Vien, RVN, Rtd., Captain Hung Manh Dinh was located. Captain Dinh took over the command of the Tran Quang Khai and with the ship overloaded with hundreds of refugees, escaped to the Philippines when Saigon fell.

Captain Hung Manh Dinh now lives with his family in the

United States, and when interviewed, he offered to send the story of the escape and his coming to the United States. However, nothing has arrived, and when reminded he says, "Soon it will come, I must be very careful. It would be bad to have something wrong."

It seems that many Vietnamese who escaped and came to this country are fearful of talking about the war. Whether it concerns their part in it, or whether it concerns prisoners of war , they seem afraid of saying something that might make trouble for themselves or their relatives.

During the war, Captain Dinh and his family had their home in Saigon. His son, who is training to be an engineer, remembers going to parties aboard the Tran Quang Quai, and from his description of the family home and the school he attended, they must have been in comfortable circumstances until the fall of the city.

With the US troops out of Vietnam, the South Vietnamese feared that the truce would not last long. While President Nixon had said that the US would intervene if the Communists broke the truce, public opinion in the United States was so strongly against any further involvement in Indo-China, that a bill enacted by Senators Clifford Case and Frank Church to block funds for any such military activities, was passed by the Senate on June 4th. 1973.

It soon became obvious that neither President Nguyen Van Thieu or President Le Duc Tho intended to abide by the truce. According to reports by the CIA, there were still approximately one hundred and forty thousand North Vietnamese in South Vietnam and the South Vietnamese feared that more and more were infiltrating daily.

In spite of the agreement, there seemed little hope of lasting peace.

Henry Kissinger, who had worked as negotiator, had become very depressed about the situation. Kissinger knew that Thieu was indecisive and corrupt and unlikely to withstand attacks from the North.

By now the American Embassy in Saigon was considerably reduced.

The new Ambassador, Graham Martin, was a seasoned diplomat who had begun his career under President Roosevelt. A liberal democrat and strongly anti-communist, it was thought that he would do well in Vietnam. Unfortunately, his health was not good. An automobile accident had left him physically weak. This meant that he did not control and advise the jittery and inept Thieu who needed strong guidance and reassurance.

By now, anti-American feeling in South Vietnam was growing stronger and stronger. The people felt abandoned and hopeless. Poverty was extreme leading to a breakup of old values and family tradition.

The helpless at either end of life were abandoned and left to die when there was not enough food to go round.

In 1974 the failing economy, inflation and corruption meant that the majority of the soldiers were unable to provide for their families and the morale of the Army fell heavily. President Thieu's wife and the wives of other high officials in the government made fortunes from bribery and illicit trading. Seeing them and the government officials living in luxury when they were starving, drove the homeless refugees to angry despair.

After President Nixon had resigned in August 1974, Congress reduced the Military aid appropriation to South Vietnam, from one billion to seven hundred million dollars. Meanwhile the North Vietnamese were planning the takeover of the whole country.

A brilliant General, Tran Van Tra, who had trained in China and the Soviet Union, was one of the brains behind the plan. In December l974 the Communists began their attacks and by January 6th 1975 they had captured Puoc Binh, the capital of the Puoc Long province.

By March 1975 it was obvious that the Viet Cong would take over the whole country. On March 10th, General Van Tun Dung had taken Barmethuot with 10,000 men. The people of South Vietnam remembering only too well, the massacre of the Tet offensive in 1968, were terrified, and, fearing the same treatment , they fled south.

As the month wore on Saigon was filled with desperate refugees frantically trying to escape the communists. Although there was an air of disaster in the city, many people continued to go about their business and the House of ladies who make men Happy, was still well patronized.

Little Star, like the others ladies, was terrified of what might happen when the enemy took the city.

"Will they kill us all?' she asked.

"Not in the beginning," answered Summer Rose, "They will use our bodies until they can be used no more and then leave us to die in the dust."

"What can we do? Is there no place we can go?"

"There is no place left." Summer Rose said hopelessly, "The Americans are gone and help us no more."

Little Star sat quietly thinking of what could be done. She wondered if Pretty Flower had left with her American or whether she was still in Saigon. Pretty Flower would know what to do, she said to herself."

Since she had been in the House of ladies who make Men Happy, Little Star had not seem much of Pretty Flower, the American her friend lived with, stayed longer in Saigon than most because he was an advisor to the Army of South Vietnam, but it was nearly a year since she had last seen Pretty Flower.. I will go and see if she is still here, Little Star decided.

So she went to the Lady in Charge and told her she wished to go and visit with her friend.

"I will be back in a very little time, Madame," she said.

"It is no longer safe to be in the streets, there are many bad people."

"I will be careful. It is only a short way."

The Lady in charge liked Little Star. She had always been obedient and humble, doing whatever was requested of her, so she reluctantly agreed to Little Star's request, warning her to be very careful.

Little Star felt sure she would be able to get to Pretty Flower's house easily, but when she stepped into the street, she was unprepared for the noise and the pushing and shoving of the crowds.

People seemed to have lost their humanity in their desperate need to escape. Little Star felt herself swept along with the crowd until she was well past the place where Pretty Flower lived.

It was impossible to escape. Somehow, she managed to get to the edge of the mass of people and, seeing the open door of an empty shop just ahead, she slipped through it.

Trembling with relief to be out of the noise and struggle of the crowd, she leaned on the empty counter top to catch her breath.

Then she heard a footstep behind her. Terrified, hardly daring to breathe, she looked around the dark, empty, space and saw the figure of an old man standing looking at her.

"What do you want?" She faltered.

"I want nothing. I only ask to shelter here for a while."

Relieved, Little Star answered, "That is what I want also. There are so many in the street I could not walk."

"Where do you go? Do you live in this place?"

"No," she answered, "I live not far away but I was looking for my friend, but she might be gone, I think."

The man came nearer and Little Star could see he wasn't really old, just feeble. He was very thin and his face badly scarred.

Something about him was pleasing to her. She was no longer afraid.

"What is your name?" he asked. "You are like someone I once knew."

"My name is Little Star."

"Ah, it is a good name. The one I knew was called Thuy. Thuy Ha she was called, but she is dead."

Little Star's heart nearly stopped, "Thuy Ha! That used to be my name long ago when I lived in another place. Can it be that another has the same name?"

"I do not know, she was beautiful, but younger than you. She helped my mother look after my son, but she died. they all died. Only I am left and I am useless as you see."

Can it be? Can it possibly be? Little Star thought excitedly. No, it cannot be. On was strong and handsome, it cannot be. Yet .....

"What is your name?" she asked not daring to hope.

"On Quai." he said, "I am of no importance."

"On," she cried, "I am your Thuy Ha. I did not die. They took me to the American's hospital and made me better. On, dear On, I am so happy to see you. I thought you were dead, burnt up in the house."

On stared at her, then he grasped the counter to hold himself up and Little Star realized the shock of finding her was almost too much for him. Anxiously, she reached out to comfort him. Putting her arms around his bony shoulders she held him close.

"It is so wonderful to find you again. My heart has been like stone since the day the house burned. Now we are not alone, we can help each other."

Tears were running down On's cheeks, "Forgive my weakness, I have been so sad and lonely all this time. I can hardly believe I have found you and you are alive."

"Let us rest on the floor and then you must tell me what happened. I was sure you were burned in the house with your mother and son."

Resting on the floor, On wiped his eyes and explained, "My mother and my son were in the house when they were killed but I had gone to the well for water. When the bomb fell it threw me into the air and I hit the ground and broke many bones. Someone took me to a hospital close by but they had little to help me, so they put me in a boat and American ship take me to hospital here."

"I also, the same. Maybe we in hospital the same time and did not know. How long you were in the hospital?"

"They kept me until I could walk by myself, but I had no place and no work. I am ashamed, I beg from people in the street. You have work?"

"I also am shamed. I work in the House of Ladies who make Men Happy. There was no other work that I could do, so I stay there and save money to go back and bury my mother in her ancestral place."

On was silent and Little Star feared he was thinking she was such a bad woman that he would not speak to her and her heart cried out in pain.

Then, as if feeling her anguish, On took her hand in his, "I am sorry you suffer so much and I am sorry I have no way to help you. It makes me very sad."

Clasping his hand tighter, Little Star said, "Do not be sad. Let us be happy we have found ourselves. It is a present from the Gods."

"You are right. My strength, perhaps, will return and I will work and take care of you. You will be my Thuy Ha again." and he kissed her gently.

"I will help you to grow strong, do not worry." The noise in the street was growing louder.

"We cannot stay here." On said, struggling to his feet. "There will be more fighting. We must find somewhere to hide."

"I must go and tell the Lady in Charge that I go with you."

"Do not leave me, we may not find each other again. It is not possible to go back to the Lady in Charge with all the people fleeing the city. Stay with me and let us escape together."

Looking up at On, Little Star saw the pleading in his eyes and she knew she could never part from him again. It was a miracle that brought them back together.

"I will stay with you always." she said, her eyes shining with the realization that they loved each other. Together they would face whatever lay before them.. Surely the miracle that had brought them together would protect them.

"We will go back to the place of our ancestors. We will find a way. The land will still be there and we can build a hut together." Suddenly On felt his strength returning.

"Yes, yes, we can walk by night when all is quiet. and, outside Saigon, in the countryside, some will help us."

And so they rested together ignoring the tumult in the streets, until night fell. Then, assured by their new found love, they started their journey back home.

On March 30th, Easter Sunday, the Communists captured Danang, the second largest city in Vietnam. Already overflowing with desperate refugees from Hue, when several thousand Communists flooded into the suburbs, there was nothing but utter chaos.

The airport, the beaches and the docks were littered with dead and dying shot or trampled to death as they tried to escape. Many had drowned as they tried to wade to the barges and little boats, others had been shot by their own soldiers racing to save themselves.

People, still clinging to the ladders of planes and helicopters as they took off, fell to their death on the airstrip.

Anxious to take Saigon before the rainy season, Communist troops were already moving towards the capital. Once this was in their hands, they knew all Vietnam was theirs. Lu Doc Tho himself, arrived from Hanoi to take charge of the attack .

Although there were six thousand Americans still in Saigon, Ambassador Martin had not started evacuating them or any of the large number of South Vietnamese who were working for them. Finally, under pressure from Washington, the emergency plans for withdrawal were started.

With Admiral Nigel Caytor in charge of the evacuation, a fleet of helicopters lifted people from the city to the aircraft carriers off shore. Because the airport was under constant Communist rocket fire, it was not feasible to airlift from there. Those who were present tell of the indescribable horror of these tragic days as the refugees fought for a place on the helicopters or tried to get to the ships.

South Vietnamese officials and high ranking Army officers commandeered helicopters, filled them with their families and friends and landed on the carriers in such numbers that once emptied, they had to be pushed overboard in order to make room for the US Navy and Marine helicopters to land on their own ship.

Decks were absolutely covered with refugees. Sick and dying lay together, women in labor next to cases of malaria. The sick bays were overflowing. Crews did all they could for the people, giving up their bunks to the severely wounded.

"All you could hear was children crying and the wounded screaming with pain. You can't never forget something like that." a Navy corpsman said.

President Thieu had abdicated in favor of his Vice President, Tran Van Huong, but he quickly passed his authority to General Minh who was only to keep it a very short time.

On April 29th, Communist tanks swept into the Palace courtyard and a crew member from one of them ran into the Palace and hung the flag of the Viet Cong from the balcony signaling that Saigon had fallen.

The Commander of the tank group, Colonel Bui Tin, as ranking officer of the Viet Cong tank squadron, accepted the surrender from General Minh on April 30th.

The following day the streets of Saigon were silent and empty except for the dead. The ships and boats were gone from the harbor, the helicopters no longer filled the sky.

The Tran Quang Khai, with every inch of space overflowing with refugees was at sea bound for the Philippines. She arrived off the coast of the Philippines at the end of May. A sad and unhappy ship.

Captain Dinh's family had left Saigon before the Communists took over and were already en route to the United States where the Captain joined them later.

The refugees remained huddled aboard the ship waiting for the Philippine government to give them permission to land. Eventually, they were placed in refugee camps to await disposition.

The costs of this war were enormous. Not only in money. In addition to the military casualties in Vietnam, there were nearly 2 million civilians killed, 800,000 children orphaned and 83,000 amputees. The economy of the country was ruined, the social fabric almost completely destroyed. Thousands of refugees fled the country.

The South Vietnamese blamed their defeat on the American withdrawal and the limiting of military funds.

A total of 2,100,000 US men and women served in Vietnam. Of these 58,152 were killed and 153,303 were wounded so seriously that they had to be hospitalized.

In spite of the common belief that casualties were mainly draftees, 70% were volunteers.

The morale of the US Army was so low by 1974, that many were only concerned with their own survival and evaded going into combat. Fragging, the name given to the practice of murdering officers with fragmentation grenades, became a problem. Relations between blacks and whites had become very tense.

The use of drugs was so widespread that an official report states that a third of the troops were addicted. These troops came home to be the parents of today's teenagers. If the Vietnam veterans had been given more help, more understanding, more training, would some of the addiction, increasing violence and crime of today have been avoided?

This war has been analyzed by an array of specialists military, civilian and political. Most have decided that it was a mistake.

Perhaps the remark of a seaman 3rd class summed it up when he said, "I heard as Kennedy had good intentions when he went in there, like Nixon and Johnson after him had, but they say as that's what Hell's made of and Nam sure was that."

## VIETNAM MEMORIAL

When in November 1980, a competition for a Vietnam Memorial design was announced, it was not only professional architects and sculptors who entered, but also men who had served in Vietnam.

One of them was David Priddy who served as admissions and dispositions officer at the 91st Evacuation Hospital, Vietnam, and then at the HQ of the 44th Medical Brigade.

Priddy never forgot the tragic sight of the broken, bleeding bodies that were brought for admission to the hospitals. Remembering them, he developed a design called the RISING STAR MEMORIAL OF VIETNAM VETERANS. The explanatory text given below, describes his deep feelings and desire to honor those who suffered and died.

"The Rising Star Memorial of Vietnam Veterans is a classically simple design representing the aspiring hopes of our nation.

It is to be constructed of white marble with level pathways all around. The height to be 30 ft. at the center, sloping towards the feet of the star, ending in a seven ft escarpment in order to prevent climbing on the memorial.

"The names to be carved in alphabetical order on the faces of the points in half inch letters in a six foot wide band running around the star. In memory of our Vietnam veterans and those who died while serving there, it is appropriate that a rising star that represents our nation, our country and those who gave their lives for it, be placed between the Washington Monument and the Lincoln Memorial.

"In flower beds between the points of the star, plantings will give a contemplative ambiance to the memorial.

"As a former Vietnam veteran serving in the medical corps, some of the names to be placed on the memorial, I know, and others I saw take their final breath for their country.

"It is with pride and the hope that we will not forget them and all who served, that I submit this God inspired design to my country."

While his was not the winning design, Priddy's was among the finalists. see Photograph with Mai Lin, the winner on page ---

Like many others who served in Vietnam, Priddy had mixed feelings about the war, but, he said he decided to give of his best while he was there.

Parachutist Sabatini of Newport Rhode Island, describes his feelings in a similar way.

"I was called on to serve my country and I gave it my best shot. Yeah, it was tough. You never knew what was waiting for you when you jumped out of that plane, but after I gave it a year, I signed up again. It was better over there than the way vets got treated over here at the time."

Now the women who served in Vietnam have their own Memorial statue. Diane Carlson Evans from Minnesota, who served as an Army nurse in Vietnam, has been the moving spirit behind the drive to honor the women vets. Finally, after many years, the statue by nationally known sculptor, Glenna Goodacre, was placed 300 feet south of the Vietnam Wall and 300 feet southeast of the Hart statue.

War is always cruelly hard on women, whether they are serving in the war zone themselves or waiting at home working and keeping the family together.

Many of the men who returned were so haunted by their experiences that they were unable to lead a normal life. Wives longing for the return of a loved one found themselves living with a stranger.

Physical injuries can be seen and understood. Injuries to the mind and spirit are hidden and not always recognized.

As the Vietnam war lingered on, morale fell lower and lower.

Not only did men not know what they were fighting for, but they were unsure of who was the enemy. It could be the man or woman who had offered food or shelter the day before. It could be a child, an old woman - so all became the enemy. Then came the guilt and remorse when it was discovered that the innocent were killed with the guilty.

Back home in the States, those who served were blamed and

ostracized, when in reality, they were but pawns in a losing game.

Most had given their best and more than 58,000 gave their lives.

Hopefully, lessons were learned that will serve us well in the future.

# WITH THE

# PHILIPPINE NAVY

## 1976-1987

Now the Bering Strait aka Tran Quang Quai, was scarcely recognizable. Her decks were covered with trash and filth from the hundreds of refugees who had scrambled aboard in their desperate efforts to escape from Saigon.

Equipment and machinery were wrecked. Heads stopped up.

Kitchens unusable, the water purifying unit which had not been properly maintained and managed by the Vietnamese, was no longer working. The ship was in such bad shape that, after inspection, the Coast Guard said they did not want her back. It would be too costly to put her back in service.

Al Olsen, Jr. Senior Coast Guard Officer in the Philippines said, "the ship brought in several hundred refugees. It was rat infested and in a filthy, deplorable condition."

After inspecting the ship, P. A. Hogue, Acting Chief Officer of Coast Guard Operations said, "We do not desire the ship returned to the Coast Guard inventory."

So the Bering Strait, aka Tran Quang Khai, came under the disposition of the United States Navy once again.

For a while she languished deserted and empty, then, in December 1975 she was acquired from the United States government under the Military Sales Act and formally transferred to the Philippine Navy on April 6 1976. She was then towed to Bataan Shipyard Engineering Company for repairs and rehabilitation.

A helicopter pad on her fantail was added in order to accommodate a Navy helicopter. Finally, on August 21st 1983, the Bering Strait, aka Tran Quang Khai, was renamed the BRP Diego Silang after one of the great heroes of the Philippines, and commissioned into the Naval Defense Force of that country.

As the Diego Silang, the ship's career was an exciting and dangerous one. It would require a whole book to describe it.

She was given the following missions: Conducting anti-submarine operations. Providing support to merchant convoys and other combatant ships. Giving rescue and disaster assistance. Providing Naval Gunfire support in Military Operations. Chasing Pirates and Gun and Drug runners.

The Diego Silang was used also for training cadets of the Philippine Naval Academy and student officers and Ensigns undergoing Seaphase Training during their Naval Officer Qualification course.

As Rear Admiral Mariano Dumancas, Flag Officer in Command of the Philippine Navy, wrote to Innis, "her entire stint with us was indeed distinguished, commendable and in more ways deepened its hold in our hearts and memories as a symbol of great naval tradition."

Now the Bering Strait's Naval career is over. She was decommissioned in November 1987 and mothballed as a reserve of the Philippine Navy. Shortly after, she was transferred to a civilian business group who own the R.I. Caillian Enterprises.

It would be a more fitting end if the USS Bering Strait were taken back to the waters she was named for and became a museum in Beringea, the public park which the United States and Russia have agreed to make of the Greater and Lesser Diomede Islands. These islands line the stretch of water marking the International dateline and divide East from West.

Ebi continued to keep in touch with Innis. He now has his own Law firm in Tokyo with several partners doing business in the United States, Asia, Saudi Arabia, Switzerland and the United Kingdom.

Hearing that Innis had a heart attack and was in hospital, Ebi came to visit him. It was an emotional meeting. They had not seen each other for many years. Ebi could not help thinking back to their first meeting in 1945. Then, Innis was a vigorous, handsome young Naval Officer and Ebi was a thin, worried boy. Now, Innis was thin and weak from his illness and Ebi a vigorous, successful lawyer.

Taking Innis' hand, Ebi said, "All in my firm are keeping to the Golden Rule which, long ago, you exemplified for me so well."

In 1991 Ebi came to Arlington National Cemetery to pay his last respects to Innis. Kneeling at the gravestone he said a Buddhist prayer for the crews of the Bering Strait and the Philippine Sea and for the continued strengthening of the Bridge to Peace and Goodwill which, together, they had brought into being.

*Crew 15, VPB 22.*

*91st Evacuation Hospital.*

# PROGRAM
## TURNOVER CEREMONY
## 1 JANUARY 1971

Arrival of Guests

Arrival of Commander Coast Guard Squadron THREE and Commander Coast Guard District 14 Representative

Arrival of Chief of Naval Operations, Vietnamese Navy and Commander U. S. Naval Forces, Vietnam

Invocation

Remarks by CAPT R. E. HOOVER, Commander Coast Guard Squadron THREE

Remarks by CAPT J. W. MOREAU, Commander Coast Guard District 14 Representative

Remarks by VADM J. H. KING, Jr., Commander U. S. Naval Forces, Vietnam

Signing of Turnover Document

Ship decommissioning

a. Lower Colors of United States of America (United States National Anthem)

b. USCG personnel debark

a. VNN crew embarks

b. Hoist Colors of Republic of Vietnam (Republic of Vietnam National Anthem)

Remarks by Rear Admiral TRAN VAN CHON, Chief of Naval Operations, Vietnamese Navy

Awards

Benediction

Reception

*Ship's Patch after Vietnamese renamed her Dragon Two.*

*Mai Lin architect of Vietnam Wall and David Priddy.*

# APPENDIX

## USS BERING STRAIT, AVP 34

The Bering Strait (AVP 34) was laid down on June 7 1943 at Houghton, Washington, by the Lake Washington shipyards. She was launched on 15 January 1944 sponsored by Mrs. George F. Cornwall, wife of the managing editor of *The Timberman*, which was published in Portland Oregon. On 19th July 1944 the Bering Strait was commissioned at the builder's yard with Commander Walter D. Innis in command.

### DIMENSIONS AND CHARACTERISTICS

| | | |
|---|---|---|
| Displacement ................ | 2800 tons | |
| Dimensions .................... | Length | 311 ft. |
| | Beam | 41 ft. 2 ins. |
| | Draft | 13 ft. |
| Propulsion machinery .... | Four 1600 HP diesel engines | |
| | Twin screws. | |
| Speed ............................ | 8.5 knots. | |
| Range ........................... | 13,000 miles. | |
| Fuel capacity .................. | 16,000 gallons diesel oil. | |
| Complement .................. | 367. | |
| Armaments .................... | 3 5", 8 40 mm, 8 20 mm., | |
| | 6 .50 cal. mg., 2 dct. | |

(Barnegat Class)

VH3/P20

Serial: 106

# RESCUE SQUADRON THREE
FLEET POST OFFICE
SAN FRANCISCO, CALIFORNIA

13 August 1945.

From: The Commanding Officer, Rescue Squadron THREE.
To : The Commanding Officer, U.S.S. BERING STRAIT.

Subject: Aviation Maintenance Unit of the U.S.S. BERING STRAIT - Commendation of.

1. It is the desire of the commanding officer, the pilots and the aircrewmen of Rescue Squadron THREE to extend their sincere congratulations and appreciation to the aviation maintenance personnel of the U.S.S. BERING STRAIT for their cooperation and excellent performance of duty during the many months in which Rescue Squadron THREE aircraft were maintained by your ship.

2. The number of missions flown by this squadron over a sustained period was well beyond that normally expected of its type and was made possible by the teamwork, efficiency and willingness of all hands in the V-division of the U.S.S. BERING STRAIT. The fact this unit maintained an operational availability of 81% of planes assigned during the first six weeks of the operation, is adequate testimony of the efficiency of the division as a seaplane maintenance unit. In addition, the determination of the personnel of this unit led to the accomplishment of an exceptional amount of work on the water including the changing of floats, flaps, bombardier's windows, wing tips, and engines, none of which have ever been considered routine operations.

3. It is requested that a copy of this letter be inserted in the service record of each of the men of the aviation maintenance division.

W. D. BORVILLIAN.

The following message was sent by the Commanding Officer of the BERING STRAIT in reply:

"THIS COMMAND DEPARTS PRESENT ASSIGNMENT CONSIDERING IT AN HONOR AND A PRIVILEDGE TO HAVE BEEN ASSOCIATED WITH THE MAGNIFICANT OPERATIONS OF YOUR WING AGAINST THE ENEMY X MAY THE ANGEL OF GOOD FORTUNE ATTEND ALWAYS THE COMMANDING GENERAL AND THE GALLANT FLIGHT CREWS OF THE 313th BOMBARDMENT WING"

# BERING STRAIT (AVP 34)
## WEDNESDAY 19TH JULY 1944.
## FROM THE LOG:-

The ship was placed in commission with suitable ceremonies by Captain H.K.Stubbs, USN, Assistant Supervisor of Shipbuilding, Seattle, WA in accordance with orders from Commandant 13th Naval District..12.20 the ship was turned over to Commander Walter D. Innis, US Navy, who read his orders, assumed command and posted the watch.

The following officers reported aboard for duty,

Lt. Elmo M.Chase, D-V(G)USNR,97367;
Lt. William L. Echols, D-V(S), USNR, 254722;★
Lt. Roderick C. Blatchford, MC-V(S), USNR, 361246;
Lt.(jg) William E. Housel, SC-V(G),USNR, 135371;
Lt.(jg) Ralph S. Michael, Jr., D-V(G),USNR 162273;
Lt.(jg) Albert T. Meisner, US Navy,198379;
Ensign Springer H. Moore, Jr.,C-V(S), USNR, 280691;
Ensign Jack G. Dunn, US Navy, 355580;
Ensign Harry G. Lane, US Navy,355766;
Ensign Delmas C. Snow, US Navy, 355997; ★
Ensign Gordon L. Jarvis, US Navy, 364322;★
Ensign Robert E. Robinson, A-V(S) USNR, 373019;
Boatswain Joseph T.Adams, US Navy, 349915;
Machinist Vincent P. Wilde, US Navy, 342693;

The following named men were received:

| | |
|---|---|
| Aills, Billy J. | 939 10 82 |
| Aiston, William H. | 375 93 44 |
| Alexdander, John E. | 849 27 86 |
| Allen, James T. | 356 49 52 |
| Alvarez, Julian R. | 887 72 67 |
| Anderson, Keith V. | 859 25 25 |
| Ashley, Jack B. | 849 28 28 |
| Averette, Caarl W. | 838 60 61 |
| Baltezar, Herman C. | 554 86 87 |
| Bark, Carl W. | 866 85 04 |
| Barnett, Hubert L. | 939 10 70 |
| Barnett, Millard O. | 413 58 71 |
| Baron, Roland E. | 943 26 87 |

| | |
|---|---|
| Barr, Frederick Jr. | 299 87 24 |
| Bates, R. V. | 939 10 77 |
| Beasley, Oscar H. Jr. | 648 98 82 |
| Bellina, Philip V. | 847 56 98 |
| Belseth, Vernon S.K. | 621 43 08 |
| Berghuis, Henry E. | 871 60 96 |
| Berry, Tommy H. | 680 35 22 |
| Billings, Robert C. | 368 10 94 |
| Bishop, Richard F. | 283 15 11 |
| Bowdon, Brigham W. | 368 81 28 |
| Bowie, Walter A. | 828 72 46 |
| Brekke, Christian A. | 329 10 00 |
| Bridge, William C. | 611 00 54 |
| Briggs, William R. | 621 36 71 |
| Brigham, John H. | 849 28 17 |
| Bronson, Raymond B. | 660 50 65 |
| Bouwer, George W. | 665 46 43 |
| Brown, George A. | 846 34 10 |
| Brown, William A. | 939 35 59 |
| Browning, George W. | 849 27 71 |
| Bruno, Lawrence C. | 378 60 47 |
| Butler, Donald T. | 664 31 12 |
| Bykonen, Edward E. | 866 73 31 |
| Cagle, Jack H. | 890 96 15 |
| Cain, Donald N. | 805 83 52 |
| Campbell, Bertram R. | 406 99 02 |
| Carlyon, Joseph E. | 338 12 05 |
| Carpenter, Harold C. | 964 42 50 |
| Catanach, Marcos R. | 889 70 98 |
| Cates, Charlie B. | 967 77 01 |
| Challstrom, Robert W. | 386 92 77 |
| Chisham, George H. | 628 08 15 |
| Christensen, Russell L. | 730 78 80 |
| Clark, Loyd R. | 888 09 51 |
| Clark, Melvin M. | 975 01 13 |
| Clark, Ronald D. | 820 03 65 |
| Cobb, Ross L. | 564 02 41 |
| Coburn,Carl H. | 975 01 17 |
| Clay, Homer W. | 939 10 68 |
| Claypool, Conard C. | 287 36 22 |
| Collins, Ellsworth L. | 866 65 55 |
| Conklin, Bruce B. | 757 95 31 |
| Cox, Howard J. | 358 00 61 |

| | |
|---|---|
| Crawford, James R. | 883 47 67 |
| Crews, James B. | 641 29 37 |
| Crider, Claud D. | 967 76 96 |
| Cunningham, Fred W. | 878 86 42 |
| Davis, John R. Jr. | 956 52 75 |
| Davidson, Orville | 387 04 09 |
| Della monica, James M. | 378 58 67 |
| Dismore, Horace O. | 885 35 77 |
| Doner, Charles E. | 564 61 12 |
| Donahue, Robert E. | 941 13 09 |
| Donaldson, James N. Jr. | 311 20 61 |
| Donavan, John F. | 871 62 48 |
| Dronyk, Joseph. | 356 10 39 |
| Eastman, William R. | 393 61 95 |
| Ellis, Henry M. | 939 10 59 |
| Ellison, Harold (n) | 880 42 98 |
| Epperly, John W. | 875 60 46 |
| Ferrel, James C. | 857 18 31★ |
| Ferris, Joe F. | 849 27 70 |
| Firmin, Curry J. | 848 01 11 |
| Fish ,Barton L. | 963 98 07 |
| Fishel, Clinton E. | 620 40 71 |
| Fleischman, Harvey L. | 306 60 10 |
| Fontana, Roy A. | 387 04 25 |
| Fulbright, Boyd L. | 890 96 35 |
| Gaesler, Harold F. | 967 65 93 |
| Gallant, James S. | 262 27 04 |
| Garcia, Marcelino A. | 625 98 91 |
| Gonella, Mario J. | 808 06 44 |
| Goretti, Pete L. | 687 04 24 |
| Gregory, William J. | 880 38 75 |
| Grover, William T. | 329 41 53 |
| Golder, Wylie O. | 347 00 01 |
| Gray, Gail M. | 864 82 59 |
| Greene, Edward D. | 287 49 82 |
| Guillory, Sidney J. | 840 01 03 |
| Gumatatotao, Augustin U. | 421 01 67 |
| Hall, Maurice C. | 316 64 03★ |
| Hamilton, Charles E. | 964 42 49 |
| Hand, John L. jn. | 649 97 78 |
| Hanes, George R. | 555 94 36 |
| Hanser, Vernon R. | 843 39 87 |
| Hanson, Harold N. | 206 83 10 |

| | |
|---|---|
| Haproff, William T. | 879 03 74★ |
| Harmon, Richard A. jn. | 782 04 38 |
| Hass, William G. jn. | 329 53 06 |
| Hathaway, Thomas E. | 854 42 14 |
| Hayes, William R. | 967 80 04 |
| Hicks, Lewis E. | 829 44 10 |
| High, Robert W. | 633 82 51 |
| Highfield, Albert O. | 885 36 03 |
| Highfill, Theo(n) | 967 60 66 |
| Hilterty, Daniel P. | 651 56 29 |
| Hilton, Homer E. | 634 04 19 |
| Hilton, Leslie L. | 849 27 67 |
| Hines, Jack L. | 848 79 71 |
| Hodson, Harold L. | 629 09 89 |
| Hough, George R. | 620 62 12 |
| Houston, Stanley C. | 368 81 12 |
| Howard, Hoyt M. | 893 61 34 |
| Hue, Albert J. | 923 21 74 |
| Hughlet, Orvel E. | 967 80 12 |
| Hukkanen, William B. | 663 57 41★ |
| Huston, Edward D. | 858 24 98 |
| Ingram, Lloyd, E. | 885 21 21 |
| Johnson, Jack (n) | 662 11 48 |
| Jones, Joe (n) | 849 97 18 |
| Kabarec, Joseph M. | 810 49 47 |
| Keeler, Donald E. | 800 55 33 |
| Kellett, James T. jn. | 647 55 89 |
| Kelley, Morris C. | 847 68 21 |
| Kelly, Rex E. | 630 34 19 |
| Kersey, James R. | 844 96 57 |
| Kerwin, Leo F. | 650 14 01 |
| Killough, David N. | 840 88 85 |
| Kingsley, Kenneth L. | 300 46 18 |
| Kinsey, Milton E. | 967 76 61 |
| Kline, Ralph M. | 246 43 12 |
| Knowlton, Kenneth L. | 664 37 65 |
| Kutterer, Thomas R. | 943 45 73 |
| Lake, Dareld B. | 368 81 17 |
| Lantz, Harold J. | 874 15 08 |
| Lawrence, Arthur H. | 816 34 08 |
| Lay, Elwin K. | 671 19 94 |
| Lindener, Clifford J. | 386 57 14 |
| Loeser, John J.jn. | 819 07 45 |

| | |
|---|---|
| Long, Merlin D. | 867 37 01 |
| Madere, Ralph P. | 644 08 48 |
| Mabes, Earl L. | 266 14 21 |
| Maginnis, Charles H. | 655 27 56 |
| Malouff, Louis J. | 562 56 04 |
| Manley, James B. | 624 24 81 |
| Martin, Russell C. | 291 78 63 |
| Martin, Shelby "D" | 670 61 60 |
| Mathis, Lyal M. | 849 27 99 |
| McGuire, Roy L. | 844 34 94 |
| McCollam, Joe (n) | 650 14 56 |
| McCord, Donald K. | 819 15 47 |
| McDonald, Charles | 860 05 79 |
| McRill, John L. | 853 07 36 |
| Melton, Henrie D. | 616 06 47 |
| Mercer, James E. | 886 99 70 |
| Miller, Ralph S. | 871 20 41 |
| Moore, "H' "T". | 967 58 91 |
| Monroe, Vernon O. | 877 12 35 |
| Morrison, John W. | 356 52 98 |
| Morsaint, Donald E. | 381 21 88 |
| Munro, Charles S. | 837 05 85 |
| Nelson, John T. | 840 55 78 |
| Nichols, Roy (n) | 612 05 66 |
| Nichold, Willie L. | 849 28 00 |
| Nokes, Glen C. | 654 53 53 |
| O'neil, Robert F. | 378 05 34 |
| Ornduff, Leonard A. | 860 06 17 |
| Oshakken, Richard B. | 871 21 94 |
| Owens, Owen (n) | 651 52 68 |
| Parker, Robert L. | 356 18 33 |
| Parker, William H. | 614 46 56 |
| Peltier, Richard J. | 846 96 49 |
| Phelps, Charles M. | 634 72 61 |
| Poindexter, Gilbert R. | 842 65 23 |
| Pmeroy, Joseph L. | 803 30 76 |
| Puckett, Glen W. | 847 44 13 |
| Ratols, Antonio (n) | 633 13 44 |
| Reeves, Lester R. | 291 52 23 |
| Reis, Adam W. | 321 89 72★ |
| Richardson, Willie "B" | 637 17 71 |
| Riddlesburger, Elbert L. | 671 21 62 |
| Roark, Leonard L. | 844 75 57 |

| | |
|---|---|
| Robinson, Bina R. | 840 75 57 |
| Ruff, Loid W. | 346 49 89 |
| Russell, Sera H. | 275 10 59 |
| Russo, Joseph (n) | 250 73 83 |
| Schmidt, Henry (n) | 385 06 74 |
| Serur, Joseph (n) | 616 26 45 |
| Shaw, Nathan C. | 862 55 37 |
| Sherrard, Lee H. | 201 23 46 |
| Shipley, Marion L. | 867 07 48 |
| Shumate, Carl K.jn. | 375 89 05★ |
| Siddens, Gerald J. | 337 59 94 |
| Small, Moses (n) | 831 30 58 |
| Smith, Octave(n) | 645 19 61 |
| Sopke, Norman F. | 883 38 19 |
| Spatz, Hevert(n) | 801 28 22 |
| Springer, Alvin L. | 321 41 75 |
| Staley, Clarence L. | 662 45 18 |
| Stanford, David E. | 839 60 73 |
| Stapp, Kenneth L. | 838 19 29 |
| Stidham, James E. | 614 07 11 |
| Street, Willis H. | 638 22 19 |
| Such, Walter T. | 724 74 04 |
| Swartz, James J. | 626 70 02 |
| Thomas, Robert E. | 847 95 32 |
| Thomas, James R. | 849 27 83 |
| Thompson, William H. | 895 09 69 |
| Tomerlin, William F. | 629 81 18 |
| Trullinger, Jerome R. | 371 69 27 |
| Tudor, Walter C. | 265 61 63 |
| Turpin, Leroy (n) | 755 87 71 |
| Vargas, Juan (n) | 293 46 08 |
| Webster, Howard S. | 865 35 30 |
| Wesson, Daniel D. | 967 71 47 |
| Wehrli, Wallace H. | 321 40 85 |
| Whitsett, Alfred W. | 655 30 43 |
| Williams, Thomas R. | 371 93 32 |
| Williamson, William L.jn. | 624 24 50 |
| Witt,Theodore R. | 634 42 48 |
| Wunder, Alexander (n) | 883 82 54 |
| Young, Victor L. | 873 51 43 |

Joined Ship Nov. '44 - Shwartz, Marvin★

★ Those with star provided information for this book.

## LIST OF MOST OF B-29 SURVIVORS PICKED UP BY THE BERING STRAIT 1945.

Those with star supplied personal stories for this book.

Edward Albraicht, Sgt.
Howard Atkin, 2nd Lt.★
Robert Aspinall, T/ Sgt.
A.E. Austin, Lt.
Marvin Binger, Sgt.
Claude Blackwell, T/Sgt.
William Brabham, 2nd Lt.
B.G. Budd, Cpl.
Samuel Burch, T/Sgt.
Melvin Cash,1st. Lt. ★
Thomas Cerro, Cpl.
William Cook, S/Sgt.
Ernest Deutch, 2nd Lt.
Robert Driscoll, S/Sgt.
Hugo Drum, S/ Sgt.
A.W. Fletcher, Cpl.
Bernard Gallinger, Corpl.
N.S. Garrick, Cpl.
Richard Gillman, Sgt.
Carl Gustavson, 2nd Lt.
John S. Halloran 1st Lt.★
James Halsey,S/Sgt.
Richard Hansen, 2nd. Lt.★
Muriel Hargrove, 1st. Lt.★
Everett Holt, Sgt.
Mary, widow of William Hupman,Sgt.★
Frederick Kays, 2nd Lt.
Philip Knutson,Sgt.★
Floyd Larson, Corpl.★
Sigmund Lewandowski, Sgt.
Donald Lehman, Corpl.
Bernard McCaskill, Capt.

Clifford MacComber, Lt.Col.
Leon Melensky, Sgt.
David Nesmith, M/Sgt.
Philip Neverman, Sgt.
Stanley Odon, Cpl.★
Morris Palmer, Sgt.
Peterson - passenger, B-29 K-375.
Carl Ptalzgrat, Sgt.
Joseph Ptazskowske, 2nd Lt
Robert Ping, Col. ★
Donald Reed, 2nd Lt.
Julius Rivas, Sgt.
John Schoonmaker, S/Sgt.
Sol Serkin, Sgt.
Paul M. Shuford, 2nd Lt.★
John R. Slevin, 2nd Lt.
Charles H. Smith,
Elmer Stapler, 2nd Lt.
Frank Sult, 2nd Lt..
Benjamin Townsend, 2nd Lt★
W.T Trivette, 2nd LT.
Galen Westmoreland, S/ Sgt.
H.W. Wing, 2nd Lt.
R.M.Wiegel, 2nd Lt.

A4-3/FF12 UNITED STATES PACIFIC FLEET
16-sr. FORWARD AREA, CENTRAL PACIFIC

SERIAL: 01298 16 April 1945

CONFIDENTIAL
From; Commander Forward Area, Central Pacific.
To: Distribution List.

**SUBJECT: SURFACE ASPECTS OF AIR-SEA RESCUE**

1. The information contained herein is based on the experiences of the USS BERING STRAIT (AVP-34) while serving under this command as an air-sea rescue vessel. During the period in which these experiences were gained, the BERING STRAIT acted as an air-sea rescue station ship, conducted searches and worked with Dumbo aircraft to effect the rescue of numerous downed aviators in the northern MARIANAS area.

2. This material is being disseminated to commands in the Forward Area who are immediately concerned with the surface aspects of air-sea rescue. Certain of the BERING STRAIT's experiences which have a universal aspect into rescue picture for the distressed as well as the rescuers are being disseminated separately in air-sea rescue bulletins.

3. To effectively accomplish its mission as an air-sea rescue station ship, a vessel does not necessarily have to rescue survivors; it can serve in many other ways to support the operation.

(a) Weather reports should be sent in to the controlling air base at prescribed intervals when the location of the ship with relation to enemy bases permits.

(b) An efficient C.I.C. team closely coordinated with communications gives the station ship additional value as a navigational aid. Many returning bombers showing emergency IFF were in need of nothing more than a vector to home base, which can be given more readily and more accurately by a ship on advanced station. Likewise, the ship serves as a valuable relay point between plane and base, not only for bombers but for Dumbos as well.

(c) To be efficient in what might well be called preventative air-sea rescue measures, the station ship must track every aircraft continuously. It should make every attempt to contact aircraft showing emergency IFF, or failing this, to communicate with an escorting aircraft, offering all possible assistance such as weather, position, and navigational vectors. It should report to the appropriate base and to air-sea rescue group or unit headquarters the positions of planes in distress when they pass off the radar screen, listening for confirmation of their safe arrival at home base. Count the number of outbound bombers as seen on the radar screen, estimate time of return, and check off the number returning. Those on time usually will be all right, but the late ones will keep the station ship busy. If ditching is inevitable, try to effect rendezvous between plane and ship, or if this is impossible, between plane and a Dumbo in the vicinity.

4. The air-sea rescue station ship is in an excellent position to evaluate ditching positions given by aircraft and to act accordingly. Many times the nearest base, although able to obtain accurate bearings, cannot get good ranges, and, at the same time, ditching aircraft are themselves often unsure of their positions. The following example is illustrative:

(a) A bomber reported himself in trouble in the vicinity of MAUG islands, and ditched shortly thereafter about 40 miles NNE of the station ship's position. Prior to the actual ditching, the ship had established communications with a companion plane. A half-dozen ditching positions (all different) were received from various sources, including the ditching plane, the escorting plane, and nearby bases. When the escorting plane corrected his report, which had been based on a reciprocal bearing, the ship was able to evaluate it as correct because it agreed with the air plot in C.I.C., and rescue was effected two and a half hours later without the aid of Dumbo or any signals from survivors except from a flashlight (Navy type) pinned to one man's lifejacket, and sighted at 100 yards. Seven crew members perished in the ditching; the five who survived were swimming, some without lifejackets inflated. Had their position been in doubt, some or all of these men would have drowned before a lengthy air-surface search could have found them. Early rescue was possible because of the ship's ability to evaluate the communications heard and the maintenance of an alert C.I.C.plot.

5. By early knowledge, through radar and communications, of the prospective ditching of a distressed aircraft, the station ship can save lives by vectoring the plane so that ditching can take place alongside the ship. At night or in heavy seas the ship must plan in advance what action it ca, and will, take to assist ditchings. The BERING STRAIT worked out two such plans:

(a) The normal night ditching plan was successfully carried out with a distressed bomber which had lost all means of communications, the lights and the movement of the ship guiding the plane to a landing and immediate rescue of all hands. The use of lights to show the state of the sea, height and length of swells, direction of the true wind, are of tremendous value when the tactical situation permits their employment. Running lights aid the plane in determining the ship's course,which should be directly into the wind.The red masthead light is an obstruction marker. Searchlights depressed on the water allow the pilot to see for himself the conditions of the sea, they should be used so as to indicate course, silhouette the ship, and afford reflection on the waves; control must be exercised to avoid directing the searchlight on the plane and blinding the crew.

(b) Because of duty on air-sea rescue station when surface winds reached 30 knots, the BERING STRAIT worked out a plan for ditching under this condition. This plan was merely an elaboration of the "cast recovery" maneuvers of a cruiser. Although never put to the test for ditching, similar methods have been used by AVPs and destroyers to enable seaplanes to take off in extremely rough water conditions, and it is believed it would be equally effective in improving conditions for ditching. In addition to the usual maneuver of steering 45 degrees on one side of the wind at 15 knots, changing course through the wind to 45 degrees on the other side of the wind, reducing speed to 10 knots in the turn to prolong the slick, the BERING STRAIT's plan called for dropping two smoke pots in the turn so as to line up in the wind, and draining oil through the scuppers. The procedure could be repeated once or twice to enable to plane in trouble to see the effect created and gauge his approach and let-down for the near-precision landing necessary. The ship could swing on around away from the upwind line thought the slick, completing a circle and thereby have the ditched plane ahead of him and never get more then 500 yards away from it.

6. Searches for survivors by surface craft, initiated soon after the ditching, may be effective provided the exact area of ditching is known. Coordinated search by Dumbo and ship is, of course, the most effective method. The normal plan used by the BERING STRAIT was to steam along the line of most probable drift at a speed which enabled the Dumbo plane to pass directly over the ship at twice the radius of visibility used from the last position of passing over the ship on sweeps normal to the course of the ship. This method gives the plane an accurate reference to check his navigation, and further assures the ship being near to rescue survivors located at the earliest possible time.

7. For communications, VHF is an essential for any air-sea rescue station ship. Likewise, there would be provision for voice communication between the ship and base. The BERING STRAIT made use of the TCE (40 watts) on 4475 Kc for this purpose, and had extreme difficulty in receiving and transmitting at certain times of the day. This ship recommends a 200 watt transmitter be provided both for the station ship and the base controlling it. The BERING STRAIT further recommended ten-channel VHF equipment be provided for the station ship, and suggested that a separate channel for air-sea rescue alone be established because of overcrowding on 140.58 mc. CW frequencies and equipment can be used to establish station positions and the like, but voice communications are an essential when actual rescue operations are underway, or ditchings imminent.

8. During its air-sea rescue operations, the BERING STRAIT make the following evaluations of survival equipment:

(a) The life raft corner reflector was picked up on ship's surface radar at five miles.

(b) Raft lights were visible at night at five miles, pin-on type flashlight at 100 yards.

(c) The Gibson Girl antenna balloon was visible at ten miles.

(d) Mirrors were very effective.

(e) Bearings were obtained on a radio buoy dropped by a plane; although the characteristic letter signal was not detected, good bearings were taken on the "hum" which was received.

9. Once survivors are located, rescue is best accomplished by use of embarkation nets on the ship's quarter, even when a small boat is employed to reach the rafts. Stretcher cases are more easily handled with the nets, using manila slings; ship's crew members can be of more assistance to weakened or injured survivors at the nets than on a ladder.

G.P. KRAKER,
Chief-of-Staff.

DISTRIBUTION:
Com MARIANAS-IWO JIMA Surface Patrol & Escort Group (15)
Com CAROLINES Surface Patrol & Escort Group (15)
Com Air-Sea Rescue Group (5)
ComGenXXIBomCom (5)
ComStratAirFor (2)
ComGenAAFPOA (2)
ComFairwng ONE (15)
OpNav 16V (1)
CinCPac (2)
ComAirPac (2)
ComAirPacSubComFwd (2)
ComDesPac (2)
ComFIFTHFleet (5)
ComSEVENTHFleet (5)

AUTHENTICATED:

J.W. Dinkelspiel,
Flag Secretary.

## SURVIVORS PICKED UP BY SQUADRON VH3

Commanded by Lt. Commander Bonvillian, based aboard the Bering Strait.

R.W.Allan, 1st Lt.
A.D.Anton, Lt.
P.F. Avant, Capt.
E.R. Bailey, Amm2c.
R.A Ballard Ens
Glenn H. Bergen, Lt.
H.A. Brislown, Amm3
Charles Canter, T/sgt.
F. Coffee, Am3c.
- -Cohan, Arm2c.
Lois Coloin, Ens.
L.L. Colvin, Ens.
V.J. Colo, Ens.
C.H. Collins, Aom2c.
A. G. Cooper. Ens.
- Cory, Arm2c.
R.J. Cowger, Lt.
R.B. Cromwell, 1st Lt.
- Cozzons, Lt.(jg)
J. Denison, Lt. (jg)
H.J. Derr, Capt.
- Dulnize, Amm2c.
R.W.Forth, Sub Lt. RVVR.
J. Forbes, Lt.
R.D. Flodquist, Ens.
O. Galilei, Aom3c.
Alfred Godfrey, Lt.(jg)
C.G.Gordon, Leading Seaman, RNVR.
- Grist, Lt.
L.E. Graine, 2nd Lt.
C.R. Hamlin, Pvt.
G.W.Head, Lt.
Merle M. Hershey, Lt.
- Hudspeth, Ens.
W.S. Hutchins, Ens.
M.J.Ireland, Arm3c.
R.F. Johnson, Amm2c.

K.M.Keeton, 1st. Lt.
- Kemp, Lt. (jg)
R.G.Koeller, Ens.
D.R. Kingsley, 1st.Lt.
E.C. Levesque, Amm2c.
- May, Lt.
W.H. Marr, Lt(jg)
R.J. McInnis, Ist Lt.
H.S.Miller, Lt.(jg)
A. Moos, Lt.(jg)
D.N.Myers, Amm2.
O. Payne, Lt.(jg)
Walter L.Peckham, 2nd Lt.
B. Phillips, 1st. Lt.
C.C. Platczyk, Amm3c.
W.A. Reeks, Sub Lt. RNVR.
C.M. Reynolds, Lt.
M. Replogle, Lt.
R.L.Rice, Ens.
G.E Roberts, Lt.(jg)
F.S. Royce, Ens.
Earl Russell, 2nd Lt.
W.R. Sankey, Ens.
Paul A Shaefer, 1st.Lt.
D.R. Sonner, Arm2c
L.T. Stattins, Lt.(jg)
R. Straws, Ens.
H.W. Sturtevant, Lt.
C.A. Sherman, Cpl.
C.P.Smith, Lt.Cdr.
J.R.Thacker, Arm3c.
P.F.Thompson, Arm2c.
C.E.Ware, Lt.(jg)
R.J. Warner, Lt.(jg)
F.F. Warren, Lt.
L.D.Welch, Lt.(jg)
R.H.Went, Ens.
D.E. Whitefield, 1st. Lt.
R.L.Wood, Cpl.
L.E. Zemanck, Ens.

10 men from USS Braine, DD 630, rescued from water and flown to Kerama Retto for treatment.

## USS PHILIPPINE SEA CV 47

The Philippine Sea, (CV 47) was laid down on August 19th, 1994 at the Bethlemen Steel Co. shipyard Quincy, Massachusetts. She was launched on 5th of September 1945. Mrs. Albert B. Chandler, wife of the governor of Kentucky, christened her. On the 11th may 1946, RADM Morton L. Deyo, Commandant 1st Naval District turned CV-47 over to Captain Delbert Cornwell who placed her in commission.

### DIMENSIONS AND CHARACTERISTICS

| | |
|---|---|
| Displacement ............ | 27,000 tons. |
| Dimensions ............... | Length 888 ft. |
| | Beam 147 ft. |
| | Draft 28 ft. 7 ins. |
| Speed ........................ | 33 knots. |
| Complement ............. | 360 Officers and 3,088 enlisted. |
| | 80 plus aircraft. |
| Armaments ............... | 12 - 5 inch guns, 18 - 40 inch guns. |

(Essex Class Carrier)

*Members of crew Philippine Sea, Ebi second from left.*

## CHRISTMAS GIFT FROM THE CREW OF THE PHILIPPINE SEA DECEMBER 1950.

While most of those aboard contributed, the following played a major part.

Captain W. D, Goodney USN

Commander Walter D. Innis USN

Commander Robert F. Jones USN, TF Operations Officer

Chaplain Dick Barnes

Father Harold Mead

Clancy, James, Bo'suns mate, USN★

Davis, Charles, YN3X, USN★

Dirodus, Jerry, AO2 - V30★

Johnson, D.R. M, Chief PO★

Le Baron, Alan, YN1st, USN★

Thompson, Benjamin SK1S-1, USN★

★Those with star provided personal recollections for this book.

Others who played an important part in the arrangements were

Alexander Ruthven, President, Michigan University

Edwin Stason, Dean of Michigan Law School

R. Smith, Professor of Law

## THE UNITED STATES COAST GUARD

Since its beginnings in 1790, the U. S. Coast Guard has continued growing in size and importance. It is the principal Agency for maritime law and safety in American waters and the high seas.

Officers and men of the Coast Guard constantly put their lives at risk rescuing passengers and crews from ships in distress and when working with the Customs and Narcotic Bureau and the Department of Justice in attempts to prevent drug smuggling into this country.

Since 1912, the Coast Guard has been conducting the International Ice Patrol providing warnings to ships and planes of dangerous weather conditions.

In addition, the Coast Guard maintains more than 39,000 navigational aids such as lighthouses, lightships, radio beacons, buoys and loran, greatly adding to safety at sea and in the air.

While the Coast Guard is well known for its life saving efforts, its contribution in time of war is not always recognized. Under the Navy in time of war, the Coast Guard has played a vital part in battle areas and this book makes an attempt to show some of their contribution to the war in Vietnam.

*Bering Strait renamed Diego Silang, with the Philippine Navy.*

## RE - USS BERING STRAIT AKA TRAN QUANG KHAI AND DIEGO SILANG

Officers responsible for repairs and reconditioning of the ship BRP Diego Silang,(PF 14) in Bataan and in Cavite shipyards were, CDR Vincente C. Escala, Jr LCDR Ramon C. Aquino, CDR Jaime Orcine, LCDR Joaquin L. Limon Jr., CDR Guerero E. Guzman.

Officers commanding the ship after commissioning were, CDR Robert V. Garcia, Capt. Ernesto S. Ramos, Capt. Federico B. Lardin, Capt. Danilo Avellanosa, Capt. Antonio G. Suratos, Capt. Danilo E. Pizarro.

Information contained in this section of the ship's history was provided by the following, Ambassador Nicholas Platt, American Embassy , Manila.

Ambassador Peter Koch, Netherlands Embassy, Makati.

Rear Admiral Mariano J. Dumancas, Flag Officer in Command, Philippine Navy.

QM1(SW) John M. Trail, Manila.

G. Eugene Martin, American Embassy, Manila.

Susan Hurley Bennet, Washington D.C.

## SOURCES

Main sources of information are from the Ship's Logs, Operational reports, Ship's histories and Operational archives.

From interviews with the ship's Officers and Enlisted personnel and their families.

From interviews with survivors of ditched B-29 crews rescued by the USS Bering Strait and family members and from members of the air crews aboard.

Interviews with Officers and Enlisted personnel of the USS Philippine Sea, CV 47. and from S. Ebihara.

Also from Officers and men of the US Coast Guard who served aboard the Bering Strait during the Vietnam War.

From Rear Admiral M. J. Dumancas, Jr. Flag Officer in Command of the Philippine Navy and his staff.

## BIBLIOGRAPHY


Accoce and Quest, *A Man Called Lucy*, Coward McCann.

Agoncilla and Guaerrero, *History of the Filipino People*, R. Garcia.

Bethel, N. *The Great Betraya*L, Hodder and Stoughton.

Cagle, M. W., *The Sea War in Korea*, Naval Institute.

Candrew and Gordievsky, *KGB, the Inside Story*. Harper Collins.

Churchill, W., *The Second World War*, Cassell.

Costello, J., *The Pacific War.*, Rawson Wade.

Dull, P. S. *A Battle History of the Japanese Navy*, 41-45 Stephens.

Fitzhugh and Crowell, *Crossroads of Continents*. Smithsonian.

Heffernan, R. *US Navy in World War II*, Chartwell Books.

Howard, S. *From Sea To Shining Sea*, Random House.

Karnow, S. *Vietnam, A History*, Penquin Books.

Morna, Lord, *Winston Churchill-The Struggle for Survival*, Constable.

Morison, Samuel, *The Two Ocean War*, Little Brown.

Puller, Jr., Lewis J. *Fortunate Son*, Bantam.

Romulo, Carlos P. *I Walked with Heroes*, Holt, Rinehart, Winston.
Wheeler, K. *The Road to Tokyo*, Time Life.

PERIODICALS

DAV Magazine.
Janes Defense Weekly.
London Times.
Naval War College Review.
Naval Institute Proceedings.
Retired Officer.
Shipmate.
Veterans of Foreign Wars Magazine.
World War II Magazine

## ACKNOWLEDGMENTS

---

The Honorable John Marsh, Jr.
Colonel J. Whitehouse, US Army Rtd.
Admiral John Yost, US Coast Guard Rtd.
and Staff of Coast Guard Historical Center.
Colonel Arthur Forster, USAF.
Sgt. Barry Spink ,Air Force History.
John Veda, Director, Navy Department Library and Staff.

# INDEX

## Symbols



## A

# D

## E



## F



## G



## H

# I



# J

## K



## L



## M

## N

## O



## P

## Q



## R



## S

# T

## U

## Z

## MEMORIES AND PHOTOGRAPHS

*The following pages are included for your own memories and photographs.*